# Redesigning English

## new texts, new identities

## The English Language: past, present and future *course team*

**The Open University**
Sally Baker (liaison librarian)
Pam Berry (compositor)
Helen Boyce (course manager)
Martin Brazier (cover designer)
David Calderwood (assistant project controller)
Joan Carty (liaison librarian)
Hazel Coleman (editor)
Lene Connolly (print buying controller)
Christine Considine (editor/editorial co-ordinator)
Anne Diack (BBC producer)
Margaret Dickens (print buying co-ordinator)
Sue Glover (editor)
Sharon Goodman (author/book co-ordinator)
David Graddol (author/book co-ordinator)
Martin Kenward (assistant project controller)
Julie Laing (BBC production assistant)
Avis Lexton (secretary)
Rob Lyon (designer)
Paul Manners (BBC producer)
Gill Marshall (editor)
Janet Maybin (author/book co-ordinator)
Barbara Mayor (author and course manager)
Neil Mercer (author/book co-ordinator)
Ray Munns (cartographer/graphic artist)
Kay Pole (developmental testing co-ordinator)
Pam Powter (course secretary)
Cathy Rosario (editor)
Lynne Slocombe (editor)
Gill Smith (editor)
Linda Smith (assistant project controller)
Joan Swann (course team chair)
Nikki Tolcher (main compositor)
Iva Williams (BBC production assistant)

**External assessor**
Professor Peter Trudgill, University of Lausanne

**Assessors for this book**
Professor Roger Fowler, University of East Anglia
Professor Theo van Leeuwen, London College of Printing and Distributive Trades
Professor Ulrike Meinhof, University of Bradford
Dr Kay Richardson, University of Liverpool

**Developmental testers and critical readers**
Kim Beckley
Nigel Blake
Susan Gander
Gilberto Giron
Anthea Fraser Gupta
Lindsay Hewitt
Diana Honeybone
Karen Hovey
Mike Hughes

The four volumes of the series form part of the second level Open University course U210 *The English Language: past, present and future.* If you wish to study this or any other Open University course, details can be obtained from the Central Enquiry Service, PO Box 200, The Open University, Milton Keynes MK7 6YZ.

For availability of the video and audiocassette materials, contact Open University Educational Enterprises Ltd (OUEE), 12 Cofferidge Close, Stony Stratford, Milton Keynes MK11 1BY.

# Redesigning English

## new texts, new identities

Edited by
Sharon Goodman and David Graddol

The Open
University

LONDON AND NEW YORK

First published 1996
by Routledge
11 New Fetter Lane
London EC4P 4EE

Simultaneously published in the USA and Canada
by Routledge
a division of Routledge, Chapman and Hall, Inc.
29 West 35th Street, New York, NY 10001

Published in association with The Open University

Edited, designed and typeset by The Open University

Printed and bound

A catalogue record for this book is available from the British Library

Library of Congress Cataloging-in-Publication Data applied for

ISBN 0 415 13124 3 (paper)
ISBN 0 415 13123 5 (hardbound)

## Book editors

**Sharon Goodman** is a lecturer in the Centre for Language and Communications at the Open University School of Education. She is a linguist whose interests include language and power, stylistics, media studies and the relationship between visual and verbal communication.

**David Graddol** is a lecturer in the Centre for Language and Communications at the Open University School of Education. He is an applied linguist with an interest in cultural and political aspects of language and discourse. He is co-author with Joan Swann of *Gender Voices* (Blackwell, 1989), and has published several papers on changing forms of textuality related to technological innovation.

## Other original contributors

**Allan Bell** combines work as a researcher in mass communication and sociolinguistics with freelance journalism and media consultancy. He is Senior Research Fellow in the Department of Linguistics, Victoria University, Wellington. His research interests and publications cover media language, public discourse on the global environment, language style and New Zealand English, and include *The Language of News Media* (Blackwell, 1991).

**Anthea Fraser Gupta** is a lecturer in the School of English, University of Leeds (formerly a senior lecturer in the Department of English Language and Literature at the National University of Singapore). She is primarily a sociolinguist with a particular interest in the acquisition of Singaporean English, and in its historical development, an area explored in her book *The Step-Tongue: children's English in Singapore* (Multilingual Matters, 1994).

**Theo van Leeuwen** is Professor of Communication Theory at the School of Media, London College of Printing and Distributive Trades. His research interests include visual communication, language and music in the media, and he is co-author with Professor Gunther Kress of *Reading Images: the grammar of visual design* (Routledge, 1996).

**Stephanie Markman Marriott** is a lecturer in the Programme in Literary Linguistics at the University of Strathclyde. Her research interests include broadcast talk and the sociolinguistics of the media, and she is currently working on a book on the language of live television.

**Simeon Yates** is a lecturer in the Social Sciences Faculty at the Open University. He has written on social and linguistic aspects of computer-mediated communications. Currently he is researching the effects of new communication technologies in the production of TV news.

# CONTENTS

# INTRODUCTION

*Sharon Goodman and David Graddol*

This book examines the new forms of text that have appeared in English in the twentieth century as a consequence of technological innovation and social change. A central theme of the book is the idea that new kinds of text reflect and help construct changing identities and social relations. The English language, indeed, plays a key role in the global restructuring of social and economic relations that has been collectively referred to as 'the postmodern condition'.

We live in a world in which the validity or interpretation of communication depends crucially on an understanding of when and where the speaker/writer was when the text was created. Indeed, the word 'time' is one of the commonest words in the English language. Allan Bell, in Chapter 1, examines the changing structure of time as represented in one of the oldest of the 'new media' – news journalism. He shows how news stories abandoned a chronological narrative structure in the late nineteenth century, as a distinct genre of news reporting emerged which satisfied the new requirements of readers – who no longer had the leisure or patience to reach the end of a long story in order to discover the outcome – and the requirements of a more complex institutional production process, where sub-editing means news stories must be designed so that they can be shortened without losing key information. News stories illustrate a number of other textual qualities that became more frequent in other genres as the twentieth century progressed. Bringing together many voices – sources, witnesses, earlier stories on the same topic – leads to forms of heteroglossic text in which the concept of authorship is rendered problematic.

Sharon Goodman, in Chapter 2, discusses the increasingly visual nature of English texts. At the height of the eighteenth century the perfect serious text was a tombstone of elegant typography. Pictures, even simple engravings and line drawings, were a signifier of popular and lower class taste. This sense of the vulgarity of visual communication carried over into social anxieties in the twentieth century, first for comics and then for television. In the late twentieth century, developments in technology have brought about a reversal of fortune for visual communication. The increasing availability of tools for creating visual texts – and the means to disseminate them globally – have engendered a change in the status of the visual. Sharon Goodman discusses the return of the visual semiotic to English texts in the postmodern age, and the ways in which words, typography and pictures are woven together to form multimodal texts. One of the readings associated with the chapter, by Theo van Leeuwen, extends this discussion into the area of film.

When one thinks of new, global communications technologies it is likely to be the Internet which first comes to mind, and this is considered by Simeon Yates in Chapter 3. The Internet has spawned so many new genres – from asynchronous communications by e-mail to on-line interactions (Internet Relay Chat) between people scattered across the world who have never met, and who present themselves through imaginary identities – that it demands closer linguistic scrutiny. English was one of the first European languages to benefit most from standardization and the development of the new modes of representation provided by scientific English. Now English seems likely to benefit most from the creation of the new genres associated with the new communications media. It may be possible, technologically, to communicate across the Internet in languages other than English, but will all languages be allowed to develop the linguistic resources required for the range of distinctive Internet genres? And, since people's identities are constructed in part through their interaction with texts, are English-speaking 'netizens' forming a global social elite who have privileged access and experience of the global village?

One often noted feature of the postmodern world is the blurring of boundaries – not just in geographical space but also in social identities. The trend towards a global market and consumer society is one that has had transformative effects at a cultural level, and no arena shows better the mixing of genre and conflicts of social identity than the kind of information texts produced to inform clients and consumers. Sharon Goodman, in Chapter 4, explores some of the hybridizing processes of 'informalization' and 'marketization' that have affected many genres of public language, and the contradictory effects on the producers and receivers of such texts, from university prospectuses to sales talk.

The thesis of globalization suggests that English – which is the first language of capitalism – will enter the linguistic repertoire of all parts of the globe but will enter new relationships with local languages and cultures, and meet new forms of local resistance, which in turn will lead to a redefinition and shift in status of both English and local languages. In Chapter 5 David Graddol explores some of the conflicting trends in global English, from the early twentieth-century aspiration that English could become a universal language bringing peace and wealth to all nations, to the global restructuring of social and economic inequality that is being brought about by global economic trends, assisted by communications technology. It shows that globalization, whatever else it might be, is not about the creation of a uniform global culture and language.

The readings which accompany each chapter's main text have been chosen to exemplify key points made in the chapters, often by exploring related kinds of data, or comparing English texts in different parts of the world.

*Redesigning English: new texts, new identities* is designed for readers who have an interest in English, but who do not necessarily have any detailed knowledge of linguistics or other forms of language study. It can be read independently but it is also the last in a series of four books designed for an Open University undergraduate course: U210 *The English Language: past, present and future*. We occasionally refer readers to these books, as well as to *Describing Language* (Graddol et al., 1994), for further discussion of topics touched on here.

---

Features of each chapter include:

- *activities*: these provide guidance on the readings or suggestions for tasks to stimulate further understanding or analysis of the material;

- *boxed text*: boxes contain illustrative material or definitions or alternative viewpoints;

- *marginal notes*: these usually refer the reader to further discussion in other parts of the book, or to other books in the series, or to *Describing Language*; where necessary, they are also added to explain conventions used in the text;

- *key terms*: key terms in each chapter are set in bold type at the point where they are explained; the terms also appear in bold in the index so that they are easy to find in the chapters.

# TEXT, TIME AND TECHNOLOGY IN NEWS ENGLISH

*Allan Bell*

## 1.1  INTRODUCTION

This first chapter considers some of the ways in which the English language is used in international news. English has been extraordinarily important in the development and diffusion of news practices and news conventions, as the forms of modern journalism were largely developed in the English language. It was the rise of daily newspapers in English-speaking countries that helped define the nature of modern news and news stories. Still more strongly, it was the emergence of international news agencies, overwhelmingly in English, that both defined and disseminated these forms throughout the world. Stories from these agencies make up a large proportion of the content of most newspapers, and the agencies are leading purveyors of news and custodians of news style. The English language dominates the exchange of news around the world, particularly through the major international agencies such as Reuters and Associated Press. Translation into other languages is time-consuming and expensive. Although the agencies do a lot of translation, the need for this cuts news flows by at least half, according to Oliver Boyd-Barrett (1980). In short, if you do not have access to English, you miss out on most of the news disseminated throughout the world.

The chapter deals with the way the English language is used in news stories, mainly as they are published in daily newspapers. It looks especially at the discourse structure of news stories – that is, how the various language elements that make up a news text are put together. In particular, it focuses on time as one crucial dimension of the news story, and how this is expressed in news English, through different levels of language structure. The chapter examines how the time structure of news stories is different from time in other kinds of story. It looks at how shortness of time affects the way news stories are actually put together, and how news workers embed stretches of text from a wide range of sources to produce a story.

## 1.2  ENGLISH, NEWS AND TIME

The first and most far-reaching change to the means of news distribution – the telegraph – became widespread in the mid nineteenth century and combined with other developments such as the creation of international news agencies. The telegraph has been a crucial technological influence on news practices and forms, establishing the period in which news and news work assumed its modern pattern: a quest to get the story first, before one's competitors, and the use of a nonchronological format for writing stories. Technological developments in the pursuit of timeliness continue to impel news coverage towards 'present-ation' – that is, closing the gap between the event and its telling, with the goal of displaying events in 'real time'.

The pattern of news work operates to the rhythm of, usually, daily deadlines. On these are imposed shorter and longer cycles, with different hours of the day producing different mixes of news, and different days of the week producing differently defined news for publication or broadcast. In the western model that dominates world media, the basic cycle of news is a 24-hour one. Newspapers appear daily, and even broadcast media that transmit hourly bulletins also have flagship news programmes that serve as the main recapitulation of the previous 24 hours' news.

Time is a defining characteristic of the nature of news English. It is a major compulsion in news gathering, and has an influence on the structure of news discourse. The journalist's basic rubric of 'the facts' to be included in a story holds time as a primary element. *When* is high among the 'five Ws and an H' that journalists are taught to cover: who, what, when, where, why and how.

The news is one particular kind of story, and I approach it primarily in terms of the way news stories (particularly in the press) order the events they report. Time is a basic element of a story, and stories are arguably central to human experience. They come in many forms: romances, Westerns, fables, parables, gospels, legends, sagas. One feature of stories, however, appears to be so shared between cultures that it is practically a defining characteristic of what counts as a story: events tend to be told in the chronological order in which they occurred. Cognitive psychologists such as William Brewer, who study the ways in which people understand stories, make the distinction between event structure and discourse structure – that is, between the order in which events actually happened and the order in which they are told in a story (Brewer, 1985, p. 167). There is only one real-world event structure, but many possible discourse structures. Telling a story in chronological order is apparently the 'natural' way because it matches the discourse structure to the event structure.

A useful way to begin examining news stories is to look at the extent to which they differ from other kinds of story. To do this, I make some comparisons with the way people tell stories of their own personal experience in face-to-face conversation. Personal narratives have been studied in particular by the American sociolinguist William Labov (Labov and Waletzky, 1967, pp. 12–44; Labov, 1972), who has analysed the structure of personal narratives and separated them into six elements:

Labov's study of conversational narratives is also discussed in Chapter 1 of the second book in this series, *Using English: from conversation to canon* (Maybin and Mercer (eds), 1996).

1   The *abstract* summarizes the central action and main point of the narrative. A storyteller uses it at the outset to pre-empt the questions 'What is this story about? Why is it being told?'

2   The *orientation* sets the scene: it addresses the questions 'Who, when, what, where?', establishing the initial situation or activity of the story, and sometimes sketching out events before or alongside the main narrative events.

3   The *complicating action* is the central part of the story proper, answering the question 'Then what happened?'

4   The *evaluation* addresses the question 'So what?' Narrative has a point, and it is the narrator's prime intention to justify the value of the story he or she is telling, to demonstrate why these events are reportable.

5   The *resolution* – 'What finally happened?' – concludes the sequence of events and resolves the story.

6   Lastly, many narratives end with a *coda* – 'And that was that'. This is an additional remark or observation that bridges the gap between narrative time and real time, and returns the conversation to the present.

These six elements occur in the above order in personal narratives, although evaluation can be dispersed throughout the other elements. Only the action and some degree of evaluation are obligatory components of the personal narrative. By applying this framework, we can see the ways in which news differs from other stories. I will take as an example a typical story from an international news agency.

Figure 1.1 shows the text of a story from Reuters. The story originated in Peru, and is given here as it was published in New Zealand, in Wellington's *Evening Post* newspaper. The time structure of the story's events is listed in the column on the right. Time zero is the present tense of the story, which I define as the time of the lead event in the lead sentence: Higuchi's departure to hospital. Times prior to this are labelled Time –1 for the event immediately preceding, moving back up to Time –6 in this story, the earliest occurrence in the reported background. The story also reports on events subsequent to Time 0, labelled Time +1 (Higuchi's diagnosis), and so on.

| *Sentence number* | | *Time structure* |
|---|---|---|
| | **Protest cut short** | |
| S1 | LIMA, Jan 18. – The estranged wife of Peru's President Alberto Fujimori was taken to | 0 |
| | hospital today just 24 hours after she began a | –2 |
| | hunger strike to protest at her party's | |
| | elimination from congressional elections. | –3 |
| S2 | Doctors said she was suffering from | +1 |
| | tachycardia, or an accelerated heartbeat. | |
| S3 | Earlier, [deposed first lady Susanna] Higuchi, | –1 |
| | sitting under an umbrella in a scorching | |
| | summer sun outside the National Electoral | |
| | Board's headquarters, had pledged to press on | |
| | with her protest. | |
| S4 | The electoral board said on Monday Higuchi's | –3 |
| | Armonia-Frempol party had not qualified | |
| | for the April Congressional vote because it | +2 |
| | failed to present a full list of candidates for | –4 |
| | the 120-member legislature. | |
| S5 | Board member Manuel Catacora said today | 0 |
| | that since Higuchi had presented her party's | –4 |
| | congressional slate just 10 minutes before the | |
| | filing deadline, a provision allowing parties five | 0 |
| | days to correct any error did not apply. | |
| S6 | Higuchi, a 44-year-old civil engineer, has been | –5 |
| | estranged from Fujimori since August when | |
| | she protested an election law that banned her | –6 |
| | from running from [*sic*] public office. – Reuter | |

*Figure 1.1   International news agency story as published in the* Evening Post, Wellington, *20 January 1995. (The text in square brackets in S3 is taken from the caption to the photograph published with the text of the story)*

## Abstract

The first sentence of a news story – known as the 'lead' or 'intro' – functions as its abstract. It summarizes the central action and establishes the point of the story. The story in Figure 1.1 has a triple abstract. The lead sentence covers a sequence of three events, but in reverse chronological order. The result (Higuchi's departure to hospital) precedes the cause (her hunger strike), which itself precedes the prior cause (her party's disqualification from the elections). Double abstracts are frequent in news stories, and triple abstracts are not uncommon in the drive to pack maximum news impact into the lead sentence. They are typically linked by time expressions, usually *after* for a sequence (as in Figure 1.1) and *as* for simultaneous events. These time expressions commonly imply a cause-and-effect link. In S1 of Figure 1.1, this link is obviously justified – Higuchi's hunger strike is the cause of her hospitalization. In other stories, however, the causation implied through the use of *as* or *after* does not always seem warranted.

In press news, there is also the headline – an abstract of the abstract. The lead sentence is the journalist's primary abstract of a story, although to the reader the headline appears as the first abstract. The headline is in fact a last-minute insertion, written by a sub-editor rather than the journalist. Time is virtually never expressed in headlines, so it is not surprising to find no time expression in *Protest cut short* in Figure 1.1.

## Orientation

For journalists, the basic facts are: who, what, when and where; they are given in concentrated form at the beginning of a story, but may be expanded further down. Where other kinds of story routinely take time out at the beginning to set the scene, describing the characters and the setting, news stories present their orientation while they are already telling the story events.

In Figure 1.1, time zero is explicitly identified in the lead sentence, with other earlier or later time points specified in later sentences (see Table 1.1). Some time

**Table 1.1**
Time expressions in the story in Figure 1.1

| Sentence | Story time | Time expression |
|---|---|---|
| Dateline | 0 | Jan 18 |
| S1 | 0 | today |
|  | 0 | just 24 hours after … |
|  | −2 | … she began a hunger strike |
| S3 | −1 | earlier |
| S4 | −3 | on Monday |
|  | +2 | April |
| S5 | 0 | today |
|  | −4 | just 10 minutes before the filing deadline |
| S6 | −5 | since August when she protested … |
|  | −6 | … an election law that banned her |

references in news stories situate events in calendar time, by reference for example to a particular day or month: *on Monday* or *since August*. Others place events in relation to each other, such as *just 24 hours after she began a hunger strike* in S1 and *just 10 minutes before the filing deadline* in S5. Still others are **deictic** – that is, they refer to time in its relation to the present, such as *today* or *yesterday*. International agency stories such as that in Figure 1.1 are 'datelined' at the top for place and time or origin. So *LIMA, Jan 18* specifies the calendar time at which the story was reported, and the deictic *today* in the lead sentence locates the present time of the story at that same point of calendar time. Deictics take their meaning from the viewpoint of the speaker who uses them. It is noticeable that *today* in this story (and of course in many other international news items) has a different meaning for the journalist who wrote the story than for the story's readers in New Zealand. *Today* refers to 18 January, when the story was written, but the story was published in New Zealand two days later on 20 January (although because New Zealand time is 18 hours ahead of Peru, the events are in fact little over a day old). Because of the difference between time of writing and time of reception, a deictic like *today* can really only be used in the first sentence of a story near the specification of the date to which it refers. If it were further down the story, the reader would be confused as to whether it referred to time of writing (18 January) or time of publication (20 January).

**Deixis** refers to language features that anchor statements in relation to space (e.g. *here, there*) or time (e.g. *now, then*) relative to the speaker's viewpoint (see Wales, 1989, pp. 112–13).

❖   ❖   ❖   ❖   ❖

**Activity 1.1**   *(Allow 40 minutes)*

Choose a short news story (up to ten sentences long) from an English language newspaper you are familiar with. Identify and list the time expressions it contains in the way shown in Table 1.1. Try to establish the chronological order of the events in the story.

❖   ❖   ❖   ❖   ❖

## Action

At the heart of a narrative is the chain of events that occurred: the action. This is always told in chronological order. (See Labov's definition of narrative below.)

### Labov's definition of narrative

We define narrative as one method of recapitulating past experience by matching a verbal sequence of clauses to the sequence of events which (it is inferred) actually occurred. For example, a pre-adolescent narrative:

1  a   This boy punched me
   b   and I punched him
   c   and the teacher came in
   d   and stopped the fight.

An adult narrative:

2   a   Well this person had a little too much to drink
    b   and he attacked me
    c   and the friend came in
    d   and she stopped it.

In each case we have four independent clauses which match the order of the inferred events. It is important to note that other means of recapitulating these experiences are available which do not follow the same sequence; syntactic embedding can be used:

3   a   A friend of mine came in just
        in time to stop
        this person who had a little too much to drink
        from attacking me.

Or else the past perfect can be used to reverse the order:

4   a   The teacher stopped the fight.
    b   She had just come in.
    c   I had punched this boy.
    d   He had punched me.

Narrative, then, is only one way of recapitulating this past experience: the clauses are characteristically ordered in temporal sequence; if narrative clauses are reversed, the inferred temporal sequence of the original semantic interpretation is altered: *I punched this boy/and he punched me* instead of *This boy punched me/and I punched him.*

   With this conception of narrative, we can define a *minimal narrative* as a sequence of two clauses which are *temporally ordered*: that is, a change in their order will result in a change in the temporal sequence of the original semantic interpretation. In alternative terminology, there is temporal juncture between the two clauses, and a minimal narrative is defined as one containing a single temporal juncture.

   The skeleton of a narrative then consists of a series of temporally ordered clauses which we may call *narrative clauses*. A narrative such as 1 or 2 consists entirely of narrative clauses. Here is a minimal narrative which contains only two:

5   a   I know a boy named Harry.
    b   Another boy threw a bottle at him right in the head
    c   and he had to get seven stitches.

This narrative contains three clauses, but only two are narrative clauses. The first has no temporal juncture, and might be placed after *b* or after *c* without disturbing temporal order. It is equally true at the end and at the beginning that the narrator knows a boy named Harry. Clause *a* may be called a *free clause* since it is not confined by any temporal juncture.

(Labov, 1972, pp. 359–61)

Labov found that a defining characteristic of personal narrative as a form is the temporal sequence of its clauses. That is, the action is invariably told in the order in which it happened – 'matching a verbal sequence of clauses to the sequence of events' (Labov, 1972, pp. 359–60). Telling it in a different order would mean that it had happened in a different order.

News stories, by contrast, are seldom if ever told in chronological order. The time structure of the story in Figure 1.1 is very complex, with nine points in time identified in the analysis. The story as a whole divides into three sections: S1–2, S3–5 and S6. The lead sentence alone covers three events and times, as we have seen. Each of the three sections represents a cycle through events taking us further back in time, presenting in reverse order of actual occurrence (plus a couple of excursions into the story's future time) the chain of events that have culminated in the lead event of this story. The earliest events are reported last of all, with the final sentence describing events from some six months earlier, which are the antecedents to the present occurrences. The chronological order of events in Figure 1.1 is shown in Table 1.2. The glance forward to the future end-point of this process – the elections in April – is a completely standard representation of the ongoing nature of most news stories. So also is the official pronouncement (S2 Time +1) following the lead event, in this case the doctors' diagnosis.

**Table 1.2**
Chronology of events in the story in Figure 1.1

| Story time | Calendar time | Action |
| --- | --- | --- |
| −6 | Before August 1994 | The law bans Higuchi from the elections |
| −5 | August 1994 | Her protest estranges her from Fujimori |
| −4 | Before Monday 16 January 1995 | Her party files an incomplete candidate list |
| −3 | Monday 16 January | Her party is disqualified from the elections |
| −2 | Tuesday 17 January | Higuchi begins a hunger strike |
| −1 | Wednesday 18 January | She pledges to continue her protest |
| 0 | Wednesday 18 January | She is taken to hospital |
| +1 | Wednesday 18 January | Doctors diagnose her condition |
|  | [Friday 20 January | Publication date in New Zealand] |
| +2 | April 1995 | Date of upcoming elections |

❖ ❖ ❖ ❖ ❖

**Activity 1.2**   *(Allow 30 minutes)*

Analyse the time structure of the story you used for Activity 1.1 and list its events in chronological order in the way shown in Table 1.2. You may find that having to be explicit about the events and their ordering changes some of the chronology you outlined in Activity 1.1.

❖ ❖ ❖ ❖ ❖

## Evaluation, resolution and coda

Evaluation is the means by which the significance of a story is established. In personal narrative, evaluation is what distinguishes a directionless sequence of clauses from a story with a point and a meaning. In the case of the fight stories studied by Labov, the point is often the self-aggrandizement of the narrator. Evaluation pre-empts the question 'So what?' It gives the reason why the narrator is claiming the floor and the audience's attention.

News stories also require evaluation, and its function in them is identical to that in personal narrative: to establish the significance of what is being told, to focus the events and to justify claiming the audience's attention. Like all news stories, that in Figure 1.1 stresses repeatedly the importance of what has happened, particularly in the lead sentence with its vocabulary of news value: *estranged, President, taken to hospital, just 24 hours after, hunger strike, protest, elimination, elections.* The lead sentence is a nucleus of news evaluation, because the function of the lead is not merely to summarize the main action. The lead focuses the story in a particular direction. It forms the lens through which the remainder of the story is viewed.

Most kinds of story move to a resolution: the fight is won, the accident survived. News stories often do not present such clear-cut results (although journalists prefer the conclusiveness that a result offers). When they do, as noted above, the result will be in the lead rather than at the end of the story. In this example, the nearest thing to a resolution is Higuchi's departure to hospital. But this of course is only the latest step in a continuing saga: the news is more like a serial than a short story. While the beginning of a news story is everything, the ending is nothing. This is a challenge to the 'storyness' of news, because we expect stories in general to end at the end. Brewer (1985) found that narrative sequences that lacked an outcome were not even classed as stories by his (US) informants.

Nor is there a coda to the news story. In personal narrative, the coda serves as an optional marker of the story's finish, returning the floor to other conversational partners, and returning the tense from narrative time to the present. None of these functions is necessary in the news, where the floor is not open, and where the next contribution is another story.

## The way it was

Labov's analyses show that in personal narrative if you change the order of narrative clauses, you change the order of events. In news English, order is everything but chronology is nothing. As news consumers we are so accustomed to this approach that we forget how deviant it is compared both with other kinds of narrative and with earlier norms of news reporting. Research on news narrative styles by the US sociologist Michael Schudson shows that the nonchronological format developed in American journalism in the late nineteenth century. Stories of the 1880s covering presidential State of the Union addresses did not summarize the key points at the beginning, but by 1910 the lead as summary was standard (Schudson, 1989).

The extract below is part of a story from the *New Zealand Herald* of 11 June 1886. It reports the eruption of Mount Tarawera, a volcano located near Rotorua, some 200 km to the south-east of Auckland. The eruption caused considerable loss of life and reshaped an extensive area of the New Zealand landscape. This is a typical disaster story (albeit closer to its readers than most), which might be found in any newspaper around the world today. But here it is narrated in absolute chronological order.

**June 11, 1886**

At an early hour on Thursday morning a noise as of the firing of cannon was heard by many Auckland residents.

From the continuousness of the firing, the loudness of the reports, and the apparent occasional sound resembling salvoes of artillery, many people both here and at Onehunga were under the impression that a man-of-war, probably the Russian Vestnik, had run ashore on the Manukau bar and that these were her signals of distress.

Vivid flashes, as from the firing of guns, were also seen both at Onehunga and also from the cupola of the Herald Office, which served to almost confirm the impression that there had been a marine disaster. At about 8.30 a.m., however, it began to be circulated about town that a catastrophe, far surpassing in horror even the most terrible of shipwrecks, had taken place.

The first news was, through the courtesy of Mr Furby, the officer in charge of the telegraph department, issued by us in an extra and consisted of the following message, sent from Rotorua, by Mr Dansey, the telegraphist there, who manfully and bravely "stuck to his instrument" in the face of the most dreadful danger:

"We have all passed a fearful night here. At 2.10 a.m. there was a heavy quake, then a fearful roar, which made everyone run out of their houses, and a grand, yet terrible, sight for those so near as we were, presented itself. Mount Tarawera suddenly became active, the volcano belching out fire and lava to a great height. A dense mass of ashes came pouring down here at 4 a.m., accompanied by a suffocating smell from the lower regions.

"Several families left their homes in their nightdresses with whatever they could seize in the hurry, and made for Tauranga. Others more lucky, got horses and left for Oxford."

The historical story begins at the beginning and proceeds with a straight chronological narrative. Its lead sentence describes the first sounds of the eruption as heard by people living in Auckland, where the *Herald* is published. By contrast, the modern news lead sentence on such a story would run something like this: 'Mount Tarawera erupted last night sending residents fleeing …'.

**Activity 1.3**   *(Allow 30 minutes)*

Rewrite the nineteenth-century story above in the order and style in which a modern journalist would write it.

**Comment**

The orientation of the Tarawera story to its readers' fragmentary experience of a distant news event is quite remarkable to the modern reader. Instead of going straight to telling what has happened at Tarawera, the story narrates how Aucklanders experienced the signs of the eruption – the sound and sight of explosions – and how they interpreted these phenomena. We learn of the actual cause only, so to speak, when the news arrives in town. This contrasts with the anchoring of the Higuchi story in the time and place where it happened and was reported, rather than where it was to be read. The assumption that all the readers of this nineteenth-century story are in a limited geographical area is not one that can be made for any news story nowadays. The direct quotation from the telegraph report in the fifth and sixth paragraphs is, however, anchored at the point of origin through the place deictic *here: We have all passed a fearful night here.* The technology of the telegraph began to redefine time and place in the news by its rapid provision of information from distant places.

❖   ❖   ❖   ❖   ❖

## 1.3   DISCOURSE STRUCTURE OF NEWS ENGLISH

By analysing the structure of news stories compared with that of other stories, we can see that the most striking characteristic of news discourse is the nonchrono-logical order of its elements. The Dutch discourse analyst Teun van Dijk has called this the instalment method (1988b, p. 43), by which an event is introduced, then returned to in more detail two or more times. We can see this pattern in the way the story in Figure 1.1 introduces Higuchi's disqualification from the elections in the lead sentence (Time –3) and expands on it in S4.

The radical discontinuity of time between sentences imparts a general lack of cohesion to the news story. This is typified by the fact that each news sentence is usually also its own paragraph, so there is no larger unit of text organization. As in Figure 1.1, there is routinely no flow of time sequence from one sentence to the next, and a lack of devices such as adverbs to express linkages between sentences. The news story jumps from one statement to the next, offering somewhat isolated chunks of information in each sentence.

In many kinds of writing it is common to link one sentence to another with time adverbs such as *then*, or markers of cause and effect like *therefore*, or conjunctions such as *however* or *and*. Words such as these mark the cohesion of a text. They serve to flag continuity from one sentence to the next and help the reader to understand the development of the narrative or argument. News stories usually lack these signposts, so that cohesion between sentences is unclear or non-existent. It may be genuinely in doubt what events within the story belong together (as for S3), at what point location actually shifted, or what material is attributed to whom. The lack of cohesion is accompanied by a lack of resolution at the end of the story, as I have already noted.

Time is not the only dimension that structures news stories in English; I briefly describe here a more general framework for analysing the discourse structure of news, using an approach adapted and expanded (Bell, 1991) from van Dijk (e.g. 1988b). A news story normally consists of an abstract, an attribution and the story proper (Figure 1.2).

- The abstract consists of the lead sentence of the news story and, for press news, also a headline (as in Figure 1.1). The lead covers the main event, and possibly one or more secondary events. This necessarily entails giving some information on actors and setting involved in the event.

- The attribution – where the story came from – is not always explicit. It can include a credit to a news agency (for example to Reuters news agency at the end of S6 in Figure 1.1) and/or a journalist's byline. It may also state place and time, as the dateline *LIMA, Jan 18* does in that story.

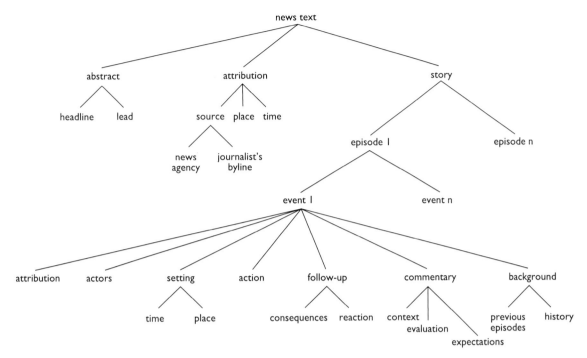

*Figure 1.2   Outline model discourse structure of a news text*
(Bell, 1991, p. 171)

- Episodes and events: the body of the story itself consists of one or more events. Related events may be grouped together and treated as a more general episode.

- Events must describe the actors involved and the action that takes place. They also usually express the setting (time and place), and may have an explicit attribution.

As well as the above elements, which present the central occurrences, there are three additional categories of material in a news story: background, commentary and follow-up. These represent the past, the (non-action) present and the future of the events described in the main action of the story and are all exemplified in Figure 1.1.

The category of background covers any events prior to the current action – the story's past time. These are frequently previous events that probably figured as news stories in their own right at an earlier stage of the situation, as undoubtedly did the background from August 1994 given in S6 of Figure 1.1. If the background goes back beyond the near past, it is classed as 'history'.

Commentary provides the journalist's or news actor's observations on the action in the present time period; it is an assessment of and a comment on events as they happen (rather than the actual narration of the events themselves, or other parties' verbal reaction to them). In Figure 1.1 it is represented by the electoral board's evaluation of why Higuchi's party was disqualified (S4–5).

Follow-up covers the story's future time – any action subsequent to the main action of an event. It can include verbal reaction by other parties or nonverbal consequences – for example, the doctors' diagnosis (S2) and possibly the elections to be held in April (S4). Because it covers action that occurred after what a story has treated as the main action, follow-up is a prime source of subsequent updating stories – which are themselves called 'follows' by journalists.

**Activity 1.4**   *(Allow 20 minutes)*

Choose a longer story from an English language newspaper (about 15–25 sentences long). Can you identify examples of background, commentary or follow-up in this story? Describe how they relate to the main events. Do you think the background represents the main point of a previously published story? If so, write a lead sentence that might have been used on that earlier story.

The structures of news stories also seem to be quite standardized in cultures other than Anglo-American ones, and in languages other than English. Van Dijk's (1988a) analysis of newspaper stories in many languages found few significant differences in news values or structure. In a comparison between different treatments of the assassination of Lebanese President-elect Gemayel in 1975, he found that stories in Spanish, Chinese and Swedish all followed a similar pattern to English language news. There were some differences between newspapers in the first and third worlds. The greatest differences, however, were between 'quality' and 'popular' papers, for instance within West Germany and the UK. The popular *Bild Zeitung* (literally 'picture paper') used a more chronological news order for dramatic effect. The similarities are clearly in part or in whole due to the domination of English language models of news stories, and global patterning on western (particularly Anglo-American) models.

## 1.4   TIME IN NEWS WORK

I have discussed the nonchronological order of news stories, and the discourse structures that they follow, and pointed out that news was not always written like this. That raises an obvious question: why are modern news stories written with this deviant time structure? Why are they written in an order that both research and intuition indicate is harder to understand, when one of the main features of a news story is supposed to be that it is easily understandable? The answer lies in a combination of journalistic values, journalistic practices and technological developments, and I now turn to look briefly at these factors.

### News values

The values of the media control the way in which news is presented. We can account for the way news stories are structured only with reference to the values by which one 'fact' is judged more newsworthy than another. The foundation study of news values was undertaken by the Scandinavian media researchers Galtung and Ruge (1965), and their categories have been found to be valid and enlightening for a wide range of news types in many countries. I adapted and added to their categories in Bell (1991), distinguishing between content-related and process-related values. Time is important in a number of them.

Recency or immediacy means that the best news is something that has only just happened. Recency is related to the concept of frequency – how well a story conforms to news work cycles, how close something falls to an achievable deadline. Events whose duration or occurrence fits – or can be made to fit – into a 24-hour span are more likely to be reported than other events. So the murder is more newsworthy than the police investigation, the verdict more than the trial.

Unexpectedness, however, means that the unpredictable or the rare is more newsworthy than the routine. It is the reverse of frequency, which attempts to tame the rhythm of events to fit the cycle of media deadlines. Closely related to unexpectedness is novelty. 'New' is a key word in advertising, and novelty is one of the main factors in selecting what is newsworthy.

**Activity 1.5**   *(Reading A)*

Read extract 1 from 'When? Deadlines, datelines, and history' by Michael Schudson (Reading A). Schudson gives examples of how news values affect the reporting of events, and of how journalists attempt to cope with stories in which the outcome is unclear.

Schudson notes that the best news has an ending that can be anticipated, and that journalists like to be able to identify where they are in a story – at the beginning, the middle or the end. This is closely linked to the issue of journalistic cycles.

## Deadlines and cycles

To say that immediacy, novelty and other time-related concepts are news values is not, however, a sufficient explanation of their importance in news and news work. Why is time such a dominating news value? To shed light on this issue we need to look at the practices of news work, the processes by which news is produced, rather than the content of the news text. In section 1.5 I detail some of the processes by which news workers create a story, and the sources they draw on. First, I identify several news values that relate to the production and processing of news rather than to its content. They all have a time element – either present (co-) or future (pre-) time. Among the most important are: continuity, competition, predictability and prefabrication.

Continuity means that once something is in the news, it tends to stay there. Stories have a life cycle, a time period during which they can stay alive in the news. Politicians and other would-be news makers know well that news breeds news. Once one news outlet has a good story, all its competitors want it too.

Competition is the urge to be first with the news. Every news outlet wants a first, an exclusive, or at least wants not to miss out on the stories that other media have. There is a paradox here between the desire of the media to get a scoop, and their desire to cover what other media are covering – continuity.

Read extract 2 from 'When? Deadlines, datelines, and history' (Reading B),
Schudson's account of the newsroom's obsession with the scoop.

The drive to get the news first – by a few minutes or even a few seconds – is
embedded deep in the news ethos. Getting it first is a reason for self-
congratulation, and being scooped a cause for mourning. Yet the rush of the
deadline is largely self-inflicted. It is a fetish of the profession, as the sociologist
Philip Schlesinger shows in his participant observation study of news practices in
the BBC (Schlesinger, 1987). There is no evidence that the audience really
expects such timeliness, but news workers expect it of themselves and expect to be
evaluated by it. As Schudson says in Reading B, the audience couldn't care less
who gets the scoop.

   Predictability is important for news operations, because it enables the planning of future work time. An event is more likely to be covered if it can be
prescheduled for journalists than if it turns up unheralded. The canny news
maker uses this knowledge to schedule the timing of an event according to news
deadlines. Paradoxically, the predictable nature of much news gathering is in
contrast to the high value placed on news as the unexpected.

   Finally, there is the factor of prefabrication – the pre-existence of ready-made
text such as press releases, speech notes, reports and, particularly, earlier news
stories on a topic. Journalists can take these over to process them rapidly into a
story. The more closely these prefabricated texts conform to news style, the more
likely it is that they will appear in the news. I look in more detail below at how
journalists use prefabricated text to make new stories. In the visual channel, the
existence of high-value news footage of an otherwise low-rating story can take it on
to the television news.

   Time dominates news work in a way it does few other professions: the product
must be ready by a set time or it is useless. The restaurant business comes to mind
as a parallel, for meals must be ready on time as well as good to eat. Schlesinger's
study rightly characterizes news work as 'a stop-watch culture' (1987, p. 83). All
newsrooms are the same in this respect. They operate against the clock, measur-
ing daily achievement by the ability to produce a required number of stories for
the deadline. The stimulus of the deadline helps compensate for the humdrum
nature of most news work, but deadlines also encourage high productivity, the
maximum number of stories being produced in the minimum time. Journalistic
deadlines are genuinely terminal. The paper must be put to bed, or the bulletin
broadcast at a certain time. The would-be journalist who cannot meet deadlines is
as unemployable as the chef who takes all evening to cook one meal.

## 1.5   PRODUCING NEWS ENGLISH

Having examined some of the features of English language news texts, I now turn
to look at how 'news English' is produced. The process by which news is generated
has an effect on the nature of the product. News English is production-line
language: it is a response to the demand for productivity against the clock, and the
outcome of the involvement of a chain of news workers who handle the news text
as it moves along that production line.

The news is seldom a solo performance. News media offer the classic case of language produced by multiple parties. Journalists, editors, printers, newsreaders, sound technicians and camera operators are just some of the people who can directly influence the form of news discourse. Scholars in a number of communication-related fields, particularly the sociologist Erving Goffman (1981), have taken an interest in the different roles that people may take in producing composite discourse such as news. The composite nature of news stories is a very explicit example of what the soviet literary theorist Mikhail Bakhtin (1981) has called **heteroglossia** – the mixing of many voices – to which we will return in a moment.

## Authoring

The 'author' is the main character involved in producing discourse. All news production focuses on an individual journalist writing stories. I distinguish this originating, usually sole, author of a text from 'editors' – those numerous others who operate on what an author has drafted, whether or not they have 'editor' as part of their job title. Authorship is seldom genuinely shared. However, describing the journalist as the originating author of a story is an extreme idealization. After all, the basic stuff of news is what people tell a reporter. Much of what a reporter writes is therefore paraphrased or quoted from somebody else's words. That much is obvious, but journalists draw on written as well as spoken sources. Very few stories consist entirely of wording newly generated by journalists from their own observations or verbal interviews. Much news comprises updates and rewrites of previous stories. In some media the basic news-gathering practice is the following up of stories that were 'diaried ahead' (noted for a follow-up story) the last time they were covered. In addition, many stories contain material selected and reworked from documents generated by news makers or other media. Journalists draw on both spoken and written inputs for their stories. My own analyses and experience yield the following classification of input sources:

- interviews, either face to face or by telephone;
- public addresses;
- press conferences;
- written text of spoken addresses;
- organizationally produced documents of many kinds: reports, surveys, letters, findings, agendas, minutes, proceedings, research papers, etc.;
- press releases;
- earlier stories on a topic, either from the journalist's own newspaper or from other media;
- news agency copy;
- the journalist's notes from all the above inputs, especially the spoken ones.

The journalist's main spoken source is the interview (and notes taken from it), and most interviews are conducted over the telephone rather than face to face. Secondary sources are public addresses of all kinds, and press conferences, which are a combination of both address and interview. Some stories are entirely cut-and-paste jobs from such sources.

## Editing

The processing of news involves the complex and rapid movement of copy (the actual text of the news story) between individuals within a newsroom. Even in a small newsroom, stories are handled by perhaps four different individuals, and may follow a complex and often cyclical route: from the chief reporter who assigns the story, to the journalist, to the sub-editor, back to the chief reporter, to the newspaper editor, and back to the sub-editor again. The role of editors is crucial because of the number of them who handle a journalist's story. On a standard, medium-sized daily newspaper, a journalist's story may pass through the hands of up to eight news workers, each making alterations and producing a new version.

While copy movement within a newsroom may seem complex enough, most news in fact weaves a much more intricate path to its consumers. News media publish more copy that has been generated by other, external, news agencies than by their own in-house journalists. The average international news item published anywhere in the world has probably been through at least four separate news-rooms. At each stage, copy is received, put through the newsroom's editing process and transmitted to the next receiver, where the cycle is repeated.

## Heteroglossia in news English

Bakhtin viewed texts and utterances as being made up of multiple 'voices' from all kinds of genres, styles and dialects within a language. His concept of **heteroglossia** was developed in particular through his study of the many styles of voice used in the novel (Bakhtin, 1981). The term covers everything from the explicit, sourced quotation of others' voices within a text or speech, to the subtle hints of their origins that words continue to carry with them, which flavour the utterances in which they are used. Bakhtin examines the variety of voices that are drawn on in the nineteenth-century comic novel, and the ways in which they are incorporated in the novelist's text. But he also argues more widely that 'at any given moment of its historical existence, language is heteroglot from top to bottom' (1981, p. 291). The social history of a word remains present even when the word is spoken in a context very different from previous ones. The diversity of voices might be concealed below the surface of a discourse, or be more openly drawn upon, as in Charles Dickens's parodies of the speech modes associated with official, commer-cial, ceremonial and other spheres. Bakhtin (1981, p. 303) cites as an example the 'parodic stylization of the language of ceremonial speeches (in parliaments and at banquets)'. This passage is from Dickens's *Little Dorrit*:

> Mr. Merdle came home, from his daily occupation of causing the British name to be more and more respected in all parts of the civilised globe, capable of the appreciation of world-wide commercial enterprise and gigantic combinations of skill and capital.
> (Dickens, [1855–7] 1979, p. 386)

Here the use of elevated vocabulary and expressions such as *the British name* and *all parts of the civilised globe* flag this as drawing on a ceremonial speech-making style.

News text provides a clear illustration of Bakhtin's concept of heteroglossia. Inputs to the finished text can range from overt and acknowledged direct quotation, to the subtle, unacknowledged use of wording from a bureaucratic document. When journalists reproduce unacknowledged wording from bureau-cratic reports or meeting agendas, they carry into the news text the taste of

Bakhtin's work is also discussed in the second book in this series, *Using English: from conversation to canon* (Maybin and Mercer (eds), 1996).

those original contexts just as surely as when they quote sources openly. The journalist, therefore, is as much a compiler as a creator of language, and much news English consists of previously composed text reworked into new texts.

This is, of course, a main means by which journalists meet the productivity demands of their employer. A standard quota of stories ranges between four and ten per day. Generating that amount of fresh text is impossible, so the generous adoption of old text is required. The usually smooth, unified surface of most news stories thus conceals a variety of origins. But the individual journalist remains the main channel via which diverse sources converge into a single flow of copy. Editors hold journalists responsible for wording that they reuse, as well as wording that they generate themselves. A journalist sanctions the language culled from other sources simply by adopting it.

## Embedding in the news text

The way in which journalists insert into their stories text that already exists is only one example of a basic feature of media communication, which I label **embedding**. Embedding is a type of heteroglossia in which one speech event is incorporated into another. This happens most obviously in broadcasting, where recording technology enables actual strips of a news maker's speech to be embedded into a newscaster's or reporter's script instead of being quoted at second hand.

The concept of embedding draws on Erving Goffman's notion of 'footing' (1981) – that is, a speaker's alignment to what he or she is saying. Even in everyday conversation, speakers are constantly quoting other speakers or representing other voices. In so doing, they take a different alignment to what the represented speakers say than they do to their own self-generated words. They embed words from these other speakers in their own talk, but they may not fully own the opinions expressed in such embedded statements. Indeed, they may embed another's statement specifically to disown its sentiments. Goffman's book *Forms of Talk* is concerned in large measure with the embedding of one kind of utterance within another. He writes: 'a speaker can quote himself or another directly or indirectly, thereby setting into an utterance with one production format another utterance with its own production format, albeit now merely an embedded one' (Goffman, 1981, p. 227). Narrators of all kinds of story are constantly embedding strips of others' talk and quotations from others' speech into their stories. The narrative structures of novels as analysed by literary theorists are obvious sites of embedding.

So far I have described the production of news language as taking place in a linear fashion, with news copy being passed from one news worker to the next along the assembly line. However, we can view the process in another way: as layered in the vertical dimension rather than segmented horizontally. From this point of view we can regard all earlier versions of a story as embedded within the final text. Each successive handling of the copy produces a potentially different text, which is input to the next stage of the process. Each layer implies not just the text and its content but the full speech event that generated it. The speech event includes the participant sender and receiver, and the time and place it occurred.

The many layers of editing are not generally evident in final news copy, since editors aim to produce a unified text that conceals their intervention. But the final text may bear detectable traces of the embedded texts from which it came. For example, copy generated by an international news agency may express a distance in miles, with an exact conversion to kilometres given in parentheses. Recipient sub-editors in a country that uses metric units may use only the converted value and describe a place as being '129 kilometres west of London'. Such exactitude reads strangely. It is explicable as the conversion of '80 miles' to a precise metric equivalent. Since '80' in the original copy was assuredly a rounded number in the first place, an approximation (130 km) would read more naturally in the metric conversion.

The concept of embedding is extraordinarily important for understanding the language of news discourse. Journalists are rarely on the spot for unscheduled news events, so other people's accounts are the journalists' stock-in-trade for reporting events. Further, news is what people say more than what they do. Much – perhaps most – of what journalists report is talk not action: announcements, opinions, reactions, appeals, promises, criticisms. Most news copy is therefore reported speech – although it may not be overtly attributed as such.

**Activity 1.7**   *(Allow 20 minutes)*

For one of the stories you selected in a previous activity, try to identify the sources of information that have an explicit attribution (e.g. people quoted). Identify the parts of the story that seem to come from each of these sources. Is all the information in the story credited to a particular source? Where do you think the information that is not obviously attributed to a specific source has come from?

## Prefabricated text

Although talking to news makers forms a major part of reporting the news, documents play a large part, too. The documentary inputs are of two main kinds: those already written in the style of news, and those not written in the style of news. The second group consists mainly of official documents of some sort: reports, agendas, judgements and the like.

Journalists favour written sources that are already prefabricated in an appropriate news style and that therefore require the minimum of reworking. These come in three kinds: news agency copy, press releases and earlier stories on the same topic. News agencies provide most of the copy on any newspaper. Most agency stories will be run almost verbatim, but some will be assigned to a journalist to find a new or local angle using the agency story as a basis. The press release was invented in the USA at the beginning of the twentieth century. Now it is a staple of journalism, openly despised but heavily used by news workers, and providing the basis of a high proportion of published news stories. Still more highly favoured are earlier stories on the same topic. These may be from the journalist's own newspaper, but often come from other media. News media feed voraciously on each other's stories. While always trying to find something new to update and begin the story, an evening newspaper will often reproduce the bulk of a story published by its morning competitor. Text from a continuing story may come round again and again in a format that has changed little.

Pre-existing text can play an important role in news workers' judgements about what is news. Texts that are already cast in news format and style stand a much better chance of selection than texts that are not appropriately packaged.

Having worked as an organizational press officer, I have often seen journalists ignore a suggestion about a story that they might follow up themselves. They will, however, reproduce the story faithfully when it is supplied as a ready-made press release a week or two later.

The three kinds of pre-packaged news distinguished above have a head start on other news inputs. A story that is marginal in news terms but that is already written and available may be selected ahead of a much more newsworthy story that has to be researched and written from the beginning. So the usability of press releases gives the advantage to those potential news makers who can afford to pay someone to write for them – generally official and commercial entities. In addition, the use of earlier news copy embedded into updated stories favours publication of something that has already been in the news – that is, continuity, in terms of the news values outlined earlier.

## How journalists use sources

Apart from stories published verbatim from press releases or agency copy, most stories are, then, based on more than one input. Covering a speech by a government minister is a frequent news-gathering routine. In constructing a story from the speech the journalist will draw on sources such as:

- the written text of the minister's prepared speech;
- (the journalist's notes of) the minister's speech as actually delivered, which may diverge anywhere between 0 and 100 per cent from the prepared speech;
- a press release containing those points of the speech the minister wants reported;
- an interview after the speech with the minister.

To these four main sources may be added advance written briefing materials, prior verbal indications from the minister's press secretary on the content of the speech, an official report released at the time of the speech, subsequent telephone calls to interested groups for comment on the minister's statement, and so on. The situation is further complicated because most source documents are themselves composite productions, with text from earlier documents embedded within them.

A record of an interview or spoken address is kept by the journalist. The record may be verbatim in the form of a tape recording, a selective but more or less verbatim shorthand transcript, or highly selective longhand notes. This material may appear in a story in the form of direct quotation, indirect quotation, or unattributed information. It may be paraphrased or summarized. Direct quotation – that is, text that is enclosed between quotation marks – is supposed to be verbatim. Much that appears in the form of indirect quotation is paraphrased, and much unattributed information draws heavily on what a news maker has said. Written documents may similarly be used either for quotation or to provide background information.

Researching how journalists work and what inputs they use is not easy: getting access to the material is an obvious problem. I have been able to take advantage of records of my own work as a journalist. In one fairly ordinary story I wrote, concerning the introduction of the gorse mite into New Zealand to control gorse,

I found I had dealt with two main persons as sources, a scientist and his research group leader, and used no fewer than eight inputs:

1    Notes from a brief preliminary face-to-face interview with the leader of the group of scientists who had been researching the introduction of the mite.

2    Notes from a later telephone interview with the same group leader.

3    The 350-page Environmental Impact Assessment on the effects of introducing the gorse mite. This is itself a highly composite document, drawing heavily on earlier reports. In particular it stresses that three previous impact assessment documents 'should be consulted before reading this EIA' – and it embeds these as appendices.

4    A draft press release written by the main scientist involved in doing the work.

5    A covering letter from this scientist, which accompanied the press release.

6    A copy of a press release (and published clips) issued the previous year at an earlier stage of the assessment.

7    Notes from my telephone interview with the scientist (and follow-up questions in subsequent phone calls).

8    Amendments to my draft story made by both the scientist and the group leader.

The story was 24 paragraphs long. Of these, nine were based mainly on the spoken inputs (interviews) and fifteen on written inputs. Figure 1.3 gives the first few paragraphs of this story as published (verbatim) in one newspaper, and shows how the eight inputs were used to build the text of the news item. The processes I see at work in Figure 1.3 include the following:

1    Selection from the available inputs and corresponding rejection of most of the written material in order to handle the size of the EIA and the number of other inputs.

2    Reproduction of source material. I found that the later paragraphs, which provide detail and background, tend to reproduce wording from input texts in contrast to the wholesale blending and rewriting evident in the early paragraphs.

3    Summarization in early paragraphs of information to be detailed later (compare S7 and S9).

4    Generalization and particularization. In S7 we see a shift from the particular to the general, and from the general to the particular in the description in S5.

5    Frequent restyling and translating of information expressed in scientific phraseology to less technical wording.

## 1.6  TIME AND TECHNOLOGY IN NEWS ENGLISH

I began this discussion of the nature of news processing by looking at the technological development that first made rapid news dissemination possible – the telegraph. In this section I look at changes in news technologies, their relation to time, and their effects on the character of news English. This section also looks at the effects of technology on the English of another form of 'reporting' – the televised sports commentary.

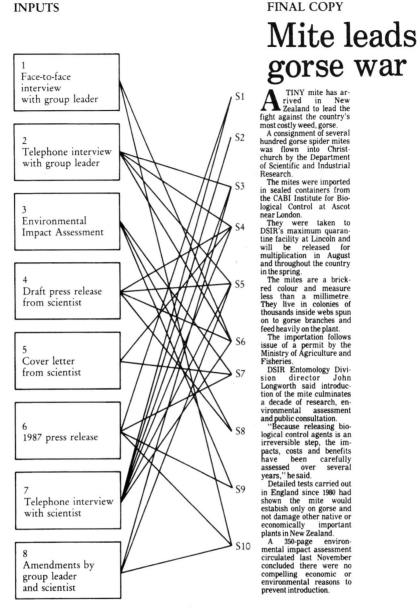

INPUTS

FINAL COPY

# Mite leads gorse war

A TINY mite has arrived in New Zealand to lead the fight against the country's most costly weed, gorse.

A consignment of several hundred gorse spider mites was flown into Christchurch by the Department of Scientific and Industrial Research.

The mites were imported in sealed containers from the CABI Institute for Biological Control at Ascot near London.

They were taken to DSIR's maximum quarantine facility at Lincoln and will be released for multiplication in August and throughout the country in the spring.

The mites are a brick-red colour and measure less than a millimetre. They live in colonies of thousands inside webs spun on to gorse branches and feed heavily on the plant.

The importation follows issue of a permit by the Ministry of Agriculture and Fisheries.

DSIR Entomology Division director John Longworth said introduction of the mite culminates a decade of research, environmental assessment and public consultation.

"Because releasing biological control agents is an irreversible step, the impacts, costs and benefits have been carefully assessed over several years," he said.

Detailed tests carried out in England since 1980 had shown the mite would estabish only on gorse and not damage other native or economically important plants in New Zealand.

A 350-page environmental impact assessment circulated last November concluded there were no compelling economic or environmental reasons to prevent introduction.

1 Face-to-face interview with group leader

2 Telephone interview with group leader

3 Environmental Impact Assessment

4 Draft press release from scientist

5 Cover letter from scientist

6 1987 press release

7 Telephone interview with scientist

8 Amendments by group leader and scientist

S1 S2 S3 S4 S5 S6 S7 S8 S9 S10

*Figure 1.3    Embedding of inputs to construct the text of a news story (adapted from* The Daily News, *New Plymouth, 4 August 1988 by Bell, A., 1991)*

At the beginning of this chapter I indicated that the invention of the telegraph was the first crucial step in the development of modern news practices and forms in the pursuit of immediacy and productivity. The US media sociologist James Carey (1987) traces the rise of modern forms of news English in nineteenth-century America, particularly the concept of time. He argues that the penny press, which began in the USA in the 1830s, took its concept of time from trade and business, the cycle of which is the day, with its never-ending repetition of prices, goods and transactions. It imposed this daily cycle of commerce on other spheres of social life. By the 1860s, the telegraph cemented what the penny press had begun, as the turnaround time on news shortened radically. So journalistic achievement became defined as being the first rather than the best.

**Activity 1.8**   *(Reading C)*

Read James Carey's account in Reading C of the links between the development of the telegraph and news practices.

**Comment**

Carey considers that such a concept of time – orientation to the daily, to the most recent, to being first – is a key factor in the news's non-attention to the question why, its lack of explanation and context. So the journalistic concept of when – of immediacy as a news value, of the scoop as the professional goal – defeats the coverage of the why and how.

The computerization of news writing and processing has redefined the work practices of journalists. The recycling of existing news text in new stories is increasingly likely to occur. Print journalists now input their stories direct to their newspaper's central computer system. Typesetting is eliminated, and with it several distinct steps in news production. News copy received from external news agencies or correspondents is also fed straight into a newspaper's computer, with no need for rekeying on site. In addition, the computer archiving of previously published issues enables journalists to reduce turnaround time and increase their productivity.

A combination of technological advances in and legislative deregulation of the broadcasting industry is leading to more outlets and more competition, and this is also reshaping broadcast forms and styles. Deregulation, primarily of frequencies and ownership, is opening the television spectrum to private operators in countries where public television has been the norm. In this highly competitive environment the way in which news is framed and presented is changing. The old public-service approach to programming was to set off one programme clearly from the next, marking the junctions and encouraging audiences to choose whether or not to watch. Stig Hjarvard (1994) describes how public television scheduling in the UK and other European countries is moving away from this kind of segmented programming format to a commercially oriented flow of programmes designed to lock in the attention of viewers to a particular station.

This process is further along in New Zealand, where public television has always carried advertising. It is at its most obvious in the placement of advertisements. Although there may be as many as five advertising breaks (each several minutes long) within an hour-long programme, no advertising is screened between programmes. The end of one programme leads straight into the start of the next. The intention is blatantly commercial – to avoid giving the 'consumers' a chance to get away during the transition between programmes. It is the exact opposite of a purely public-service approach, which would offer the audience maximum uninterrupted viewing by running advertisements between rather than within programmes.

What effects do such practices have on broadcast news? News has long been regarded by both audiences and media personnel as significant far beyond the rather small amount of time it actually occupies (generally less than 10 per cent of a station's air time). News bulletins structure programming and audience time, and are scheduled at transition points in the personal day. News is becoming a serial, along the lines of fictional television forms like soap operas or situation comedies (Hjarvard, 1994). It is shifting from recapitulating the day's events to continuous updating, with television adopting the practice of hourly bulletins that has long been used on radio. This reaches its peak in the continuous news services, again part of the radio scene for at least 20 years, but comparatively recent in television.

The emphasis on getting the news first impels news work towards the ultimate goal of offering coverage in real time. Development of the technology for this is closely linked with war and war reporting. It took its first major step with the telegraph during the American Civil War, and attention is now focused on the technology of the satellite. Coverage in real time – prototypically in CNN's reporting of the 1991 Gulf War – is closer, although it requires further qualitative technological developments to make it more common. Having said this, though, live coverage requires the predictability of situation that I listed earlier as one of the factors in news selection, and most news is not specifically foreseeable in this fashion.

The move to live coverage in broadcast news takes news reporting from the past tense to the present. Studio presenters interview news sources and journalists live on air. The role of scripting is diminished, and with it the tightly developed format of the modern news story. Ironically, the achievement of real-time coverage would mean that the inverted news chronology and structure I have described would become obsolete. But such coverage is of course only partial, provides a small minority of regular broadcast coverage, and is by definition impossible in print. So the classic news story, with its violation of chronological order and fragmented paragraphs, will remain a staple as long as we have printed news and as long as most broadcast news remains retrospective rather than live coverage.

The final activity of the chapter looks at this issue – the move from past to present – in a different but related context. As I said above, the tense used in live coverage of news changes from the past to the present. In Reading D Stephanie Marriott takes a detailed look at the changes to forms of English brought about by the live coverage of sporting events. A sports commentary can be broadcast either as the action happens, as part of the live coverage, or later, to accompany an action replay. The reading looks in detail at the way deictic expressions are used in both situations. You may find it helpful to refer back to the discussion of deixis in Section 1.2.

**Activity 1.9**   *(Reading D)*

Read Stephanie Marriott's 'Time, space and television commentary' (Reading D) in which she points out that it is the advances in available technology – the microphone, the video recorder, the television camera – that have brought about these new uses of English.

## 1.7   CONCLUSION

This chapter has dealt with the way in which news stories in English are written, particularly in relation to time. A feature common to all kinds of story is their chronological time structure: events tend to be told in the order in which they happened. But news stories follow a radically different ordering. They generally begin with the most recent event and cycle back through earlier events, giving information in instalments. Modern news discourse has developed this time structure through a combination of the news values of recency and novelty, the journalistic practices of the deadline and the scoop, and technology that increasingly allows coverage to be live, in real time.

News media also offer the classic case of language produced by multiple parties. The processing of news involves the complex and rapid movement of stories through the hands of many news workers. Much of the news consists of previously composed text embedded and reworked into new texts. This composite character is a very explicit example of Bakhtin's heteroglossia – the mixing of many voices. The push to offer coverage live, or in as close to real time as possible, took its first major step with the telegraph 130 years ago. Attention is now focused on the technology of the satellite, with repercussions for the format the news will take.

## Reading A

# EXTRACT I FROM 'WHEN? DEADLINES, DATELINES, AND HISTORY'

*Michael Schudson*

Nearly everything else may vary, but this is constant in hard news: an orientation to the past twenty-four hours. Time is the scaffolding on which stories are hung, and the day is the chief unit of time. The result, of course, is that events in the world that are or can be made to appear timely, that is, linked to some development of the preceding day, are more reportable than events that move by less discernible rhythms. These events are more easily justified for front-page attention by an editor who does not have room for all the stories he or she would like to include.

But it is clear that the fact that something happened yesterday is not sufficient to make it news. Sometimes newsworthiness has to do not only with timeliness but with the ease with which an event can be placed in a cycle or rhythm of time. Election stories are easy to report not so much because something newsworthy happens each day in an election campaign (although, of course, candidates do their best to see that this is so), but because journalist and reader alike know the election date and know when the story will *end*. Because everyone knows the story will end the first Tuesday after the first Monday in November, every speech, every poll, every alliance, every debate, every gaffe can be weighed and measured against a day of judgment. The reporter, the editor, and the reader all know *where they are* in the story – near the beginning, the middle, or the end. The election story has a cadence, a rhythm, and is easier to read and absorb because readers can tap out the beat.

The most notorious consequence of journalism's love for stories whose ending they can anticipate is the 'horse race' style of covering elections. Sometimes, even in the best of newspapers, the result is a caricature of itself:

> Sen. Gary Hart of Colorado made it two in a row Sunday, with a come-from-behind victory that snatched away Walter F. Mondale's front-runner status.
>
> Hart's upset victory in Maine's Democratic caucuses gave him vital additional momentum just five days after his surprise triumph in the New Hampshire primary and nine days before the crucial Super Tuesday contests in nine states.
>
> (*Los Angeles Times*, March 5, 1984)

Election reporting can always count on an end point to give news a location in time that most reports do not have.

Reporting on legislative activity is correspondingly more difficult much of the time. This is well illustrated in a *Los Angeles Times* story of May 25, 1985, headlined, 'Did Senate Vote Deal Fatal Blow to Future of MX?' The answer is: the reporters cannot be sure. They write, 'The lopsided Senate vote to limit deployment of the MX missile to 50 unless the Reagan Administration can find another basing plan dealt a profound and perhaps fatal blow to the future growth of the MX program.' *Perhaps* fatal? Well, the Pentagon portrayed the vote as a victory, since some senators had sought to limit deployment to forty missiles, not fifty. 'But,' the reporters tell us, 'the Senate decision Thursday represents one of the extremely rare occasions in which Congress has made a clear – and possibly successful – effort to sharply curtail a major weapons program already under way.' But defense appropriations have a way of returning to the floor of Congress. A bill once introduced and defeated may be introduced again. Compromises can be made. Adjustments can be arrived at. A story about failed or failing legislation, especially budgetary legislation where judgment is not 'yes or no' but 'more or less' is not a story with beginning, middle, and end. It is a P.D.Q. Bach spoof of a Beethoven symphony: how many endings are there? how many times will it roar to a climax only to return for one more reprise of the opening theme?

The sense of an ending that gives body and rhythm to a story need not be a date like the first Tuesday in November. It can be a clear-cut finish without a date. In hostage crises, the hostages will either be released safely or killed. The Iranian hostage crisis was mentioned every night on the evening news for fifteen months. It was not *timely* news – it was old hat. Most days it was not timely *news* because nothing new or different had happened. But the gravity of the opposition of the two outcomes – freedom or death, rescue or humiliation – provided a dramatic structure that kept the story a story.

This is what the press handles best: stories that are timely, that have anticipatable end points, and that have end points that figure in simple, binary possibilities – the election or the game will be won or lost, the Dow-Jones will go up or down, the defendant will be judged guilty or not guilty, the criminal is apprehended or at large, the patient survives or dies, the child is missing or has been found. Stories that are more complex than this – the budget, for instance – if they are to be covered well at all, are translated into a binary opposition of this sort: the president is going to get his way or he is going to lose to the Congress. The media found a comfortable way to report President Reagan's tax revision initiative when they discovered in Representative Dan Rostenkowski a skillful and attractive antagonist to set against the president.

Source: Schudson, 1987, pp. 97–9

---

## Reading B

## EXTRACT 2 FROM 'WHEN? DEADLINES, DATELINES, AND HISTORY'

*Michael Schudson*

Getting the news fast and, ideally, getting it *first* is of passionate interest to journalists. On November 22, 1963, the UPI White House reporter, Merriman Smith, sat in the middle of the front seat of the pool car in the presidential motorcade in Dallas. When he heard gunshots, he jumped to the phone and started dictating. His Associated Press rival, Jack Bell, seated in the backseat, was helpless to get out a story. Bell demanded the phone, but Smith said he wanted the Dallas operator to read the story back to him because the connection was faulty. This was obviously a dodge to keep hold of the phone. 'Bell started screaming and trying to wrestle with Smith for the receiver. Smith stuck it between his knees and hunched up into a ball, with Bell beating him wildly about the head and shoulders. UPI beat the AP by several crucial minutes on the story, and Smith won a Pulitzer for his coverage of the Kennedy assassination.'

Daniel Schorr's on-the-scene radio reporting from disastrous floods in Holland in 1953 brought him to the attention of Edward R. Murrow, who then hired him at CBS News. Dan Rather began his rise to prominence at station KHOU Houston with live coverage of Hurricane Carla. 'Live coverage,' Rather writes in his autobiography, 'is the mark of a really good local news station.'

But why?

Why should this emphasis on getting the story minutes or seconds faster than a rival bulk so large in journalism? Once upon a time, when a dateline could be two or three or ten days past and when newspapers could differ by days or weeks, not hours or minutes, 'when' mattered. Andrew Jackson fought the battle of New Orleans because news had not reached him from the East Coast that the war with Britain was already over. That is not something that could happen today. Now, when news is a constant commodity – the wire always ticking, the radio always talking, the TV cameras nearly always available – the question of 'when' is a question journalists care about infinitely more than their readers. The pressure journalists are under to be first is generated internally in news organizations. No one in the audience gives a damn if ABC beats CBS by two seconds or not. The journalist's interest in immediacy hangs on as an anachronistic ritual of the media tribe. Getting the story first is a matter of journalistic pride, but one that has little to do with journalistic quality or public service. It is a fetishism of the present, an occupational perversion, and one peculiarly American. The American editor E.L. Godkin noted this as long ago as 1890: 'The stories which Parisian journalists tell each other in their cafés are not of their prowess as reporters, but of the sensation they have made and the increase in circulation they have achieved by some sort of editorial comment or critique; the American passion for glory in beats – meaning superiority over rivals in getting hold of news – they do not understand, or thoroughly despise.'

The American focus on the scoop serves, in part, to cover up the bureaucratic and prosaic reality of most news gathering. The news organization is, as Philip Schlesinger put it, a 'time-machine.' It lives by the clock. Events, if they are to be reported, must mesh with its temporal spokes and cogs. Journalists do not seek only timely news, if by 'timely' one means 'immediate' or as close to the present as possible. Journalists also seek coincident and convenient news, as close to the *deadline* as possible. News must happen at specified times in the journalists' 'newsday.' Politicians adept at 'making news' are well aware of reporters' dead-lines. They schedule press conferences and public appearances to coincide with reporters' filing times. The astute press secretary in government or in the private sector schedules events to accord with the weekly round of the press, knowing on which days there will be the least number of stories competing for front-page attention. Much of the news the press reports is given to it by public officials who can pass it out routinely or with fanfare, urgently or casually, all at once or in pieces, depending on what kind of effect they want to achieve. The more the media emphasize the immediacy of news, the more subject journalists are to manipulation by public officials who know how to prey on people with stopwatch mentalities.

This reality – that news gathering is normally a matter of the representatives of one bureaucracy picking up prefabricated news items from representatives of another bureaucracy – is at odds with all of the romantic self-conceptions of American journalism. The insistence on getting the latest news and getting it first, the headlong lunge, the competitive rush that comes with a breaking story, all this is an effort to deny and to escape the humdrum of daily journalism. Moreover, the race for news – a race whose winner can easily be determined by a clock – affords a cheap, convenient, democratic measure of journalistic 'quality.' American society is too diverse and American journalism too decentralized for news organizations to measure themselves by criteria of literary elegance or intellectual sophistication. No small circle of intellectuals can influence the culture of journalism in New York and Washington the way it might in Paris. American journalists are left with competition by the clock. Their understanding of their own business focuses on reporting up-to-the-minute news as fully and fairly as possible.

Source: Schudson, 1987, pp. 81–2

---

## Reading C

# EXTRACT FROM 'WHY AND HOW? THE DARK CONTINENT OF AMERICAN JOURNALISM'

*James W. Carey*

[A] critical fact concerning the partisan press concerns the matter of time. The cycle of business is the cycle of the day: the opening and closing of trade. The press of the eighteenth and early nineteenth centuries was not technologically equipped to report on a timely, daily basis, but it shared with businessmen the understanding that time is of the essence of trade. As a result, the natural epoch of journalism became the day: the cycle of work and trade for a business class. The technological impetus in journalism has been to coordinate the cycle of communication with the cycle of trade.

… Journalism is a daybook that records the significant happenings of that day … [and] the archetype of journalism is the diary or account book. The diary records what is significant in the life of a person for that day. The business journal records all transactions for a given day. The news begins in bookkeeping. Commerce lives by, begins and ends the day with, the record of transactions on, say, the stock and commodity markets. The news begins as a record of commercial transactions and a tool of commerce. Every day there is news; every day there are stories to be told because every day there is business to be done and prices to be posted. In this sense, the origins of journalism, capitalism, and bookkeeping are indissoluble.

In the 1830s, a cheap, daily popular press – a 'penny press' – was created in the major cities. The penny press did not destroy the commercial press. The latter has continued down to this day not only in the *Wall Street Journal* and the *Journal of Commerce, Barron's* and *Business Week, Forbes* and *Fortune,* but in private newsletters and private exchanges that grew after the birth of the penny press. Such publications have edged closer to the popular press with the enormous expansion of the middle class. The *Wall Street Journal* doesn't call itself 'the daily diary of the

American dream' for nothing. But the penny press did displace the commercial-partisan press in the 1830s as the model of a daily newspaper.

While scholars disagree over the significance of the penny press, one can safely say three things about it. First, the penny press was a consumer good for a consumer society; it reflected all of society and politics, not just the world of commerce and commercial politics. The retreat from partisanship meant that any matter, however minor, qualified for space in the paper: the details not only of trade and commerce, but the courts, the streets, the strange, the commonplace. The penny papers were filled with the odd, the exotic, and the trivial. Above all, they focused on the anonymous individuals, groups, and classes that inhabited the city. They presented a panorama of facts and persons, a 'gastronomy of the eye'; in another of Baudelaire's phrases, they were a 'kaleidoscope equipped with consciousness.'

Second, the penny press displaced not merely partisanship but an explicit ideological context in which to present, interpret, and explain the news. Such papers choked off, at least relatively, an ideological press among the working class. At its best, the penny press attempted to eliminate the wretched partisanship and factionalism into which the press had degenerated since the Revolution. It tried to constitute, through the more or less neutral support of advertising, an open forum in which to examine and represent a public rather than a merely partisan interest.

Third, the penny press imposed the cycle and habit of commerce upon the life of society generally. Because in business time is money, the latest news can make the difference between success and failure, selling cheap or selling dear. Time is seldom so important in noncommercial activity. The latest news is not always the best and most useful news. Little is lost if the news of politics or urban life is a little old. Nonetheless, the cycle and habit of beginning and ending the day by reading the latest prices was imposed on social activities generally. Beginning in the 1830s, the stories of society were told on a daily basis. The value of timeliness was generalized by the penny press into the cardinal value of journalism.

The events of journalism happen today. The morning reading of the *New York Times* is important because it establishes the salience of stories for the day. It also determines salience for the television networks, the newsmagazines, the journals of opinion issued weekly and monthly. And the stories of books begin in the announcements in news columns: a family named Clutter was murdered in Holcomb, Kansas, yesterday. With the penny press, all forms of writing became increasingly a parasite of 'breaking news.'

The telegraph cemented everything the 'penny press' set in motion. It allowed newspapers to operate in 'real time' for the first time. Its value was insuring that time became irrelevant for purposes of trade. When instantaneous market reports were available everywhere at the same moment, everyone was effectively in the same place for purposes of trade. The telegraph gave a real rather than an illusory meaning to timeliness. It turned competition among newspapers away from price, even away from quality, and onto timeliness. Time became the loss leader of journalism.

The telegraph also reworked the nature of written language and finally the nature of awareness itself. One old saw has it that the telegraph, by creating the wire services, led to a fundamental change in news. It snapped the tradition of partisan journalism by forcing the wire services to generate 'objective' news that papers of any political stripe could use. Yet the issue is deeper than that. The wire services demanded language stripped of the local, the regional and colloquial.

They demanded something closer to a 'scientific' language, one of strict denotation where the connotative features of utterance were under control, one of fact. If a story were to be understood in the same way from Maine to California, language had to be flattened out and standardized. The telegraph, therefore, led to the disappearance of forms of speech and styles of journalism and storytelling – the tall story, the hoax, much humor, irony, and satire – that depended on a more traditional use of language. The origins of objectivity, then, lie in the necessity of stretching language in space over the long lines of Western Union.

Similarly, the telegraph eliminated the correspondent who provided letters that announced an event, described it in detail, and analyzed its substance. It replaced him with the stringer who supplied the bare facts. As the telegraph made words expensive, a language of spare fact became the norm. Telegraph copy had to be condensed to save money. From the stringer's notes, someone at the end of the telegraphic line had to reconstitute the story, a process that reaches high art with the newsmagazines: the story divorced from the storyteller.

If the telegraph made prose lean and unadorned and led to a journalism without the luxury of detail and analysis, it also brought an overwhelming crush of such prose to the newsroom. In the face of what was a real glut of occurrences, news judgment had to be routinized and the organization of the newsroom made factorylike. The reporter who produced the new prose displaced the editor as the archetype of the journalist. The spareness of the prose and its sheer volume allowed news, indeed forced news, to be treated like a commodity: something that could be transported, measured, reduced, and timed. News because subject to all the procedures developed for handling agricultural commodities. It was subject to 'rates, contracts, franchising, discounts and thefts.'

Together those developments of the second third of the nineteenth century brought a new kind of journalism, a kind that is still roughly the staple of our newspapers. But, as explained earlier, this new journalism made description and explanation radically problematic: 'penny' and telegraphic journalism divorced news from an ideological context that could explain and give significance to events. It substituted the vague principle of a public interest for 'class interest' as the criterion for selecting, interpreting, and explaining the news. It brought the newsroom a glut of occurrences that overwhelmed the newspaper and forced the journalist to explain not just something but everything. As a result, he often could explain nothing. By elevating objectivity and facticity into cardinal principles, the penny press abandoned explanation as a primary goal. Simultaneously, it confronted the reader with events with which he had no experience and no method with which to explain them. It filled the paper with human interest material that, however charming, was inexplicable. And, finally, it divorced the announcement of news from its analysis and required the reader to maintain constant vigilance to the news if he was to understand anything.

Source: Carey, 1987, pp. 162–6

# Reading D
# TIME, SPACE AND TELEVISION COMMENTARY

*Stephanie Marriott*

Communications technologies, such as the telephone and television, give rise to communicative contexts very different from the 'canonical' one in which the grammatical resources of English originally evolved. New and more complex spatial and temporal relations between speaker and hearer have become possible, even common. The interpretation of deictic expressions depends on a mutual understanding of 'here' and 'now'. How, then, are such expressions used when these reference points are made problematic by such things as video recording, action replay during live television sports coverage, and when speaker and listener do not share the same field of vision and cannot see each other? In this reading I examine English deictic expressions in television commentary.

Deictic expressions in English – words such as *I* and *you*, *this*, *that*, *here*, *there*, *now*, *then*, *today*, *yesterday* and *tomorrow* – are most appropriately used by speakers when they can be reasonably confident that the spatio-temporal context is shared with the hearer. Fillmore points out the extreme difficulty of interpreting a message in a bottle that reads, simply, 'Meet me here at noon tomorrow with a stick about this big'. The recipient needs to know the identity of the message producer in order to know who 'me' is; in addition he or she also needs to know *when* the message was produced in order to know which day counts as 'tomorrow', *where* the message was produced in order to know where 'here' is, and what kinds of physical movements the speaker was producing in order to make sense of the gestural deictic 'this big' (Fillmore, 1975). Deictic expressions, and gestural deictics in particular, are thus most readily interpreted in what Lyons calls a 'canonical' situation of utterance, where discourse participants are physically in the same place and face to face; in other kinds of situation, as he points out, the interpretation of such expressions is likely to become problematic (Lyons, 1977).

Television commentary, like other kinds of broadcast talk, is produced primarily for an overhearing audience, the viewer at home (Scannell, 1991, pp. 1–13). Speaker and hearer are not face to face in the same place, and in the case of commentary the speaker is not even visible to the viewer, who sees only the pictures of the event. As a consequence, commentators are unable to make use of ostensive behaviour – pointing or indicating – to pick out the elements they want to talk about. In such a situation we might expect to find a general absence of gestural deictics; yet television commentary is full of such expressions, as the extracts below from snooker and tennis commentaries will demonstrate.

### Extract 1

And I think Steve is just checking if *that top red* will go into the right hand corner pocket.

### Extract 2

Well *that's* a perfect shot by Steve, and *these* are never nice to play.

**Extract 3**

Wilander hitting the returns with such deadly accuracy. *That one* just clipped the top of the net.

The use of the italicized expressions in extracts 1–3 should present serious interpretative problems in a noncanonical situation. The speaker cannot physically point out *which* of the fifteen red snooker balls on the table is intended by the reference to *that top red*, nor which particular snooker or tennis shot is intended by the expressions *that*, *these* and *that one*.

This problem is surmounted by allowing the camera to perform ostensive acts in lieu of the speaker. By restricting their remarks almost entirely to what they can see on the studio monitor, the commentators can ensure that they share the viewer's field of vision. Speakers can assume that the objects they see are also visible to the viewer; they can assume, too, that the objects are seen from exactly the same perspective, and – in the case of live coverage – that they are seen at the same moment (Marriott, 1995). Commentator and viewer thus share the same 'here' – the 'here' of the televisual space – and the same 'now' – the moment in which the commentary is both produced in the studio and heard at home. While the invisible speaker cannot gesture to pick out a salient object, the camera can zoom and pan and thus render a particular object prominent in the common televisual ground. Gestural deictics such as *these* and *that one* can then be used to pick out shared elements.

## Replay talk and the shared 'now'

Live television commentary typically involves what Lyons (1977) calls an 'experiential' mode of description, which is used to talk about events or processes that are occurring at or around the moment of utterance. It is easy to see why this might be the case. Even though the viewer may have videotaped the broadcast for subsequent consumption, the commentator is licensed to assume that the hearer is viewing the same events, and is hearing the commentary at the same time as it is produced.

This focus on the shared 'here and now' is carried linguistically mainly by the use of the present and simple past tenses. The present tense is typically used for the description of what is going on 'now', at the moment of utterance, and for the prediction of situations in the immediate future. The simple past tense is generally used for the description of what occurred immediately before the shared 'now' of the television event. The use of these tenses effectively divides the world into two separate but causally related narrative spaces, 'now' and 'then'. In extracts 4 and 5, for instance, the alternations between past and present serve to signify a movement from a description of a past state of affairs to an analysis and discussion of the situation that has come about *as a result* of this.

**Extract 4**

Just out. Just out. So the backhand volley that just *missed gives* uh McEnroe his fourth break point.

**Extract 5**

That *was* his second choice, but uh he *may* have the angle on the green here to continue his break.

However, there is one particular kind of live commentary where the shifts between tenses do not involve the expression of a causal relationship between a past and a present event. In the talk produced during action replays, commentators switch in and out of temporal modes to describe the same linear sequence of events. In extracts 6 and 7, the shifts between past and present tenses do not parallel a real-time shift from past to present. Instead, the speakers appear to treat the material shown during the replay as though it exists *both in the past and in the present at one and the same time.*

### Extract 6

See, he just *plays* a little bit wide of the target, *doesn't* quite get the angle, *removes* the two at the front, but *missed* that all-important blue shot biting the blue four-foot circle.

### Extract 7

And it's the Englishman who finally *penetrates* his armour. He *blocks* one, he *blocks* two, but he *couldn't* block three.

In extracts 6 and 7 the commentators shift from one temporal mode to the other, despite the fact that they are reporting on a linear sequence of events: the player *plays* a little wide of the target, *removes* the two at the front but *missed* his next target, the blue shot; and the goalkeeper *blocks* one, and *blocks* two but *couldn't* block three attempts at the goal.

A consideration of the circumstances underlying this phenomenon offers us interesting insights into the ways in which televisual texts structure time and temporal relations. For a commentator who is observing the action through the monitor, the events that motivate the discourse in extracts 6 and 7 form a seamless whole: one sequence follows another sequence on the screen, each one passing through the temporal zero-point, the 'now' of the speaker. From this perspective, the events in the replay are indeed taking place at and around the present moment. However, both commentator and viewer also know that the events they are observing unfolded in real time some moments earlier, and were jointly viewed *at that time.* From this second point of view, the events in the replay occurred not 'now' but 'then'. The co-temporality of live commentary thus creates a situation in which the same sequence of events is simultaneously past and present for both speaker and hearer: past because it involves pre-recorded pictures, and present because those pictures are passing through the temporal zero-point at the moment of speech. Within this framework it is the nonlive status of the image that motivates the use of the past tense in replay talk; and it is the liveness of the commentary – its unfolding at the shared 'now' of speaker and hearer – that licenses the use of the present (Marriott, 1996).

Such shifts from current to noncurrent frames of reference are not random. Transitions from one temporal mode to the other are underpinned by a choice of one perspective over the other. Where the commentators wish to concentrate on what is occurring 'now' on the monitor, a present frame of reference is selected; where they wish to focus on the situation *as it originally took place,* they will choose a past frame of reference. These systematic shifts from one point of view to the other can be traced through an examination of the temporal shifts in extract 8, which is taken from the commentary produced during a horse-racing replay.

**Extract 8**

Commentator A    Here's this these lovely shots and uh look at him come
up long there. I think this is although this is only a
little horse he could go and jump fences one day.
Watch Brad, look at him just chasing the horse away
then grabbing hold of him, and he's got a nice short
hold of his uh reins. 's it's a that was a lovely lovely shot
in getting a horse away from a hurdle and balanced
before you pick him up. And he's really running now
...

Commentator B    Yes, what was a a good uh shot also is that Brad is
gritting his teeth and I should think shouting at
Bocaro to go, cause the voice does actually motivate
them, and Brad's teeth are gritted, he knows he's got it
but look at his grimace on his face. Now I think that
tells it all, doesn't it, the grimace from uh pain goes to
joy ...

Extract 8 opens with Commentator A making an explicit reference to the action
currently taking place on the screen (*Here's this these lovely shots*) and then
exhorting the viewer to watch what is happening 'now' (*look at him ... Watch Brad,
look at him*) before expressing an appreciation of the excellence of the *original*
camera work via the use of the simple past tense (*that was a lovely lovely shot*).
Commentator B, in turn, again praises the original camera work before shifting
into an analysis of that camera work as it reoccurs on screen at the temporal zero-
point (*what was a a good uh shot also is that Brad is gritting his teeth*) and finally again
exhorts the viewer to attend to the action on screen (*look at his grimace on his face*).

These shifts from one temporal mode to the other are marked above all by
the presence or absence of direct address. Direct exhortations to the viewer, when
they turn up in replay talk, occur only during remarks on *current* television time,
where they serve to alert the viewer to some aspect of the action unfolding at the
shared 'now'; in references to past time, where commentators are meditating
upon their own view of a past situation, they do not occur.

## Live television and co-temporality

In terms of the speaker and hearer's location in space, televised sports coverage
involves a twofold absence. Scannell (1991, p. 2) points out that broadcasting
'speaks from one place and is heard in another': viewers are thus absent from the
actual place in which talk is produced, and in the case of television commentary
they are also absent from the place in which the crowd event – the snooker match,
the horse race – is unfolding in real space. The commentators' use of 'monitor
talk' compensates for these absences by permitting the viewer to take up the
mediated equivalent of a ringside seat at the original spectacle. The viewer is
relocated as an observer at a shared spatial zero-point, the 'here' of the act of
speech, and is thus drawn into a relationship of spatial co-presence in a speech
situation whose boundaries are determined by what can be seen and heard
televisually.

From a temporal perspective, televised sport may or may not involve distanciation. If the coverage is nonlive – or if viewers are watching the programme on video – then the viewer will be distanced in time both from the crowd event and from the moment of utterance. In the event of a live broadcast, however, which is watched as it is transmitted, speaker and hearer will be jointly located at the temporal zero-point. This co-presence at the shared 'now' of the act of speech means that commentary is produced on the basis of a simultaneous viewing of and expounding upon an image in the real time of both speaker and hearer. It is this circumstance that leads to the kinds of linguistic patternings I have discussed here.

## References

FILLMORE, C.J. (1975) 'Santa Cruz lectures on deixis', mimeo, Indiana University Linguistic Club.

LYONS, J. (1977) *Semantics*, Cambridge, Cambridge University Press.

MARRIOTT, S. (1995) 'Intersubjectivity and temporal reference in television commentary', *Time and Society*, vol. 4, no. 3, pp. 345–64.

MARRIOTT, S. (1996) 'Time and time again: "live" television commentary and the construction of replay talk', *Media, Culture and Society*, vol. 18, pp. 69–86.

SCANNELL, P. (1991) *Broadcast Talk*, London, Sage.

This reading was specially commissioned for this book.

# 2 VISUAL ENGLISH

*Sharon Goodman*

## 2.1   INTRODUCTION

The previous chapter looked at English in the news media, and at how developments in technology can put pressure on English to adapt itself to suit new working practices. Technological advances have brought in their wake changes of another kind – a vast increase in the use of visual information for communicative purposes. This chapter takes a look at some of the forms of visuals that are used to communicate in English. It starts by considering the types of visual literacy that people utilize, to different ends in different contexts. It goes on to look in more detail at some English texts, and considers how visual and verbal information in these texts may interact, either to create additional meanings, or to bring to the fore a *conflict* between the two modes.

There are many different ways of looking at visual information, and this chapter will inevitably raise more questions than it can answer at the moment. Those interested in the field of visual literacy include linguists and discourse analysts, cognitive psychologists, artists and art historians, graphic designers, newspaper editors, media analysts, historians and photographers – all of whom have different reasons for studying images and focus on different aspects of visual literacy. The development of a theoretical academic framework for exploring the links between visual and verbal language is still in its infancy, and appears to have its roots in the development and diffusion of various technological innovations of the late twentieth century. In considering some of the forms that visual communication in English texts can take, the chapter focuses on three main issues:

- the fact that visual forms of communication are culturally specific, and that despite their 'natural' appearance, they are often highly conventionalized;

- the ways in which graphics and pictures can communicate, and the extent to which it is possible to make distinctions between English in the visual and verbal channels of communication;

- the ways in which visual and verbal English can *interact* within a text, reinforcing each others' messages or creating potentially conflicting meanings.

First, however, we need to consider why it is becoming so important to study visual communication.

## Visual and verbal literacies: the impact of technology

**Visual literacy** is, according to some analysts, rapidly becoming an essential skill for coping with the world of work and with social life in general (Kress and van Leeuwen, 1996; Morgan and Welton, 1986). The term 'literacy' has traditionally been used to refer to the achievement of certain standards in reading and writing, while the ability to understand and communicate in the visual channel has not been considered to be of any great importance. The earlier part of the twentieth century saw a strong tradition of prioritizing the strictly verbal over the pictorial, and because images were (and in many spheres still are) considered to be less important than writing – less meaningful or useful in everyday life – they tended to be dismissed as 'pretty pictures', a distraction from the real information in reading material, and thus unworthy of serious study. Verbal English was regarded until quite recently as the mode for serious, 'real' information.

But print media have now developed to the point where it is impossible to imagine life before graphic design, and people increasingly need to draw on knowledge of *visual* codes to interpret *written* information. Because of the increase in design software and the wider availability of computer technology, traditional definitions of literacy are no longer adequate in a world where texts communicate to us in new ways – through graphics, pictures and layout techniques, as well as through words. It is difficult these days to find a single text which uses solely verbal English. The vast majority of letters, advertisements and even government circulars in most countries use at least some form of visual information alongside the verbal language. Newspapers, for example, contain numerous photographs, diagrams and changes of typeface, and company letterheads routinely contain graphic devices such as logos or borders. In this sense, texts in English are becoming increasingly **multimodal**: they use devices from more than one semiotic mode of communication simultaneously. A letter on company notepaper, for example, often has a corporate logo (visual), the name of the company in full (verbal), and the address and telephone number (verbal). It may also have a border around it (visual), it is often printed on coloured paper (visual) and it will of course have the basic text of the letter itself (verbal). An electronic text, such as a page on the World Wide Web, may have even more modes: it may contain photographs, recordings of spoken English, or music.

Modern English texts, then, are becoming increasingly visual, and new technologies are playing an important part in bringing visual forms of communication into contact with more traditional print. One area where the visual is becoming particularly important is in the sphere of global communications. As well as appearing in more traditional visual spaces such as advertising billboards, book covers, television and film, visual information is now being regularly transmitted worldwide by fax machines and multimedia computers. Computers, the Internet and global publishing mean that visual literacy in traditionally verbal territory is becoming increasingly necessary in order for individuals to participate fully in the world of work, and to comprehend the vast quantities of available information. Some see a pressing need for people to get to grips with this new literacy:

> [in future] Not being 'visually literate' will begin to attract social sanctions. 'Visual literacy' will begin to be a matter of survival, especially in the workplace.
>
> (Kress and van Leeuwen, 1996, p. 3)

This view may seem paradoxical: there have, after all, been illustrated books (and other visual narratives such as religious paintings) for centuries. In this sense there is nothing new about visual communication. But the visual is now commonly used in spheres associated with verbal language: the workplace is a prime example. Texts in English are now likely to contain many forms of what I shall be calling 'visual English'. The term is problematic for two reasons:

- in an English language text, can we say that any picture or graphic representation accompanying English words may be called 'visual English'?
- to what extent can we refer to these as examples of 'visual *English*' – as opposed to 'visual French', 'visual Arabic', etc? Does the move towards the visual entail a move away from distinct 'languages' – in other words, is the 'Englishness' of English texts disappearing?

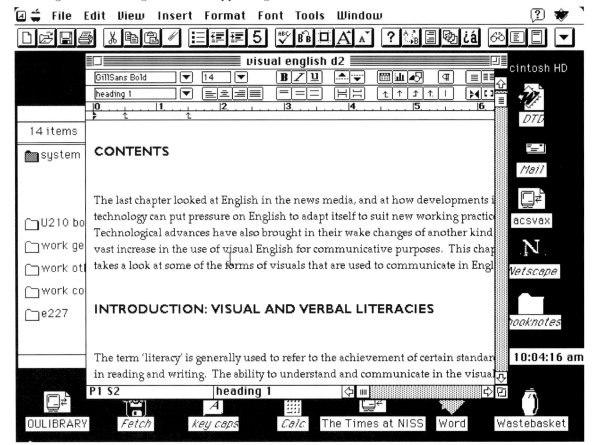

*Figure 2.1    Apple Macintosh computer screen*

## Activity 2.1    *(Allow about 5 minutes)*

Figure 2.1 shows what I see on my computer screen while I am working – a big change from ten years ago. Most of the programs, documents and functions I can perform are now shown as icons. Is this visual or verbal English?

### Comment

You may have found it difficult to decide whether some of the information in Figure 2.1 is visual or verbal. This is one of the problems we encounter in this chapter: some forms of communication require visual literacy, some verbal literacy, and some a combination of the two. Looking at the row of symbols (the second row) along the top of the screen, can you say with any certainty that these are strictly visual or verbal? Some, such as the second one which is meant to represent 'open a file' could be seen as corresponding to the verb *open*. The next one (the picture of a computer disk) represents the command *save*, but is more accurately described as a visual representation of a noun, *disk*.

Some pictures are accompanied by a verbal description. Along the bottom, and on the right of the screen are mainly programs I can run, such as Mail (electronic mail) and Netscape (for access to the World Wide Web). It is arguable that there is no need for both the words and the pictures here, and in any case the machine itself encourages me to ignore the words – by responding only if I click on the pictures.

The political and economic implications of access to technology are discussed in Chapter 3 of this book.

Desk-top computers have also had an effect on the presentation of documents. Providing people have access to the technology, they now have a great deal of control over their own *production* processes. The entire layout of documents can now be changed with ease. Photographs can be directly scanned into the text, and then resized or otherwise altered to achieve the desired effect. Once photographs and diagrams are available in machine-readable form, the possibilities are endless. Colour can be altered (or removed) at the touch of a button, and parts of a photograph can be deleted entirely. Tables, graphs and logos can be inserted, and fonts, margins and page size completely transformed. And when the desired result is finally achieved, the whole thing can be sent across the globe via the Internet – where somebody else can continue the process. Visual presentation is therefore coming increasingly under the control of the individual:

> Unlike print technology, telewriting discourages uniformity: letters, pages, columns, spacing can be changed and modified ad infinitum. Writing and design are no longer separate activities but become different moments in a single creative process.
>
> (Taylor and Saarinen, 1994, *Telewriting*, p. 11)

The problem for the image-conscious commercial or institutional enterprise is that everyone can now customize their documents, given the technology. Some are even calling this the 'new Middle Ages' – where every document produced can be individual and distinct. Much contemporary printed material is every bit as visual as were medieval manuscripts. Without detailed guidelines there is virtually no possibility that two people would produce visually identical texts. The diversification of visual presentation therefore has to be curbed in the interests of consistency – which is why there is, on my Macintosh computer at work, a folder entitled 'Approved Fonts', and strict guidelines for laying out letters and placing logos on the page. Most educational and commercial institutions now need a 'house style': a standardized prescription for internally produced documents. This is considered necessary precisely because the technology has advanced to the stage where it allows potentially for chaotic, individual styles of presentation – a risk which institutions must do their best to eliminate.

Plate 1 in the colour section shows an extract from the Open University's guide to visual presentation (Open University, 1994). If you are working in an organization, the chances are that similar guidelines are in place there too.

A glance through the verbal language accompanying these illustrations reveals an interesting use of modal verbs: predominantly *should* and *must*. It is therefore quite a prescriptive document. How do you feel about this? You may feel that guidelines need to be fairly rigid; on the other hand it could be argued that they can never be totally successful in creating complete uniformity.

Speed and convenience are two of the reasons underlying the development and wide adoption of the new tools for visual expression. Another is perhaps more fundamental: the *attraction* of images. We may find in the new technology ways of returning to the image-filled world associated with childhood – while, of course, regarding it as persuasive, coherent design! Dondis believes that people generally prefer visual representation to written explanation, noting that:

> In the modern media ... the visual dominates; the verbal augments. Print is not dead yet, nor will it ever be, but, nevertheless, our language-dominated culture has moved perceptibly toward the iconic.
>
> (Dondis, 1973, p. 7)

Intuitively it seems to be the case that images attract attention (and certainly this is the view taken by many newspaper editors), but the *types* of image that people are exposed to, and therefore learn to 'read', can vary enormously. This issue – the cultural specificity of visual representation – is considered in more detail below.

## Culture, language and 'seeing'

Semiotic systems – systems of signs – in both visual and verbal channels of communication vary with language, culture and experience. From infancy we make sense of the visual, and learn to recognize which visual codes are meaningful and significant, and which are not. It is not the purpose of this chapter to delve too deeply into the development of perception and visual literacy in children, however it is worth noting Pam Czerniewska's point (1992, p. 31) that preschool children are exposed to a vast array of logographic symbols long before learning to read (such as *P* for parking, *M* for McDonalds). Add to this what they learn about visual representation from children's books and television, and it is not surprising that even very young children have clear ideas as to which visual codes are meaningful, and what is visually 'correct'.

Children's acquisition of literacy is discussed in Chapter 3 of an earlier book in this series, *Learning English: development and diversity* (Mercer and Maybin (eds), 1996).

There are many forms of visual information that members of a culture seem to decode almost automatically, so effective is the process of internalization. Many visual semiotic systems, such as road and shop signs, are social constructs (rather than naturally occurring entities) which have been conventionalized and internationally accepted. Readily comprehensible once learned, they diminish the amount of decoding time needed, enabling us to function efficiently in the social world. Because sign systems can very quickly take on a 'natural' appearance, it takes a perceptual shift to realize that they have been learned and internalized. Faced with the signs shown in Figure 2.2, which appear on the lavatory doors in Poland, which would you go into?

*Figure 2.2*

Guy Cook points out that comprehension is often based on prior knowledge:

> Many signs are believed to be iconic because the perception of a connection between signified and signifier is so habitual that it begins to seem natural ... For a sign to be truly iconic, it would have to be transparent to someone who had never seen it before – and it seems unlikely that this is as much the case as sometimes supposed. We see the resemblance when we already know the meaning.
>
> (Cook, 1992, p. 70)

Even seeing a photograph is something that has to be learned – recognizing the people or places depicted in photographs may seem automatic, but there is evidence to show that the ability to understand them is far from natural:

Jung ... described how he visited a remote people who had had no previous contact with modern technology and showed them an illustrated magazine. Much to his surprise, they were unable to recognize that the photographs depicted people but regarded them as meaningless smudges. Finally, one of the group traced the outline of a 'smudge' and declared to a disbelieving audience that it represented a white man.
(Morgan and Welton, 1986, p. 67)

*Figure 2.3*

❖  ❖  ❖  ❖  ❖

**Activity 2.2**   *(Allow 10 minutes)*

Figure 2.3 shows some signs in use in the United Kingdom and elsewhere. What do they mean? Are they instances of visual English (that is, can we pin down the 'Englishness' of them?) or are they related to more than one language? Are they simply conventionalized international symbols? How does the visual symbol relate to a verbal word, sentence or concept (if it does)? What is its function – does it inform, prescribe behaviour, act as a visual shorthand for an English sentence? Where might you expect to find each of these symbols, and does the context in which you would encounter it influence its meaning?

**Comment**

The context is obviously crucial for meaningful decoding (how many times have you interpreted ⬆ as 'go up' instead of 'go straight on' in a shopping centre?), as is cultural significance – the symbol , for example, might be interpreted as something like 'umbrellas to keep out of the rain during monsoon' in countries where sunbathing on a sunny beach would be unthinkable. It should also be clear that the first two lines in Figure 2.3 consist of individual symbols or icons, whereas the third line is a visual shorthand intended to be read as a verbal unit (*I love New York*).

It may be that some of these symbols seem more appropriate than others to your cultural context. If you are bilingual, or live in a country where English is used alongside another language, do the visual representations used in each language differ? It occurs to me that the 'knife and fork' symbol, for example, in Figure 2.3 would not be the most obvious one for 'restaurant' in all countries.

❖  ❖  ❖  ❖  ❖

Different languages and cultures – even different regions within a single country – often develop different symbols relevant to their own needs. In some rural parts of Britain, for example, you may see a sign at the roadside which means 'beware sugar beet falling from lorries' – something less likely to be signposted in London.

A sign such as the one in Figure 2.4, displayed in British shops, would be meaningless in a country with no minimum age for the purchase of cigarettes or lottery tickets. New signs are also invented as the need arises – the Burmese capital Rangoon has recently seen the appearance of a sign depicting a betel nut chewer, with a prohibitive red circle and diagonal line superimposed over it. Chewing betel nuts is part of traditional Burmese culture, but the spitting out of the red juice is felt by the government to be messy and upsetting to tourists – so the sale of the nut has been banned and a new sign created accordingly.

Figure 2.4

New symbols are often designed in the simplest possible way for them to be readily understood. A useful tool for discussing this is prototype theory. Rosch (1978) defines a prototype as a 'typical instance of' an object or concept. Thus in Britain, a typical instance of 'bird' might be a robin, and a simplified drawing of a robin may come to signify 'bird' in visual British English. This would then come to stand for all birds, regardless of whether or not they really resembled the depiction. The process is culturally specific: a British representation of 'tree' might look something like those shown in Figure 2.5, whereas in certain parts of Africa you might find something more like the spreading branches of the acacia tree, shown in Figure 2.6.

Figure 2.5                                        Figure 2.6

Morgan and Welton (1986) note that our ideas of perspective and reality are conditioned by the culture and time in which we are living, in other words by the visual and verbal imagery that surrounds us, and also by the training we receive (by various media) in these literacies. So 'tree' in British, in Indian and in Singaporean visual English are potentially radically different.

## 2.2   VISUAL OR VERBAL ENGLISH?

As shown in Activity 2.1, one of the problems we face is in attempting to distinguish between visual and verbal English. A further complication is that the *form* of verbal English can also be considered as a visual medium: letter forms themselves can convey meaning and information. Are the shapes of the words on the page, and the spelling, part of visual English, or can we safely confine these to the purely verbal? This is a problematic area, which might lead one to consider the whole text as visual. If we admit letter shapes, spelling and punctuation into the realm of English, then we are into the field of **graphosemantics** – meaning which derives from the text's 'writtenness'. This looks not only at *what* is written, but at *how* it is written and at the relationship between the two. This section will consider some examples.

### Spelling

Recent linguistic research has shown that orthography can affect the way in which sounds are perceived. Derwing (1992) found that people may perceive phonetic differences between, for example, /rich/ and /pitch/ – an extra sound being assumed for the silent letters. It also seems that people may attach different meanings to different spellings of the same word. Bolinger's early (1946) work in the United States on 'visual morphemes' included the following citation from Raymond Macdonald Alden:

> To think, as some do, that 'gray' and 'grey' are quite different colors, and that a ghost which through the triumph of spelling reform has lost its 'h' would also have lost its terrors.
> (Cited in Bolinger, 1946, p. 336)

### Activity 2.3    *(Allow 3 minutes)*

Bolinger tested this phenomenon on his own students. He asked them which spelling of *grey* would fit best with the following sentences:

> *She has lovely* _____ *eyes*
> and
> *It was a* _____ *, gloomy day*.

Which spelling would you use for which sentence? Are you able to say why?

### Comment

Bolinger's students invariably preferred *grey* for the first (the positive connotation) and *gray* for the second (the negative). This may be a distinction which is meaningful only for speakers of American English – I myself do not feel strongly about either spelling. However, it does show that spelling is perceived as having a role to play in interpretation. Another example might be to ask yourself whether you can perceive a difference between *hello, hallo* and *hullo*.

## The semiotics of typography

The typeface in which a text, or part of a text, is set can convey vast amounts of connotative meaning – it can convey a mood, signal clues as to content or even suggest a point of view (for examples, see Carter et al., 1985, and Swann, 1991).

A glance through some of the design and typography textbooks available can reveal fascinating insights into the perceived importance of the visual presentation of print. If you look at the typeface used for different headlines in different styles of newspaper, for example, you will often find that the typeface has been carefully chosen to suit the content of the article, or the newspaper's opinion of the events being reported. There may be 'wobbly' letter forms above an article about a ghost, or 'jagged' letters for a story about an electrical storm. Handwritten-style fonts are often used by advertisers, to give the receiver the impression of a friendly, handwritten note from a friend.

### Activity 2.4    *(Allow 5 minutes)*

An inappropriate typeface can result in, at best, a poorly communicated message, and, at worst, total incomprehension. A typeface which appears to 'fit' the information, on the other hand, can give an air of coherence and 'confidence' to the words. In the examples below, do you think appropriate or inappropriate typefaces have been used? Can you find reasons for your answers?

# 𝕮𝖔𝖒𝖕𝖚𝖙𝖊𝖗 𝕬𝖎𝖉𝖊𝖉 𝕯𝖊𝖘𝖎𝖌𝖓                    –  STOP  PRESS  –

## Comment

To me, the first example (cited in Morgan and Welton, 1986, p. 31) seems to be an inappropriate typeface for the concept it is trying to convey: computers are an efficient, modern form of technology which enable people to work and communicate at high speed. Using a typeface such as Old English seems in Britain to connote old-fashioned tea shops and country villages, where little has changed over the centuries. A computer design company using this typeface is not, therefore, presenting the correct image to its customers.

The second example is in Courier, a typeface often associated with the old-fashioned telegraph machines, used to transmit news as it breaks around the world. It therefore seems to fit the information it is being used to present – a press release or urgent report. Consider how the message would be undermined if it came over the telegraph line in an alternative form:

- - *Stop Press* - -

❖   ❖   ❖   ❖   ❖

*Figure 2.7 (below)   Headmaster pupil poem by Cal Swann (Swann, 1991, pp. 46–7)*

**Headmaster**
Pupil

you know that i now **know** where you went don't you

we were in the woods

**you went to stephen kennedys house**

**i'm telling you the truth** looking at me in the eyes **and all that**

**ah no d d d don't interrupt me i warned you**

**i always find out**
**now i'm very displeased with you** **because you set out to deceive me**

**quite deliberately**

**and as i told you on friday that makes life very difficult**

cos its means every time you and m **you and i talk to**

**so can i rely on that in future**

yeah sorry about the whole thing

Changes of type can be used to imply multiple voices in a text. The impression of the presence of more than one 'speaker' can be implied through the visual presentation. Figure 2.7 is an experimental poem by the typographer Cal Swann, relating a verbal encounter between a headmaster and a pupil.

As you read, note how the type is used to indicate:

- turn taking;

- intonation and changes of tone (shouting, whispering, etc.)

Swann uses changes of type, and devices for emphasizing text such as emboldening, to express the different voices in the interaction. The headmaster's voice is in bold face, and the pupil's in small, fainter letters. The power differential in the exchange between the two speakers is thus reflected by the visual portrayal of the two voices: the pupil's is physically much smaller and less dominant than the headmaster's. Typography, therefore, has a paralinguistic function: it can portray features associated with speech such as intonation, changes of pace and even accent.

<sup>no</sup>**don't lie anna**

          we went to his house for a little while and then   he went meeting a girl

                              **yes**             **yes**

                                            **so all that messing about on friday**

**that in the end**

        **i would know what happened**

                        **and perhaps you'll believe me when i tell you that next time**

       **ah you asked me where**

                yeah  h  er  n n n n

                     **anna anna anna anna stop wriggling dear**

                                **you set out to deceive me**

**each other from now on**

              **i'm going to have to think is that right**  **am i get**  **d'you see**

                                    **d'you understand me**

**Activity 2.5**   *(Reading A)*

Read 'The semiotic construction of a wine label', David Graddol's account in Reading A of the way typefaces can be used to express different voices in another text, the label from a wine bottle. These voices, expressed through the visual semiotics of the typefaces on the label, address the reader in different ways and at different moments in the reader's encounter with the text. What institutional or persuasive voices are expressed on other products?

The connotative potential of typography suggests that content and form are inextricably linked. Burt's study of the psychological impact of typography demonstrated that while many people had no formal knowledge of typography, and could not name individual fonts, they were generally sensitive to what they called 'the atmosphere' set up by the text (Burt, 1950). Memories of hated schoolbooks printed in certain typefaces were cited, proving that typeface can function as a strong **intertextual** device (it contains allusions to, or 'echoes' of, other texts). The fact that designers, advertisers and newspaper editors take print design so seriously confirms that 'the way things look' is of critical importance. Newspaper editors are particularly vehement about the importance of visual presentation:

> Typography and make-up in a newspaper are only a vehicle for journalism; and it is journalism that is the most important. If it is poorly presented, however, good journalism loses much of its impact. First-class content, therefore, requires first-class form, and so the proper relationship of *form* and *content* is the central question of newspaper typography.
>
> (Hutt, 1967, p. 1)

The Times Roman font, for example, which first appeared in print on 3 October 1932, was designed according to very strict criteria. It had to be:

> worthy of *The Times* – masculine, English, direct, simple, not more novel than it behoveth to be novel, or more novel than logic is novel in newspaper typography, and absolutely free from faddishness and frivolity.
>
> (Cited in Hutt, 1967, p. 59)

We might accept, then, that typefaces can have a semantic function in texts in English. But what about such things as anagrams, alliteration and puns? To what extent can we talk about these occurring in visual English?

## Visual alliteration?

Alliteration in English grammar – the repetition of consonants or vowels, often for dramatic effect – can sometimes be seen in the visual as a repetition of graphic elements. A recent advertisement on television for a new film release ended with the following imperative:

# Own it now on video

This slogan is not only alliterative in the usual (verbal) sense of the term, it is also 'visually alliterative': visual repetition occurs even where there is no phonetic repetition, as shown in Figure 2.8.

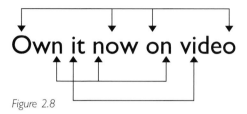

*Figure 2.8*

*Own* and *now* are of course anagrams: can we say that this adds to their meaning potential? In other words, because the two are so similar visually, do we make some sort of analogy when reading the two words?

*Figure 2.9*

Figure 2.9 shows a shop logo. Here we find recourse to a visual prototype (this shape represents a 'typical instance of' a fish, and stands for 'fish' in the collective imagination). Again, there is the equivalent to alliteration operating visually in these letters themselves, one in the icon represented by the text (the 'fish' shape), and one in the visual imagination, as shown in Figure 2.10.

*Figure 2.10*

The words *fins* and *fish* both contain four letters; three are the same in each word. The letters *N* and *H* are also rather similar visually, as they both contain two strong vertical lines.

## Visual puns

Often it is possible to uncover intentional or unintentional visual puns in images. These may exist in the typography, or in parts of a drawing or photograph. Hammond and Hughes's study of puns in 1978 revealed that pictures can contain just as many different types of visual pun as we find in the verbal English language. These range from the entirely accidental, found in revered paintings in art galleries, to those found in children's drawings, satirical cartoons in newspapers and magazines (such as a line of rats to represent *rat-race*), through to lewd picture postcards. The fact that it is possible, almost, to ignore visual puns – often they are simply not 'seen' – testifies more to dismissive attitudes to punning in English, and to lack of training in visual literacy, than to their non-existence. Some puns seem to be universal (there are visual puns on body parts and landscapes, for example, in most languages) – others are directly related to the language of the culture in which they appear.

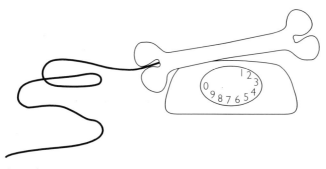

Figure 2.11

Visual puns often rely on the interaction between visual and verbal elements to bring their meaning to the fore. The advertisement in Figure 2.11 appeared on British television, advertising a phone-in programme. It is aimed at an extraordinarily narrow audience: not only is it UK specific, it is also region specific – it plays on Cockney rhyming slang associated with the East End of London, substituting *dog and bone* for *telephone*. Visual puns can often highlight the cultural (and temporal) specificity of visual literacy – Geipel (1972, p. 30) notes that even within a single language they can be very hard to decipher out of context, or years later.

   Popular newspapers, in particular, are apt to use visual puns as often as possible, and these often reinforce a point being made verbally. Figure 2.12 shows one that could only work in English.

Figure 2.12

Gaddie (1989) notes the wide diversity of intentional and unintentional or latent puns in the alphabet itself. Names of rock groups such as *U2* and *INXS* are examples, as are English nouns such as *A-frame, U-turn, T-shirt*, etc. His view is that links between letters and lookalike objects are not strictly random or accidental:

> The idea that there is some kind of strange or 'funny' connection between words that sound alike is a popular idea, but it has always been denied by the dictionaries.
>
> (Gaddie, 1989, p. 23)

Typographers and advertisers have long exploited the latent iconicity of the alphabet. To take one brief example of a typographic icon, consider the letter *X*. This seems to have become a supercharged typographic icon, at least in English. It is not widely used in the written language (i.e. there are few words that actually contain *X*). Its common use in the prefix ex-, however, has led to the widespread abbreviation X- in company signs and advertising (*X-Press Cleaners*, etc.). This is partly for reasons of economizing space, but also because it is unexpected and therefore makes it more memorable – an important function in advertising and the construction of corporate identity. *X* has a vast range of connotations. There is the (now international) rating system for film releases: *X-rated* has in its turn become diffused as a concept and acquired a whole set of its own connotations. There was a time when subliminal advertising used the technique of adding a large *X* to print and television advertisements – especially those containing landscapes. An advertisement for suntanning products, for example, would almost always contain an *X, added in* by an artist among the waves, the leaves of the trees or the sky. The *X* was barely perceptible, but there must have been reasons for its inclusion. Could it be that the letter X carries connotations of 'naughtiness' or 'temptation'? Visually at least, it is the same as the 'cross' which is used to mean 'wrong' or 'no' in schoolbooks. It can be placed over a poster to signify 'banned', 'cancelled' or 'censored'. It is used (along with the asterisk and certain other symbols) by mainstream newspapers to allow the inclusion of taboo words, even on the front page:

**B******S!**

People are sufficiently trained in this form of lexical substitution to transcode instantly the following advertising slogan:

Australians wouldn't give a **XXXX** for any other lager.

The beer (Castlemaine Four X) is ordered using its name, but the real meaning of the slogan is understood, and everyone shares the joke.

Below is a visual typographic pun which would be completely lost in the verbal. The American actor Richard Gere and his partner, model Cindy Crawford, had been subjected to a barrage of speculation in the press about the state of their marriage. In response, they published a full-page advertisement in *The Times*, saying that their marriage was still a happy one despite the rumours to the contrary. This headline was printed the following day in another newspaper:

# Cindy 4 Richard

It imitates the way that British schoolchildren used to carve their names into their wooden school desks to indicate allegiances. The headline is therefore implying that the action of publishing the advertisement was childish – and this connotation is introduced visually, by substituting '4' for 'for'. One number here is doing a great deal of work.

Where does all this leave us with regard to the boundaries between visual and verbal elements in English texts? Written English can be seen as having its own, often very complex, semantic codes, which are frequently expressed visually. We will now take a look at the idea of a visual English 'grammar', and consider to what extent it is appropriate (or possible) to speak of images in terms of a grammar.

## 2.3   SOME ELEMENTS OF ENGLISH VISUAL GRAMMAR

Many analysts of images and proponents of visual literacy claim that there is a 'grammar' inherent in images, just as there is in writing. In this section we look at some visual elements that may be seen as containing 'grammatical structures' in their own right, and consider their importance in the multimodal text. Dondis (1973) and Arnheim (1988) both provide in-depth discussions of 'visual syntax' and principles of spatial composition, for those who want to read further on the subject. Others take a functional approach and link the analysis of images to the functional theory of language associated with the work of Michael Halliday (1978, 1985). In Halliday's words, 'language is as it is because of what it has to do' (1978, p. 19). Following this view, the choice of linguistic sign – the word – and the ways in which words are combined in the clause, are related to the function(s) to which the language is being put. This view takes language as being a 'map of the world' (a way of *representing* things and events), rather than a 'window to the world' (a way of looking straight out on to the world). The implication of this is that there are alternative ways of representing the world – and that there is, by extension, no such thing as objective 'truth'. The meanings we ascribe to language are socially constructed and negotiated, or in Halliday's words:

> The particular form taken by the grammatical system of language is closely related to the social and personal needs that language is required to serve.
>
> (Halliday, 1970, p. 142)

A Hallidayan framework is useful because it adds a semantic dimension to the analysis of the text. It allows us to see differences in *meaning* between, for example, different ways of addressing people (*Mr Smith* or *John*), or different ways of describing events.

Some analysts of visual representation take a similar view: that the ways in which we represent events visually are linked to our point of view about those events, and what we want to communicate about them:

> The form of a representation cannot be divorced from its purpose and the requirements of the society in which the given visual language gains currency.
>
> (Gombrich, 1959, p. 78)

Halliday's model of language is also discussed in Chapter 1 of an earlier book in this series, *Using English: from conversation to canon* (Maybin and Mercer (eds), 1996).

Any semiotic mode (words, pictures, sound) develops resources for fulfilling three kinds of broad communicative function, or 'metafunction', in Halliday's terminology: ideational, interpersonal and textual.

---

### Halliday's communicative metafunctions – a summary

#### 1   The ideational metafunction

Every semiotic mode will have resources for constructing representations of (aspects of) the world.

#### 2   The interpersonal metafunction

Every semiotic mode will have resources for constructing (a) relations between the communicating parties (between writers and readers, painters and viewers, speakers and listeners); and (b) relations between these communicating parties and what they are representing, in other words, attitudes to the subject they are communicating about.

#### 3   The textual metafunction

Every semiotic mode will have resources for combining and integrating ideational and interpersonal meanings into the kinds of wholes we call 'texts' or 'communicative events' and recognize as news articles, paintings, jokes, conversations, lectures, and so on.

---

For every act of communication in which a given semiotic mode is used, a choice must be made from each of its systems. To form an English sentence, for example, you must choose from the system of person (first, second or third), the system of mood (statement, question, command), the system of tense (past, present or future) and so on, and all these choices combine in the one sentence, each adding an element of meaning to the whole. Similarly, in producing a picture, you must choose from the system of horizontal angle (frontal, profile or somewhere in between), the system of vertical angle (from above, at eye-level or from below), the system of distance (close shot, medium shot or long shot) and so on, and again, all these choices combine in the one picture, each adding an element of meaning.

Some elements of visual English grammar can be directly related to verbal English grammar, and it is often revealing to investigate the ways in which different modes, such as words and pictures, may express the same things, or contradict each other. Pictures and words cannot both convey all the same meanings, because not all meanings can be realized in every semiotic mode. Some things can be expressed only verbally, some only visually, and some both visually and verbally. Below we will look at a few examples.

## Direct and indirect address

Suppose we wanted to see whether the term 'direct address' can be used to describe the way that certain images communicate. Verbal direct address can be seen in:

Hey, you there, what do you think you're doing?

Direct address in pictures, on the other hand, can be seen in Figure 2.13.

Figure 2.13

Both language and pictures can be used to address directly or indirectly, but where language does it through the choice between second and third person (and in other ways also, for example through vocatives, imperatives, etc.), pictures do it by having people depicted in the image look at, and perhaps also gesture at, the viewer of the picture. (It could also be, of course, that depicted animals look at the viewer, or even things: in children's books, trains, cars and other objects may have eyes and address the viewer directly.)

Many texts these days, of course, contain both words and pictures. In a multimodal text, then, we could ask:

- does the *verbal language* address the listener or reader directly (e.g. through the use of the second person pronoun 'you')?

- does the *image* address the viewer directly (which happens if a depicted person looks at the camera, and hence at the viewer)?

and if the text has both words and pictures we could ask:

- is direct address chosen in both words and pictures or not? And if not, why?

The recruitment poster shown in Figure 2.13 has direct address in both visual and verbal modes, perhaps to reinforce the message in the strongest way possible. Other texts (often advertisements) may use direct address in the image and indirect address in the verbal text.

## Given–new structures

Given–new structures are commonly found in verbal English. Given information refers to that which is stated but already known to the participants, and new information is that which is not already known (see Wales, 1989, pp. 208–9). Wales gives the following example:

Besides being a well known literary critic (given), he also writes books on the history of aviation (new).

Given–new structures are often based on various types of opposition:

It's time to *stop* the phoney war and *start* the real battle.
(*Daily Star*, 22 January 1992)

Success is supposed to be an endangered species in this country. *Not any more.*
(*Daily Mirror*, April 1994)

Tense, nervous headache? Take Anadin.
(Advertisement)

In verbal English, such as in these examples, the given is what comes first in the clause and the new what comes last, and what, usually, has the greatest stress. In other words, given and new are realized sequentially (through 'before' and 'after'). These can be transcoded in images by use of the horizontal axis. In images, given and new are represented spatially, through 'left' and 'right'. A vast number of advertisements in English use the visual axis in this way, positioning the taken-for-granted, 'already understood' information on the left and the new information on the right. The left side of the advertisement often outlines the problem, or given situation, while the right side shows the product (and the solution), as shown in Figure 2.14.

The vertical axis can also be used as a structuring device, as shown in Plate 2. In this advertisement for Femigraine, we find visual representation of two opposing states (the 'before' and 'after' in relation to use of the product). Other

*Figure 2.14*

advertisements use the top half as the space for the 'ideal' or the 'promise' – what you will become, or have, if you buy the product. The bottom half is reserved for the 'down to earth', the 'real' (often a product description in verbal English).

## Vectors: visual transitivity?

Another grammatical element that can be seen in the visual is Halliday's theory of transitivity. **Transitivity** in Halliday's framework differs from the way the term is used in traditional grammar (where 'transitive' refers to verbs that normally require an object – *Sally cut the bread*, and 'intransitive' to verbs that do not require an object – *Sally ran*). For Halliday the system of transitivity provides a set of choices for representing 'what is going on in the world'. Put simply, it asks 'who does what to whom, and in what circumstances?' With what types of verb (processes, in his terms) are participants associated, and what does this tell us about social roles?

One of these choices is what Halliday (1985) has called the 'material process', the case in which 'what is going on' is represented as either an *action*, or a *transaction*, or an *event*. All three of these options are realized by grammatical structures. To understand this we first need to note that English requires us to analyse what is going on into two kinds of representational element, *processes* (what is going on) and *participants* (the entities involved with what is going on). For example, in reality the flying of a bird may be a single, unanalysable whole, in which the bird cannot be separated from the flying nor the flying from

---

**Outline of material processes**

*I   Actions*

There is only one participant, an actor, so that the action is represented as though it is done 'in a void', for its own sake, without anyone or anything else being involved. An example:

| Actor | Material process: action |
|-------|--------------------------|
| The soldier | fired |

*2   Transactions*

There are two participants, an actor and a goal, so that the deed is represented as having consequences for someone or something else. An example:

| Actor | Material process: transaction | Goal |
|-------|-------------------------------|------|
| The soldier | killed | innocent villagers |

*3   Event*

There is only one participant, a goal, so that whatever goes on is not explicitly represented as being done *by* someone or something. It is represented as 'just happening'. An example:

| Goal | Material process: event |
|------|-------------------------|
| Innocent villagers | died |

the bird. But if we want to speak about it in English we must analyse the event into a participant (the bird) and a process (flying). Participants can be involved in material processes in one of two ways, as *actor*, that is, as 'the one who does the deed' or as *goal*, that is, as 'the one to whom the deed is done' or 'to whom the event happens'. Three configurations are therefore possible (see box).

Clearly the above examples constitute three different representations of the same event. Which option is chosen depends on the writer and on the context of writing. Writers with a technical interest in weaponry (in a specialist magazine, perhaps) might have an interest in obscuring the pain and destruction that weapons cause. Writers who are on the same side as the soldiers might also have an interest in obscuring their army's responsibility for the death of innocent civilians, and choose the 'event' option – usually adding a circumstantial element to flesh it out (e.g. innocent villagers *died in a large-scale military action yesterday*). A very clear example of the way such ideological choices are motivated by context can be found in Trew (1979a, 1979b).

Visual transitivity can be seen in the relationships between vectors. **Vectors** can be understood as 'lines which lead the eye' in an image. They may be formed by objects or parts of objects (arms, legs, guns, branches) or by angles set up in the image, or by such elements as the direction of a person's eye. Vectors can play an important part in portraying transitivity in images – about who is doing what to whom. If, in a photograph, a line is being sent out from one person or object towards another, then it is possible to say something about the relationship being depicted – who is acting, who is being acted upon.

It is possible to represent visually the English sentences in the box above, as shown in Figures 2.15 to 2.17.

*Figure 2.15   Action: the soldier fired*

*Figure 2.16   Transaction: the soldier killed innocent villagers*

*Figure 2.17   Event: innocent villagers died*

Note that the actors and goals may be abstract shapes, for instance boxes in diagrams where concepts are related to each other, or triangles and circles in abstract art.

Vectors are also instrumental in constructing visual narratives – to show a chain of events unfolding, and to signpost the narrative path for the reader. We will look at examples of visual narratives later in this chapter.

## Modality: visualizing the 'real'

Modality is another important aspect of verbal English grammar. **Modality** in Halliday's social semiotic framework of language can be seen as, broadly, expressions of 'comment' or 'attitude' by the speaker towards a proposition, and is often realized by the use of modal auxiliary verbs, such as *should, could, ought, must* and so on. These indicate such things as obligation, permission, desirability and truth (for a fuller discussion of modality in a social semiotic framework, see Fowler, 1991, pp. 85–7). The expression of a speaker's attitude towards the truth value or reliability of a proposition can be particularly interesting to analyse. High modality (the expression of high truth value) occurs in *I know he is coming* – the speaker is expressing certainty about the other person's arrival. Low modality occurs in *He might come,* where the speaker is unsure that he will arrive. Modality may also be realized by the use of distancing strategies, as in statements such as *He says he is coming* which may indicate the speaker's doubt about the likelihood of the other person's arrival; hedges (*a bit, sort of*), and tag questions (*doesn't he?*).

Modality can be expressed visually too: some images are presented as 'more real' or 'more true' than others:

> Visuals can represent people, places and things as though they are real, as though they actually exist in this way, or as though they do not – as though they are imaginings, fantasies, caricatures, etc. And, here too, modality judgements are social, dependent on what is considered real (or true, or sacred) in the social group for which the representation is primarily intended.
>
> (Kress and van Leeuwen, 1996, p. 161)

A simple line drawing, for example, could be seen as having low modality – it may be seen as a simple sketch, or a rough outline, not intended to be accurate or proportioned. A sharply detailed, fine-grained photograph, on the other hand, could be ascribed high modality. For a start, people are trained to ascribe high truth value to photographs. Secondly, photographs often contain large amounts of detail, so seem to show more of the world 'as it is'.

Diagrams, however, can also portray high modality because they purport to show more of what a photograph cannot, such as the inclusion of electrical circuits, or mental processes – what is actually 'there' and 'real'. Diagrams can be used to portray what is normally only heard, or imagined. Take a scientific diagram like that in Figure 2.18.

This drawing is about as abstract, as 'reduced' in every respect, as possible. There is no detail in the representation, no background, no colour, no representation of depth, or of light and shade. Low modality, in other words. Yet scientists might *not* regard the diagram as unreal, because they might define reality not on the basis of surface resemblance – how much the image looks like what we would normally see – but on the basis of how accurately it represents a deeper, more

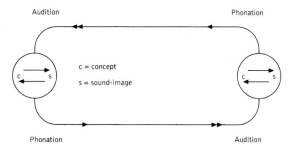

*Figure 2.18    Saussure's schematized speech circuit, 1916*

abstract or general truth based on the essential characteristics of what is depicted. In this case then, although this appears to be a highly simplified drawing of what is a complex situation, Figure 2.18 might be ascribed high truth value, because it supposedly shows us more of spoken communication 'as it really is'.

Television news, textbooks and newspapers are filled with graphs and diagrams, whether they are for displaying economic indicators, to show a chemical reaction, or to depict the military strategy of an army. The purpose of diagrams and graphics is to simplify and explain complicated information. The creation of a diagram necessarily involves, however, taking decisions as to:

- *what* to include (i.e. what is considered significant and meaningful) – and therefore what to exclude;

- *how* to present information (colour, scales on graphs, symbols on maps).

Kress and van Leeuwen note that:

> Simplicity is ... always based on a particular cultural orientation and ideological stance, and the result of intensive training. It is only once this training is achieved that images (and the way of looking at the world expressed by their structure) can appear 'natural' and 'simple', and hence not in need of analysis.
>
> (Kress and van Leeuwen, 1990, p. 15)

It is also important to recognize that there is more than one modality system, often dependent on the context in which the image appears. Just as we ascribe levels of modality to verbal English depending on the social context, the social context in which we ascribe levels of modality to images is an important factor. Colour, for instance, may have high modality in one context but low modality in another. Lynch and Edgerton's research (1988) into the visual presentation of scientific data, for example, revealed that while many scientists do not acknowledge that the aesthetic presentation of their work is important, many do in fact alter their images depending on the intended audience. The astronomers interviewed by Lynch and Edgerton all had examples of 'pretty pictures' which were produced specifically for certain readerships ('the public' versus 'the scientists'). Images were digitally processed in different ways for the two audiences – in particular many images intended for a popular, nonscientific audience included false colours. Black and white images were used by the astronomers themselves for their work, as these are easier to interpret than colour which can confuse the eye. Colour, in this case, is associated with promotion and popularization, but is a distraction from the scientific data.

**Activity 2.6**   *(Allow 10 minutes)*

Look at Plate 3, the book cover for *The Immigration Invasion*. You can decode a great deal of information from this one page. Some elements you should be looking at are:

| | |
|---|---|
| point of view: | whose point of view are we looking at, and how do you know? |
| transitivity: | who, or what, is doing what to whom in this diagram? |
| modality: | what devices are used to convince us of the truth, or falsehood, of this scenario? |

**Comment**

*The Immigration Invasion* laments the 'high number of immigrants' coming into the USA from South American countries. This point of view is reflected in the visuals as much as in the verbal English on the front cover – in fact you could say that it is not necessary to read the book in order to discover what the authors are advocating (which in this case is mass 'repatriation'). Most important of all here is the *interaction* of the visual and verbal elements – the way that the presence, and positioning, of individual elements affect and reinterpret the others.

The diagram in Plate 3 is a good example of the polysemous nature of visual representation – the way that images, like words and sentences are open to more than one interpretation. What other valid interpretations of this diagram might there be? The viewer's point of view will affect how the diagram is 'read'. The producer's point of view also affects what is included in a diagram, and how it is presented – try to visualize how this diagram might have looked, told from the point of view of the 'invaders'!

## 2.4   VISUAL NARRATIVES

So far we have been looking at individual graphic elements and single images. But longer texts have their own structure, and one way of looking at this is in terms of narrative structures. Cartoons are a good example of multimodal narratives, so we will focus primarily on these in this section.

Cartoons use most, if not all, of the devices outlined so far in this chapter. In addition they employ specific devices to convey mood, movement and narrative structure. Print cartoons share some properties with photographs, as do animated cartoons with film (the subject of Reading B). There are many genres: children's comics, teenage photo stories in magazines, adult comics, political satire in daily newspapers. Genre divisions are, as in literature, difficult to pin down, and they are breaking down further with the increasing availability of new multimedia technologies. Popular newspapers may use photo stories to portray a narrative on the problem page, and biting political satire may be achieved by using a visual style similar to that of comic books for the very young. Cartoons are also being increasingly used in traditionally nonpictorial contexts, such as job advertisements, so understanding the ways that visual and verbal codes communicate is becoming important in an increasing range of contexts.

Visual and verbal elements are so closely intertwined in cartoons that it can be difficult to separate them. Because of their visual format, cartoons provide rich resources for the representation of features common in face-to-face interaction

Figure 2.19

that are unavailable to written English. These include paralinguistic features such as facial expression, gestures and posture. There are also proxemic indicators – how characters are positioned can reveal information about their relationships and attitudes to each other – closeness, distance, antipathy and so on.

In addition, cartoons contain vast amounts of graphic information used to represent verbal English. Some of these are directly related to English phrases: we say that we 'see stars' after a bump on the head, so stars or asterisks over a cartoon character's head are understood; we say we 'have a bright idea' or 'see the light' so the pictorial representation of a light bulb is also comprehensible; we know the shapes lightning can take in the sky, so can relate ⟿ to concepts of danger, etc. There may be also be recourse to the verbal, to emphasize the visual – even a nonsense word acquires semantic significance in a visual context (see Figure 2.19).

Intonation may be expressed in a number of ways. Typefaces, in particular, can be used to show changes of pitch or stress – the size of the type and the use of emboldening, in particular, are common devices in this respect. Similarly, mixes of upper and lower case can suggest shouting and whispering respectively, as shown in Figure 2.7 (the headmaster and pupil poem) in section 2.2.

Punctuation is frequently used as a semantic device in cartoons. Exclamation marks can be added to a character's speech to indicate surprise or outrage, or punctuation marks can be used alone, indicating moments where feelings are running so high that verbal English is inadequate for expressing them (see left).

Letters can be repeated to show st-st-stammering, and clues to a character's accent can be shown by using a semi-phonetic representation of speech, such as *wot* for *what*, or *'er* for *her.*

## Creating a visual narrative

So how are narrative structures expressed visually? Movement can be conveyed as shown in Figure 2.20.

Or movement may be conveyed visually by repetitions or other devices – here is a character tossing a coin:

Figure 2.20

Figure 2.21

Cartoon narratives need to propel the reader forwards through the story, and this is often achieved through the use of vectors, as well as by utilizing the conventional verbal reading path – in the case of English, left to right. In modern print cartoons the page will be divided into a number of frames, or vignettes. This is often standardized within a particular genre, or for a particular artist – European cartoons, for example, typically use the page format and reading paths shown in Figure 2.22, which follows the left-to-right pattern for the verbal language.

Languages which traditionally do not read left to right, such as Chinese, may use either a left-to-right progression, or top to bottom, as shown in Figure 2.23.

Note that here the frames, as well as the speech, read downwards (although this is not always the case in Chinese). In any case, it is not possible to state definitively that different countries are associated with distinctive types or styles of cartoon – every country and language has a range of different styles, some of which will be influenced in turn by the styles of other countries. In addition there is always a range of purposes to which visual depiction is put – cultural, religious and educational.

Neither is the division of the page into frames the only way to create a visual

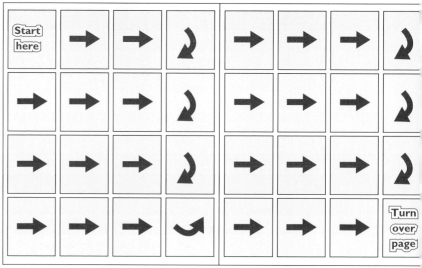

Figure 2.22

"How do you keep from getting pregnant?"

"I count days."

"Every month women have a number of dangerous days."

"For us men, every day is dangerous."

Frank treatment of relations between the sexes in Lao Chiung's adult strip, "Them."

Figure 2.23

One bottle of rice wine for my old man.

Your husband's a notorious drinker. Is one enough?

For drinking, one might not be enough.

But for hitting, one is plenty.

narrative. McCloud (1994, pp. 12–13) notes that one can see the Bayeux tapestry (an enormous linear tapestry showing the Norman conquest in the eleventh century) as a type of cartoon – it reads left to right, leading the viewer onwards as the story of the battle unfolds in chronological order. He points out that although there are no distinct frames, changes of background and subject matter are used to create a coherent story.

Egyptian hieroglyphics, too, comprise a pictorial narrative. Figure 2.24 shows McCloud's interpretation of a small section of Egyptian painting.

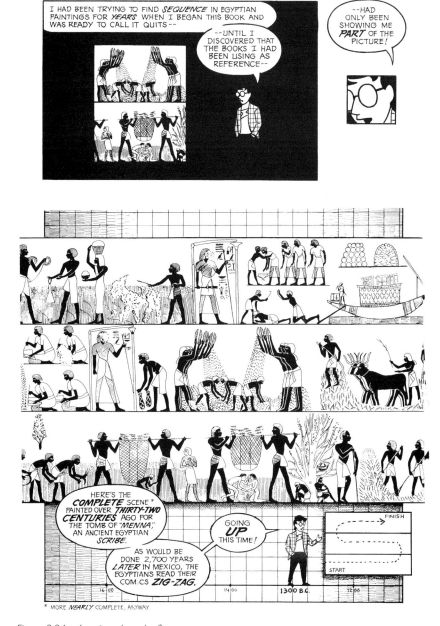

Figure 2.24    (continued overleaf)

*Figure 2.24    (continued)*

The vectors of cartoon frames themselves may encode additional information
about the next stage in the visual narrative. Plate 4 shows a page from *The
Adventures of Mighty Max*, published in December 1994; the arrangements of its
frames on the page are shown in Figure 2.25.

   The shapes of these frames set up directional vectors. The character's arms
and legs, too, are used to create vectors and thus convey directionality – the
reader's eye is led from one frame to the next by literally following the central
character, rather than by the conventional left-to-right direction in verbal English.
We as readers follow Max's zig-zag path through the story – and until we get there,
we are not quite sure where we are going next. And neither, of course, is Max – so

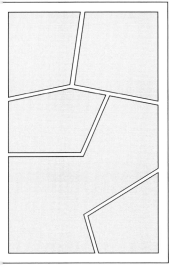

Deixis is discussed more fully in Chapter 1 of this book.

*Figure 2.25*

here the vectors have an additional function – to create links between reader and character. In more traditional reading paths, the reader knows the next step in advance (unlike the character) so is necessarily more of an observer. Here, Max and the reader share the unsettling experience.

The frame shapes can be semantically motivated: in the *Mighty Max* example the jagged and chaotic frames convey action and danger. Dondis argues that direction is one meaning-laden aspect of visual syntax: 'each visual direction has strong associative meaning and is a valuable tool in making visual messages' (1973, p. 46). He states that horizontal and vertical lines are associated with well being and stability, whereas a diagonal line is unstable, provoking and even upsetting. Curves, on the other hand, are associated with encompassment, repetition and warmth.

## Visual deixis?

**Deixis**, too, can be seen to operate in certain elements of visual English. For example, visual shapes can be used to show deictic expressions of time, such as 'then' or 'now'. Figure 2.26, from the American comic artist Will Eisner, shows how the shapes of panel borders can be used to locate the reader in the past or the present.

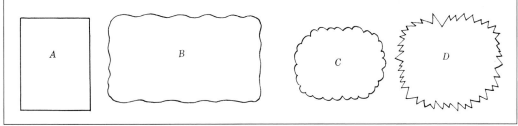

THE 'LANGUAGE' OF THE PANEL BORDER

In addition to its primary function as a frame in which to place objects and actions, the panel border itself can be used as part of the non-verbal 'language' of sequential art.

For example, rectangular panels with straight edged borders (A), unless the verbal portion of the narrative contradicts this, usually are meant to imply that the actions contained therein are set in the present tense. The flashback (a change in tense or shift in time) is often indicated by altering the line which makes up the frame. The wavy edged (B) or scalloped (C) panel border is the most common past time indicator. While there is no universally agreed upon convention for expressing tense through the outline of the frame, the 'character' of the line—as in the case of sound, emotion (D) or thought (C)—creates a hieroglyphic.

*Figure 2.26*

Colour, too, can be used deictically. In particular it can be used to indicate time and the passage of time (how do you know when it is dawn, or night-time?). Lack of colour is also significant, such as in the use of silhouettes. Black and white can often, as it can in film, convey past tense, and a transition to colour can indicate that the reader is now located in the present.

## Portraying interpersonal relationships

One of the ways in which relationships (part of the interpersonal metafunction) may be represented in images is through the camera angle. Kress and van Leeuwen believe that the horizontal angle signifies involvement or distance, and that the vertical angle can represent power relationships between the viewer and those depicted:

> In many of the illustrations in school textbooks we look down rather steeply on people – workers in the hall; children in a school yard. In such books the social world lies at the feet of the viewer, so to speak: knowledge is power. The models in magazine advertisements and features, and newsworthy people and celebrities in magazine articles, on the other hand, generally look down on the viewer: these models are depicted as exercising symbolic power over us.
>
> (Kress and van Leeuwen, 1996, p. 146)

They also note that the size of the frame itself can be an indicator of social distance – realized by the choice between close up, medium shot, long shot:

> The distances people keep … depend on their social relation … People are portrayed *as though* they are friends, or *as though* they are strangers.
>
> (Kress and van Leeuwen, 1996, pp. 131–2)

An example is shown in Figure 2.27. The viewer sees the school-children from above, and thus is literally 'looking down on them'.

Angles in drawings can operate in similar ways to those in film or photographs – aerial shots can convey power, show more information and/or slow down the narrative. The (camera) angle therefore has an important effect on pace. Empathy with Max in Plate 4 is in part created through the use of 'camera' angles: in the third frame, where he is surrounded by enemies, the reader is placed *on the same level* with him – solidarity is created through equal positioning of reader and character. In the next frame we are looking down on the scene from a more distant position, where Max is in the visual centre, surrounded by an array of large threatening characters coming at him from all sides, and – importantly – from above. He is small in this frame, and looking *up* at the impending danger, which emphasizes his vulnerability. Assuming we as readers are empathetically engaged with him, we feel powerless to intervene from this distance, and are further encouraged to read on by the last frame where Max is threatened with immediate death …

Figure 2.27

Look at the scene in Figure 2.28, where the reader is placed on the balustrade with the security guard, watching the devastating explosion below.

Figure 2.28

❖   ❖   ❖   ❖   ❖

**Activity 2.7**  *(Allow 15 minutes)*

Find a print cartoon, and look closely at:
- devices for representing movement;
- visual narrative paths: how is the reader moved on to the next frame?
- devices for creating empathy (and antipathy) with the characters – how is this achieved? Who do the characters make eye contact with?

❖   ❖   ❖   ❖   ❖

It seems that culture and the influence of the verbal language also play an important role in the layout of the page. Different languages and cultures may express visual narrative structures in different ways. McCloud noted that traditional Japanese cartoons, for example, are far more cyclical in their layout than American ones. His analysis of the cartoon techniques and narrative paths used in different countries revealed that American artists used a far higher proportion of action-to-action frame transitions than Japanese artists. This held for other 'western' countries (he studied *Tintin*, for example, and got similar results, in spite of other radical differences between French and American styles). In Japan, although artists did use action-to-action transitions between panels, they also used a striking number of subject-to-subject transitions, and moves from aspect to aspect. McCloud comments on this as follows:

Most often used to establish a mood or a sense of place, time seems to stand still in these quiet, contemplative combinations ... Rather than acting as a bridge between separate moments, the reader here must assemble a single moment using scattered fragments.

(McCloud, 1994, p. 79)

In considering the reasons for this difference, he notes that Japanese cartoons often appear in enormous anthologies, and that therefore 'dozens of panels can be devoted to portraying slow cinematic movement or to setting a mood' (1994, p. 80). But the fundamental reason, for him, is a difference between eastern and western cultural traditions (see Figure 2.29).

*Figure 2.29*

*Figure 2.29   (continued)*

## Closure: making the viewer do the work

Many forms of visual information are now encountered in the context of verbal English. Newspaper photographs, corporate logos and graphic elements are often surrounded and intertwined with print. This then begs the question of how elements in visual and verbal modes interact on the page – a central issue in multimodal texts. How do the messages of words and pictures reinforce or undermine each other, and in what ways is the reader invited to see these meanings as connected or distinct?

Creating meaning from what we see in a multimodal text involves a complex interaction of visual elements and verbal English presented to the eye, as well as contextual and background knowledge. Arnheim has noted that 'the perception of a complex visual pattern may be modified by the presence of a second pattern' (1970, p. 61), describing an experiment where observers were asked to give their impressions of two paintings of quite different style shown next to each other – when one of the pair was replaced by another, the subjects' impressions of the paintings differed enormously from the first viewing. He terms this the 'privilege of observing everything in relation' (1970, p. 62). What we see, then, depends not only upon the image itself, but also on the context and on the other images, or words, on the page.

Look at Plate 5. How are we supposed to understand this front page from a British newspaper? The articles are supposedly unrelated – but are they? It is very difficult to read them separately, given the layout of the page and the size of the headline typeface – so what possibilities for alternative meanings are being created here?

In this page layout, because of the left-to-right reading path in English, and the way the two articles are placed on the page, the two (unrelated) stories can easily become intertwined. The vector set up by the direction of Princess Diana's eyes leads the viewer to the article, and to the picture of the lion. The headline HUMAN PREY, which appears in large, bold type, is in turn followed by suspension points (…) implying that there is more to be learned from this headline, thus the reader may be again invited to make connections between the two. The juxtaposition of all the elements on the page – visual and verbal – produces a complex semantic cocktail.

Figure 2.30

❖   ❖   ❖   ❖   ❖

**Activity 2.8**   *(Allow 10 minutes)*

Figure 2.30 shows another multimodal text from a newspaper. How do verbal and visual elements interact on this page? Do they seem to be communicating the same, or contradictory messages? Do you find that one mode of communication dominates the other, or invites you as the reader to reinterpret one in light of the other?

**Comment**

Some of the elements you may have noted include the strong directional vectors and the footballer's facial expression (exertion). The camera angle is from below, so he is positioned slightly *higher* than the viewer. He is also breaking out of the frame, coming *towards* the viewer.

## 2.5   MOVING ENGLISH: THE VISUAL LANGUAGE OF FILM

So far we have been considering still images, and the ways in which images can represent semantic distinctions that in verbal English would be conveyed through grammatical structure. The two modes of communication discussed in this chapter – verbal and visual – cannot both convey all of the meanings that can be expressed individually, but there are often similarities between the two. What happens, though, when the images begin to move?

In the next reading Theo van Leeuwen describes the ways in which the dynamic nature of images in film allows new configurations of meaning in film texts. The verbal and visual languages (as well, of course, as other modes of communication such as music and sound effects) can combine in film to present us with a meaningful whole.

An important point in this reading is that it is becoming increasingly difficult to separate the various elements in modern, multimodal texts. It is practically impossible to disentangle, for example, the pictures from the words, or the music from the pictures – the text cannot be understood unless the viewer accepts that all these elements combine and interact with each other.

In order to understand how the visual and the verbal modes interact, and their differences and similarities, van Leeuwen brings them into a single theoretical framework. He uses a semiotic model (again based on Halliday) because it allows him to analyse film by looking at what structures say, rather than by trying to analyse them through their syntax. By applying Halliday's social semiotic model of language to both pictures and words in a film text, he draws an analogy between the way the visual and verbal communicate to the viewer.

**Activity 2.9**   *(Reading B)*

Read 'Moving English: the visual language of film' by Theo van Leeuwen (Reading B). Taking a social semiotic approach, as van Leeuwen does in Reading B, and looking at how visual language in film fulfils Halliday's three metafunctions of language reveals that the visual language of film can do many of the same things as verbal English. As you read, consider how far we can go in applying Halliday's model to moving images.

**Comment**

This reading poses some complex questions. Visual and verbal modes of communication in film can each fulfil similar functions (they can represent the world, they can portray interpersonal relationships and they can organize elements into texts). Van Leeuwen's last example shows that the visual and the verbal can be used to show the same thing, in his example from *Industrial Britain*. This is, of course, not always the case. Broadcast news, as he points out, has to show different information in the two modes – the pictures can only show what has already happened, whereas the words can describe the events leading up to the present moment. An interesting issue to explore is how information is represented in each mode of communication, and particularly how the information is distributed between these modes. What information is given to the visual channel, and what to the verbal?

Another interesting question to consider might be the relationship of visual language(s) to verbal languages. Would further research, using this approach, help to identify certain visual formats as being 'English' rather than as belonging to another language? Could we say, for example, that the visual mode of an American film is in 'English', and that of an Indian film is in 'Hindi'? It is difficult to decide whether a visual grammar can be said to be related to a single language. You may conclude, for example, that the dominance of English in the film industry worldwide has led to a 'universal' visual grammar of film. If so, we might note the 'demotion' of the verbal in favour of the visual, to allow people who do not share the same verbal language to communicate with others. Or you may be able to identify distinct differences in the ways different cultures and countries represent people and events visually, or in the ways they edit sequences, leading to the conclusion that there may be distinct visual grammars. Your answers to these questions will depend on how you choose to define language (and English) and on where the boundary lies – if there is one – between language and culture.

> In Chapter 5 David Graddol considers whether the dubbing of English language films into other languages contributes to the process of cultural globalization.

## 2.6  CONCLUSION

I have been arguing in this chapter that texts are becoming increasingly multimodal: employing visual and verbal (and aural) semiotic modes simultaneously. Visual literacy is therefore becoming important in spheres traditionally associated with verbal forms of English, such as writing on a computer at work or reading a newspaper. The spread of new image technologies is providing new uses for creating and understanding forms of visual English, and new reasons for people to become more visually literate.

In this chapter we have been considering some of the forms of visual information that are used to communicate in English texts. We have looked at how the meanings ascribed to visual information are to a large extent socially constructed and culturally dependent, rather than a natural or inherent characteristic of the visual form itself. Literacy in visual English, and in other visual languages, is affected by culture and also by the linguistic structure of the verbal language.

## Reading A
## THE SEMIOTIC CONSTRUCTION OF
## A WINE LABEL

*David Graddol*

The word 'text' carries with it, for many people, connotations of substantial content and seriousness of communicative purpose but the majority of texts which circulate in late modern times do not easily fit this description. For example, the packaging and labelling on food sold in supermarkets gives rise to a multitude of ephemeral texts which are in many ways typical of a consumer society. One might expect that the transient function of packaging would mean that limited resources would be expended on its design but, as all consumers are aware, this is not usually the case. A great deal of care goes into the creation of packaging and it routinely deploys a variety of semiotic resources – verbal, visual and sometimes tactile and olfactory.

One reason for this is that packaging serves several purposes, such as protecting the merchandise during distribution and storage, encouraging a shopper to buy the product, and informing the consumer of its content and potential use. It must accomplish all of these functions within a variety of constraints including legal (the law governs what must and may be said on labels), economic (such as the cost of packaging in relation to the cost of the goods, or a supermarket's requirements for display and merchandising), practical (such as the size and shape of the goods) and cultural (including the need to draw on discourses of consumer desire and to take account of social patterns of consumption). What might be perceived as its main function (that of persuading purchasers to buy) must be accomplished within a time constraint – the packaging must hail the potential purchaser from the shelves, draw attention to its presence among competitors' products, and communicate desirability both at a distance and on closer inspection.

The sophistication of packaging design thus reflects a complexity in communicative function. This point is well illustrated by the labels that can be found on the back of bottles of wine, such as that illustrated in Figure 1, taken from a Californian wine sold in California. I will examine the design of such labels more closely, showing how they address a multiple readership in complex and, at times, contradictory ways reflecting many of the ambiguities and contradictions associated with the consumer-subject in industrialized societies.

# MONT·PELLIER

### 100%
### MERLOT

Wine has been with us since the beginning of civilization. It is a temperate, civilized, romantic mealtime beverage. Wine has been praised for centuries by statesmen, philosophers, poets and scholars. Wine in moderation is an integral part of our families' culture, heritage and. the gracious way of life.

**GOVERNMENT WARNING:** (1) ACCORDING TO THE SURGEON GENERAL, WOMEN SHOULD NOT DRINK ALCOHOLIC BEVERAGES DURING PREGNANCY BECAUSE OF THE RISK OF BIRTH DEFECTS. (2) CONSUMPTION OF ALCOHOLIC BEVERAGES IMPAIRS YOUR ABILITY TO DRIVE A CAR OR OPERATE MACHINERY, AND MAY CAUSE HEALTH PROBLEMS.

750 ML

CONTAINS SULFITES

*Figure 1    The back label from a Californian
wine as locally sold*

## The multimodal nature of the label

The label shown in Figure 1 communicates its complex message by means of a variety of codes and devices in addition to the verbal channel. These semiotic modalities include:

- a code of numbers: 100%, 750 ml; numerical value of the bar code;
- the bar code;
- nibbles around the label indicating the batch and time of bottling (not shown);
- graphic design features such as rules;
- words, which are organized in space;
- typography – a visual coding of language.

The label is thus a multimodal text. As a consequence the meanings conveyed by the label are potentially complex: different messages may be conveyed through each mode, and these may reinforce each other or give rise to tensions and even contradictions – not necessarily in the basic information conveyed but in the way the reader is addressed.

## The complexity of audience address

Before it reaches the supermarket shelves the bottle will be handled by many intermediaries such as shippers, wholesalers, buyers for the supermarket, store managers and shelf fillers. At each stage the labelling must present the product in a way that ensures the best treatment so that it eventually achieves a prominent place in the store. In the supermarket it must speak to purchasers, persuading them that the product is attractive and worth the price being asked. There is thus no sole occasion on which the label serves its communicative function nor only one kind of person who will read it.

The different semiotic resources of the text are employed to address this multiple audience in a way that recognizes the different social and economic relations the text producer wishes to construct with each. For example, the bar code addresses the retailer, or rather the machines and computer systems used for stock control and pricing; the bar code also impinges on the relation between retailer and customer, since it records details of the particular transaction (location, time, quantity) in order to build profiles of consumer activity for marketing purposes. Bar codes are thus difficult things to integrate into a label design. If they are too prominent they may highlight the retailer's convenience and interest more than that of the consumer, drawing attention to the goods as revenue potential rather than as a satisfier of consumer need or desire. Unfortunately, in order to be read by automated check-out tills (and thus minimize staff costs) such bar codes need to be of a minimum size and standard placement. Practical label design must thus compromise between the two potentially competing requirements. In Figure 1 the bar code is located in the lower portion of the label, marked off from the main text by a rule.

It is not clear who is intended to read the batch information that is communicated by nibbles on the label edge. It addresses, however, some of the legal and institutional relations that govern the exchange of goods between manufacturer, distributor, retailer, customer and consumer. It is a part of the text that is not ordinarily read, but may become a focus of interest if these economic, legal and social relations are called into question – such as in the case of damaged or contaminated goods. The fact that this code is not transparent to the consumer, of course, is a part of that social relation.

### The contradictory nature of the consumer-subject

The most prominent part of the text of the label is clearly addressed to the consumer. But food buying is a complex social as well as economic activity which is highly structured according to region, ethnicity, social class and gender. A retailer's market research, for example, may show that wine in their supermarkets is bought mainly by women but drunk largely by men, or that higher price wines are bought mainly for meals to which guests are invited.

This means that the label will, at the very least, have to address the consumer-purchaser, the consumer-host, and the consumer-guest. And how does such a wine label speak to guests at the dinner table, and what does it say about the host's taste, judgement, wealth and hospitality? This will depend to large measure on the cultural practices with which the consumption of wine is associated. What, for example, is the significance of serving wine at the dinner table (in different countries, among different social and ethnic groups)? What little rituals of opening and serving are associated with it? In Britain, a supermarket brand name on the label may, for example, reassure the consumer-purchaser that a particular wine is of reliable quality and good value, but the consumer-guest may regard it as more suitable for family consumption than for a special occasion.

## Heteroglossia in the text

Heteroglossia is discussed in Chapter 1 of this book.

There is a further contradiction in the way the consumer is addressed which arises from the legislation governing label design.

The text in Figure 1, for example, contains two paragraphs: the upper one addresses the consumer as one with desires, appetites and choices. The lower text, however, addresses the reader as a consumer who has certain rights and to whom the manufacturer has certain duties of care. The result is that consumers are simultaneously told that this wine will enhance their life, and that it will damage it. This particular contradiction arises from the law governing wine labelling in California, but the words and descriptions that can be placed on wine labels are, in most countries, highly regulated. By regulating the ways in which the reader can be addressed by the text they regulate also the kinds of social relation that can be established with a reader. There is thus a contradiction which arises from the competing 'interests' established by consumer law and the manufacturer/retailer and which results in different voices being represented in the text.

The contradictions are clearly signalled by the language genres in which the two fragments are written. The persuasive text is highly evaluative, using words like *civilized* and *gracious*. It incorporates the reader in this evaluation by the use of the first person: 'wine has been with *us*', '*our* culture'. The Surgeon General's warning, in contrast, draws on language genres of information giving and objective authority. It uses modal constructions such as *should not*, terms from a formal scientific register, *alcoholic beverages*, employs a discourse of medical cause and effect, *because of the risk of birth defects*, uses impersonal address in the third person, *women should not*, or in the second person, *impairs your ability*, and includes enumerated paragraphs.

These two text fragments thus not only give contradictory messages at the surface level ('drink and enjoy' versus 'drink and die'), they also position the reader in quite different ways and attempt to construct different ideas about what it is to be a consumer. In the remainder of this reading I want to examine this heteroglossia more closely, showing how the tension between promotion and regulation affects other parts of the text and how the perception of contradiction is minimized by visual design.

## The legal restrictions

There is certain information which must by law be given on labels carried by the wine sold in the European Union (EU), such as the alcoholic strength, volume, country of origin and category of wine. There are also various kinds of optional information, such as recommendations to the consumer about:

- dishes with which the wine might be served;

- manner of serving;

- appropriate handling of the wine;

- proper storage of the wine;

- the history of the particular wine or of the bottler;

- the natural and technical conditions under which the wine was made.

If information is neither required nor optional, then it cannot be given on the label. The purpose of the legislation is to ensure that consumers know exactly what they are getting and are not misled about the quality of the wine. For example, EU law states that compulsory information, including the country of origin and category of wine, shall be given in one or more official languages of the community so that the consumer can easily understand it. EU law establishes different classes of wine, of which 'Table Wine' is one of the lowest, but in many cases this can be stated in the national language of origin. Hence a phrase such as *vin de table* is acceptable on a bottle of French wine sold in Britain and *vino da tavola* would be accepted on a bottle of Italian wine. By printing the classification in the national language, the label designers may feel that the perceived quality of the wine will be indirectly enhanced. But only standard, familiar non-English phrases can be used on wine sold in Britain. If the wine is the produce of more than one country, this description must be in English, because the regulators fear that the majority of British consumers would fail to understand if it were given in French or Italian. Indeed, it may give a false impression of quality if consumers recognized the language as being the national language of a traditional wine-producing country, but did not actually understand what it meant.

Such 'language display' in advertising is more usually associated with the English language worldwide: the perceived value of many consumer products is enhanced by being associated with a piece of English language text. In Europe, however, the use of English in connection with wine does not usually enhance the perceived quality of the product, since England is not a traditional wine-producing country.

The regulatory structure which governs label design has a wider effect on the discourse of back labels. Since quality and desirability cannot be stated explicitly, labels typically communicate indirectly through conventional discourses which have grown up around the marketing and consumption of wine in different countries. The label on a red wine bottle from France may state that the wine is an excellent accompaniment to red meat and cheese. A label from an Italian wine might add that it will be ideal with pasta or pizza. These descriptions are not directly informative: they are the conventional terms in which good red wine is described. More importantly, they allow a word like 'excellent' (which cannot be used to describe the wine itself) to be used in connection with the wine's suitability to accompany conventional foods.

There has also arisen a code of specificity about wine in which the more specific the details of the wine's origins, content and use, the better the wine is deemed to be. In part this has arisen from the *appellation* system used in France to identify the quality of wines, but it has led to a generic discourse which now extends to wine from many other countries. For example, one variety of Italian wine sold in Britain carries the following text on its back label:

### UVA DI TROIA

This wine is the result of Australian Winemaking Consultant Kym Milne MW joining forces with Italian Winemaker Augusto Càntele to produce a premium red wine from an indigenous Italian variety in the southern Italian region of Puglia.

Uva di Troia is an ancient grape variety which still exists in small quantities in Puglia. Following fermentation on skins to extract flavour, the wine was matured for 12 months in new and one year old French oak barrigues.

This elegant, medium bodied wine exhibits fruit flavours of ripe plums, balanced with toasty oak and complex, 'roasted' flavours.

This text gives highly specific information which indicates that the wine is to be regarded as being of a higher quality than is suggested by the strict legal category of *vino da tavola*, which the front label bears. The Californian label in Figure 1, on the other hand, is extremely unspecific: it finds little to say about this wine in particular but extols the virtue of wine in general. The implication is that this is really an ordinary table wine without particular character.

## The importance of visual design

The strict regulation of what must and can be said on wine labels may be one reason why visual design is so important. There are fewer legal restrictions on appearance than on words. In fact, European regulations have very little to say about visual design other than that lettering must be clear and legible, with minimum heights specified for key information, and that key information should be visible within one 'field of view' (i.e. either all on the front or all on the back).

This limited prescription does nevertheless explain one major feature of the visual design. Since basic information, such as the name, must be displayed clearly on the front label so that it is visible on a supermarket shelf, this means that *all* the key information is usually placed on the front label and the optional information located on the back.

Between the front label and the back label there is the bottle itself, containing the main contents, which has a colour and shape which conventionally indicates the style of wine. The bottle as a whole, then, can be regarded as a single text with an internal structure of front, body and back. It is interesting to note how this structure emerges from particular constraints of liquid container design, super-market design, consumer behaviour and legislation and yet also conforms to a common generic text structure. For example, the Text Encoding Initiative (TEI) which provides an international standard for the mark up of texts in electronic form, assumes that the basic structure of all texts can be described by the categories of <front>, <body>, and <back>. The text created by a wine bottle thus shares the structure of a book or a newspaper. The front label shows the title and other 'headline' information about the wine. The bottle provides the main contents, and the back label includes textual apparatus not dissimilar to the index at the back of a book, providing detailed data about contents and use.

TEI is distantly related to HTML (the mark-up language for the World Wide Web) which is illustrated in Chapter 3. Both TEI and HTML indicate the logical structure of a text, with tags within chevrons.

Visual design is used extensively to resolve some of the contradictions which arise from regulations which govern the verbal. For example, the contradiction between upper and lower text fragments in Figure 1 means that the label speaks with at least two distinct voices but the priority between these voices is clearly signalled by the placing of the promotional text at the start of the reading path. The Surgeon General's warning is marked off by a horizontal rule and relegated 'below stairs' with the other 'housekeeping' text fragments such as the bar code.

The status of the two parts of the text, promotional and warning, is also clearly signalled typographically. The persuasive, upper text is in a serif typeface called Centaur. The Surgeon General's warning is set in a sanserif face called Helvetica. Few readers will recognize the typefaces employed, but they will intuitively make very different associations with each. In order to understand how the text works at this typographic level it is necessary to understand something of the historical development of the two typefaces.

## Typographic design

The first printed books showed remarkable sophistication in typographic design. There are only 26 letters in the English alphabet, but the first founts of type produced to print English in the fifteenth century contained over 400 different character shapes or *sorts*. This was because early printers tried as far as possible to reproduce the look of handcopied books, which had by then reached a level of artistry and illustration that was extremely hard to match mechanically. Gradually, as printing technology became more mechanized and books cheaper, compe-tition from handmade books declined. But improved printing technology led, ironically, to a decline in the subtlety of page design and typography. The range of sorts used by printers reduced by over a quarter and handfinishing became increasingly rare. (Modern desk-top publishing has further reduced the range of characters used – to below 200 in many cases. It also has made more popular the spelling *font* which is used elsewhere in this chapter because of its association with newer printing technology.) In addition, there existed for many centuries a limited number of printed text types (such as books and handbills), and these tended to be set indiscriminately in whatever fount a local printer happened to have to hand. There was, in other words, little systematic distinction in the way that typefaces were employed.

However, a new typographic design order emerged in the nineteenth century, largely as a result of the increasing requirements of a consumer society for a variety of printed matter which advertised, instructed, warned and decoratively packaged the new goods of the industrial age. There was also a need in the commercial sector for specialized information giving, such as railway timetables and corporate accounts, requiring new forms of text layout and typographic distinction. The range of communicative functions of texts also became greatly extended in comparison to previous generations – from advertising hoardings which needed to persuade at a distance, to annually updated voting registers required to service an increasingly democratic society. This variety of function demanded new forms of type design. New typesetting technologies (such as the Linotype and Monotype machines) and a range of new typefaces were created in the later part of the nineteenth century to satisfy such needs.

However, it was not enough merely to invent new forms of typeface: also required were new conventions for their deployment. The limited range of standard 'jobbing' founts formerly used by printers were superseded by a wide range of founts, available in different styles (such as 'roman', 'italic' and 'bold'), each with different historical associations and conventional functions. One key distinction in modern typography is now between the traditional faces modelled on classical Roman incised lettering (which carried decorative lines known as serifs) and the simpler, more geometric sanserifs which first appeared in the industrial age. Figures 2 and 3 illustrate some of the key differences. This distinction is used to good effect in the label shown in Figure 1.

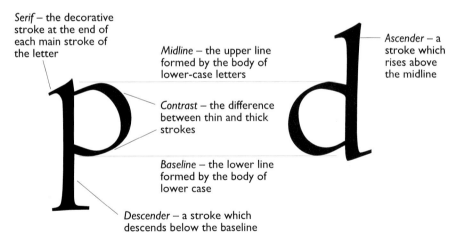

*Serif* – the decorative stroke at the end of each main stroke of the letter

*Midline* – the upper line formed by the body of lower-case letters

*Ascender* – a stroke which rises above the midline

*Contrast* – the difference between thin and thick strokes

*Baseline* – the lower line formed by the body of lower case

*Descender* – a stroke which descends below the baseline

Figure 2    *Centaur is a serif typeface modelled on handwriting*

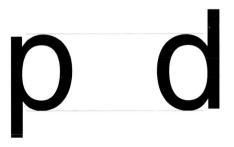

Figure 3    *Helvetica is a sanserif based on a simpler, more geometric design*

## Wine label typography

The typography of the label in Figure 1 can now be seen to be an integral part of its overall design, clearly distinguishing the two competing voices and giving them different priorities and cultural associations. Centaur, in which the upper, promotional text is set, was designed by the American typographer Bruce Rogers (1870–1957) just before World War One and released by Monotype in 1929. Centaur self-consciously attempted to create a face with 'humanist' character, based closely on handwritten models (in fact it was modelled on an early Italian typeface designed by Jenson in the fifteenth century). The genre of typeface (early, Renaissance, handwritten) as well as the particular design (twentieth-century American) helps the promotional text convey values of human agency, of culture and history appropriate for a Californian wine.

Helvetica, in which the Surgeon General's warning is set, was created in Switzerland in 1957 but its design origins lie in German realist faces of the final years of the nineteenth century. Indeed, one typographer has described Helvetica and similar faces as 'cultural souvenirs of the bleakest days of the industrial revolution' (Bringhurst, 1992, p. 189). Helvetica, however, is better seen as the outcome of a moment in twentieth-century culture which sought to produce a utilitarian typeface for objective information texts. Jakob Erbar, the Bauhaus designer of one of the first sanserifs designed for text (as opposed to display type) acknowledged that his 'aim was to design a printing type which would be free of all individual characteristics, possess thoroughly legible letter forms, and be a purely typographic creation' (cited in Tracy, 1986, p. 93). Helvetica is a typical information face, used for such things as captions, headings, motorway signs. The health warning is thus set in an impersonal 'no nonsense' twentieth-century, rationalist face which has become associated with hygiene, factuality and modernism.

In addition to the typeface there is an important political economy of space at work in the typographic design. The upper text is 'bicameral' (mixing upper and lower case) which means that the space occupied by the lettering is modulated and given rhythm by the pattern of ascenders and descenders. Furthermore, the text is slightly letter spaced, permitting it to expand generously and occupy more room. In contrast, the lower text is set in capitals and in a condensed type. Not only is there a certain meanness but also a uniformity in the use of space which helps signal impersonality.

The typographic design is thus consonant with the language genre used in each text fragment. Typography and words combine to position a reader in similar ways.

## Conclusion

I have tried to show how the genre of the back label is historically located in terms of regulatory structures, in terms of the conventional promotional discourses which have arisen within a consumer society, in terms of the cultural history of graphic design, and in the more diffuse forms of intertextual resources which promotional discourse about wine draws on. I have tried also to show the importance of visual design in the construction of labels, in addressing the different audiences and meeting contradictory needs, and in disciplining the heteroglossia which necessarily arises in such texts.

Labelling is no different from other, more conventional texts, in the way it attempts to position readers within particular social and economic relationships and in the way it speaks with several, at times contradictory, voices. Visual communication is still poorly understood, despite the fact that visual design is becoming a more prominent feature of texts in mass circulation. Packaging has been given less scholarly attention, perhaps, than its impact on people's everyday lives warrants.

## References

BRINGHURST, R. (1992) *The Elements of Typographic Style*, Point Roberts, WA, Hartley & Marks.

TRACY, W. (1986) *Letters of Credit: a view of type design*, London, Gordon Fraser.

This reading was specially written for this book.

## Reading B
# MOVING ENGLISH: THE VISUAL LANGUAGE OF FILM

*Theo van Leeuwen*

In previous publications Gunther Kress and I have developed a relatively detailed theory of the language of still images (Kress and van Leeuwen, 1990, 1996) which builds on the work of Michael Halliday (especially 1978, 1985) and other linguists and which has already been drawn upon in this chapter. The language of *moving* images has much in common with that of still images, but it also has some of its own distinct features, and it is on these that I will concentrate here. I will assume that all modes of communication (language, still images, moving images, etc.) can be used to do three things:

Halliday's three metafunctions are outlined earlier in the chapter, p. 53.

1   represent what is going on in the world (Halliday calls this 'ideational' meaning);

2   bring about interactions and relations between the communicating parties ('interpersonal' meaning);

3   form the kinds of meaningful wholes we call 'texts' or communicative episodes and recognize as cartoons, television interviews, documentaries, commercials, etc. ('textual' meaning).

Below I will describe some of the options that the visual language of film offers film makers in creating a text. Some of these options have direct equivalents in verbal English, and in these cases I refer to more formal English grammar to point to the similarities. Others have no direct verbal equivalent, but they do have a semantic function (they *mean*, either on their own or in relation to the verbal voice-over).

# Ideational meaning in the moving image

What linguists call 'lexis' is obviously important in both moving and still images: to represent people, places and things (including abstract things) visually you need a whole vocabulary of visual signs. But in terms of the 'lexical' aspect of visual communication, the moving image does not differ much from the still image. What is specific to the moving image and what makes its language different from that of the still image is:

* *motion* – both of the camera and of the people, places and things depicted;

* the ways in which images can be edited into *sequences*;

* the ways in which moving images can, and do, *combine with other modes* – with speech, music and sound effects.

## Motion and the material process

In still images, actions and transactions are realized by vectors. Moving images can also realize actions and transactions, however they do it not through vectors but through *movement*. It is not the vector formed by an outstretched hand holding the gun which realizes the action of 'aiming' but the very movement of the arm as it lifts the gun and points it. In other words, in the moving image actions are realized by actions, and transactions by transactions.

Actions and transactions are explained earlier in this chapter, p. 56.

Vectors are explained earlier in this chapter, pp. 56–7.

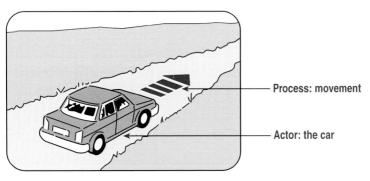

Process: movement

Actor: the car

**Action**

The car is actor and its movement along the road is a material process of action. (A 'transcoding' in verbal English could be *The car is moving along.*)

Goal: the bridge

Process: movement

Actor: the car

**Transaction**

The car is actor and the bridge is goal. The movement of the car forms a material process of transaction. (A transcoding could be *The car approaches the bridge.*)

Such actions will usually be 'figurative', recognizable as driving, walking, jumping, throwing, etc. But they may also be abstract, such as in Walt Disney's animation film *Fantasia* (1941). In such film sequences, abstract shapes engage in a kind of dance to the music of the soundtrack:

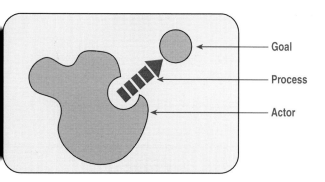

### Transaction

The big amorphous blob (actor) on the left slowly moves towards (process) the little blob on the right (goal), changing shape as it does so. Then it swallows up the little blob. (A transcoding could be *The big blob slowly engulfs the little blob.*)

In such a case we cannot say what the blobs, squiggles and other shapes represent, because they are abstract shapes. But we can see what they are *doing*.

Transactions in moving images can be realized in two ways: they can connect actor and goal:

Actor and goal are *connected* spatially, shown together in the same shot.

Alternatively, they can *disconnect* them, separating them through the editing process:

Actor

Cut to

Goal

Here we see the same participants, but they are *disconnected*, shown in *separate* shots. The beginning of the process is shown in the first shot, and the continuation in the second – in the language of film and video editing this is called a 'matched action' cut.

How is the second, 'disconnected' method different from the first one? Should we see the two shots as forming *one* unit of representation – the equivalent of a clause like *The soldier shoots the villagers* – or as *two* units, whose transcoding in verbal English would be something like *The soldier fires. The villagers get shot?* It is not easy to decide which of the two views is best, and this probably means that the truth is somewhere in the middle. On the one hand the editing brings about a disconnection between the action and its consequences which has no parallel in language. On the other hand disconnection *does* have parallels outside language – real-life parallels. The period in which this type of 'transaction' structure was developed as an element of film language also saw the development of actual transactions with a radical disconnection between actor and goal, such as long-distance telephone calls and the firing of long-range missiles.

Another difference between the two methods is that the second, 'disconnected' one can be faked. The soldier in the first shot *has* fired, but not necessarily at the villagers in the second shot. They could have been filmed much earlier or later, and somewhere else. This is not the case with the first, connected method where the soldier is definitely firing at the villagers. This difference has been discussed a great deal in film theory. Some writers preferred the second method, and saw it as proof that films do not just record reality but can *construct* reality. This was the view for instance of the Russian film makers of the 1920s, many of whom, like Eisenstein (1943, 1963) and Pudovkin (1926), were also film theorists. One of these film makers, Lev Kuleshov, conducted 'editing experiments' to show that non-existent locations could be created in this way. He called this 'creative geography'. He cut together shots of two actors meeting each other and shaking hands according to the 'disconnected' method described above. The shots were taken in quite different places, but once they were edited together it seemed they were taken in the same place. A new, non-existent place had been created out of two existing ones. In *Tarzan* films encounters with wild animals were often faked – stock shots were intercut with shots of an actor faking reactions to them in a studio. The French critic Bazin (1967), on the other hand, favoured the first method. He extolled the capacity of film to reveal reality as it is. To see a real event happening in real time, without the manipulations that editing involves, was for him the essential film experience. The scene of the seal hunt in the documentary *Nanook of the North* (Flaherty, made in 1921), for example, was not faked, said Bazin: it happened in real time, in front of our eyes.

Finally, in contrast to the still image, the moving image can realize 'events'. Shots of, say, light shimmering on softly rippling water create a sense of pure process, pure movement, in which it is difficult to disentangle process and participants, and in which participants, if they can be discerned at all, are 'caught up' in the process in a way that is neither active (actor-like) nor passive (goal-like).

## Subjective images

An element of Halliday's transitivity theory that has not yet been touched on is his recognition of several types of dynamic process. Besides material processes such as *walk, shoot, embrace,* etc. there are also *mental* and *verbal* processes. Mental processes are further subdivided into processes of *perception* (such as *see, hear, notice,* etc.), processes of *affection* (such as *fear, like,* etc.) and processes of *cognition* (such as *think, believe, know,* etc.). In verbal English there is a range of ways of expressing mental processes:

The soldier saw that *the villagers were running away*; or

The soldier saw *the villagers run away.*

In our work on still images Kress and I recognized only one kind of visual mental process and that was the 'reaction'.

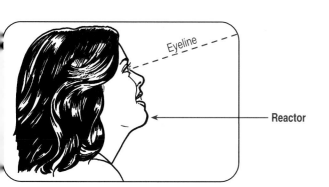

**(a)    Non-transactive reaction**

There is only one participant, the reactor, and a process which is realized by an eyeline vector. The participant, who must be human (or who is anthropomorphized and treated as human by virtue of being the reactor), looks at something which is neither included in the frame nor the viewer.

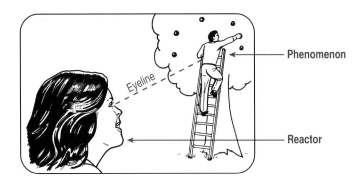

**(b)    Transactive reaction**

There are two participants, the reactor (the person, animal or thing who is looking) and the phenomenon (what the reactor is looking at), and the two are connected by the reactor's eyeline.

Reactions are therefore essentially processes of perception, with one exception:

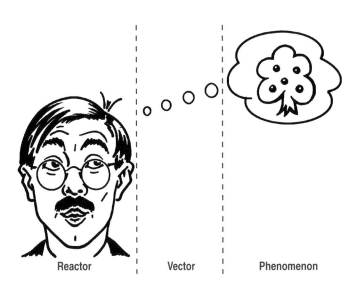

Comic strip producers have developed a 'grammatical' convention for the process of thought, the special 'thought bubble' vector.

In moving images, transactive reactions are often realized in one of two ways:

1    Connected: reactor and phenomenon are shown together in the same space:

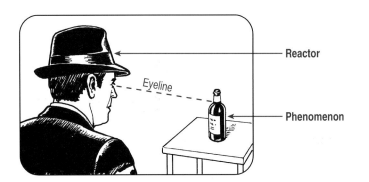

Reactor and phenomenon are shown in the same shot. Either may be foregrounded, in other words, we may look at the phenomenon 'over the shoulder' of the reactor, as in the image here.

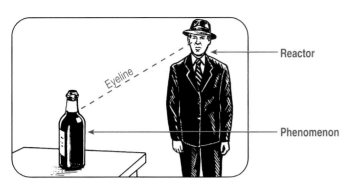

Or we may have the phenomenon in the foreground.

## 2   Disconnected: reactor and phenomenon are shown in separate shots:

### Shot 1

First shot of the 'point of view' (POV) construction: shot of the reactor.

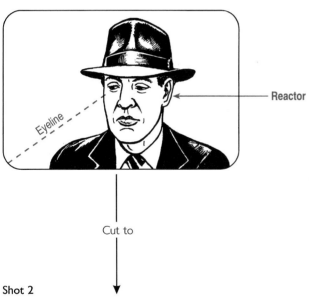

The perception process is realized by eyeline matching and by a return to the shot of the reactor.

Cut to

### Shot 2

Second shot of the POV construction: shot of the phenomenon.

The shot of the phenomenon is known as a 'point-of-view' (POV) shot in the technical language of film and video production. Matching the angle means that if, in the first shot of the reactor (above) the reactor looks down, the phenomenon should be seen from above, exactly as the reactor would see it here. If the reactor looks up in the previous shot, on the other hand, the angle of this shot should be from below, and so on.

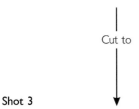

Cut to

**Shot 3**

Third shot of the POV construction: return to the shot of the reactor.

Here the direction of the reactor's eyeline should be exactly as in shot 1 unless there has been a camera movement during shot 2.

Alternative third shot to match left-to-right pan during shot 2 above.

For example, if the reactor had been looking at a moving car, instead of a bottle, his or her eyes would have followed the car (the phenomenon) while the viewers were looking at it, so that by the time we return to the shot of the reactor, the eyeline would have changed, as for example in this shot.

This second type of transactive reaction has a particularly strong 'subjective' flavour, because it allows the viewer to come face to face with both the reactor and the phenomenon.

Other mental processes in moving images also require the phenomenon (which may well be a whole sequence rather than a single shot, such as a 'dream sequence') to be preceded and followed by a shot of the reactor. For instance, the camera may zoom in on the face of the reactor in the first of the three shots, and then *dissolve* to (gradually merge into) the second shot, the shot of the phenomenon – and then return to the face of the reactor. If the reactor's eyes are closed we will probably interpret the phenomenon as a dream. If the reactor's eyes are open we might interpret the phenomenon as a memory, or perhaps as a fantasy. In other words, our interpretation of the exact nature of the mental process represented will depend on the facial expression in the opening and closing shots of the reactor, and on the modality of the shot of the phenomenon. In a memory sequence the image may change from colour to black and white, whereas in a fantasy sequence it may be distorted in some way (through slow motion, distorting lenses, colour, filtering, etc.) and this helps define just what kind of mental process it is – one that is coloured by emotion (affection) or in factual black and white, for instance (cognition).

Verbal processes in English behave rather similarly to mental processes. Again, the object can be a whole clause, whether in the form of a reactor (*The army communiqué said there were many victims*) or in the form of a 'quote' ('*There were many victims,*' *the army communiqué said*). But unlike the reactor, the sayer need not be human, as the example above shows.

Still images can realize verbal processes only through the conventional grammar of the 'dialogue balloon' and similar devices, which will always contain some kind of vector to connect the sayer with the quote (it is always a quote, visually).

Sayer                  Vector                  Quote

In moving images the verbal process is realized by synchronization between the speech and the sayer's lip movements. Without such synchronization, moving images cannot signify that the speech we hear is actually spoken by the sayer we see. Once the presence of a sayer has been established, however, dialogue may be 'off-screen' – in a scene where one person is talking to another, shots of the speaker may alternate with shots of the listener, but as we watch, we still hear the voice of the speaker. This can add much interest to dialogue scenes: we hear the words of the speaker and see the listener's reactions at the same time. But it can also be used to edit the words of the speaker without viewers noticing. This is common practice in film and video interviews.

## Dynamicizing the interpersonal

In both still and moving images the position of the camera creates a relation between the viewer and what is depicted in the image. The camera can make us look down on people, places or things, or look up at them; it can bring us close to them or put us at a distance from them; and so on. The difference is that in moving images this relationship is dynamicized. It can change as we watch: the camera can zoom into a closer shot, or out to a wider shot; it can crane up to a high angle or down to a low angle; and so on. And even when the camera is not moving, the people in the shot can move. They can walk towards or away from the camera, they can climb on a stage or walk up a flight of stairs with the camera tilting up to follow them. Or they can sit down, lie down, kneel down, with the camera tilting down, making us look at them from above.

The moving image makes social relations to people, places and things dynamic and flexible.

## Dynamicizing distance and angle

Distance can be dynamicized in two ways:

1   subject-initiated, so that the people or things in the image initiate the change of distance, by moving towards or away from the camera, and hence from long shot into close shot or vice versa;

2   camera-initiated, so that the camera causes the distance to change by moving towards or away from the people, places or things depicted in the image, either optically (through a zoom out or zoom in) or by being carried ('hand-held' camera) or moved on some wheeled support ('dollying'), often along tracks, to make the movement smooth ('tracking'). In all these cases distance will change visibly, during the shot. And as the camera distance changes, so will the viewer's imaginary relation to the people, places and things shown.

Often the expression of attitude through distance is narrativized. If, for instance, the camera moves towards the subject within a point-of-view (POV) shot, viewers will readily understand that this movement 'stands in for' the movements of a reactor who has been seen in the previous shot. Their distance from the phenomenon is thus identical to, and identified with, that of the reactor, i.e. with that of a 'character' in the film or video. In other cases, however, viewer distance will be identical to, and identified with, a point of view exterior to that of someone in the represented world – the point of view of an external narrator, explicitly imposed on the represented world by the producer of the film.

Like distances, angle can realize attitudes towards what is pictorially represented. This involves two dimensions, the horizontal dimension (from the frontal angle via the profile to the back view), and the vertical (from the low angle via eye level to the high angle).

The difference between the use of angle in still and moving images is twofold. First, in moving images angle can be dynamicized, in a way that is initiated by the depicted subject (such as a character) or by the camera. People, for instance, can turn away from the camera, from frontal view into profile. They can even turn their back to the camera. Or the camera can move around them, from frontal into profile (or vice versa). Or the two can happen simultaneously. Again, a low angle can result from an actor's position at the top of a flight of stairs (and the camera's position at the bottom) and the actor can then initiate the change by descending the stairs, moving to eye level. But (although this would be fairly rare) the camera could also initiate the change, by 'craning up' to the actor's level.

In film the angles change constantly. We tend to see any given person, place or thing from quite a number of different angles. In other words, what in still images has never moved into the mainstream, cubism, the use of multiple perspectives, has become commonplace in moving images. The only difference is that the different perspectives are shown one after the other rather than all at the same time. An example will show how such changes of angle and distance can be used to signify both the changing relations between 'characters', people we see on the screen, and the ongoing, constantly shifting relations between these characters and the viewers. In the first scene from Howard Hawks's *The Big Sleep* (1947) Marlowe (Humphrey Bogart) has been called to the house of General Sternwood (Charles Waldron) to help him deal with a case of blackmail involving his youngest daughter Carmen. As Marlowe waits in the hall to be shown in by the butler, Carmen (Martha Vickers) provocatively confronts him. The interview with Sternwood then follows. A few points are worth making:

The butler is never closer than medium long shot. In other words, throughout the scene he is not presented to the viewer as a character who might play a significant role in the drama later on, who might be worth knowing more closely.

Although the other characters are initially shown in long shot (in other words, from quite a distance, as 'strangers') the viewers then get to know them most closely, literally and figuratively, as in this medium close shot of Marlowe. They are thereby introduced as characters who *will* play a significant role in the drama.

Carmen is first seen from below, as having power (the power of sexual attraction) over Marlowe, and over the viewer. But later she descends to eye level.

As she is taunting Marlowe, she is framed in close shot – closer than Marlowe. In other words, while Marlowe 'keeps his distance', Carmen is a little more aggressive and 'comes too close'.

But as she throws herself into Marlowe's arms, the two are both in close shot, suggesting (the potential for) intimacy – and also suggesting to the viewers that they too might (in imagination) become 'intimate' with these two (i.e. know them as well as one could know only intimates in real life).

In the interview with General Sternwood, on the other hand, no shots are closer than medium shot, so that we get the impression of a relatively formal and businesslike, rather than a personal, encounter.

Finally, the shots of Marlowe in this sequence are consistently closer and from a higher angle than the shots of Sternwood (who is shown from below, in a medium shot). This makes Sternwood the more powerful of the two, but also the one who remains more distant from the viewers than Marlowe, and hence of less dramatic interest.

In news and current affairs television, on the other hand, distance and angle generally suggest the relation between the people on the screen and the viewer, rather than the relation between the people on the screen with each other. Anchorpersons are shown frontally, from slightly below eye level, and in a wider shot than most other participants in the programme. This enhances their authority. They are, literally and figuratively, 'higher up' than the viewers, and shown from a respectful distance – initial shots may even show them from a very long distance, sitting behind large, gleaming desks at the far side of an empty, palatial hall.

## Address

The distinction between 'direct' and 'indirect' address has already been discussed in this chapter. It operates in both still and moving images, but moving images can, again, dynamicize address, change it in midstream: a depicted person can turn towards the camera and then look at the lens, so moving from indirect to direct address, or vice versa. But this can only be initiated by the subject. The camera cannot initiate it, although a director can of course ask the subject to look (or not to look) at the camera.

Indirect address is the rule in naturalistic drama, in the theatre as much as in film and television. This puts the audience in the role of an unseen observer, a voyeur of what is going on in the represented world. There is no *contact* between the viewers and the characters of the stage or the screen, and the characters must behave as if they are not aware of being watched (in the case of 'candid camera' or the surveillance camera, they *are not* aware of being watched). Bertolt Brecht sought to reintroduce direct address in the theatre, especially by means of interpolated songs, and film makers like Jean-Luc Godard have followed him in this. In these contexts direct address breaks with conventions that 'naturalize' the fictional world of the stage or the screen, and makes viewers aware that they are watching a play or a movie, so that they will consciously react and think about what they are seeing, rather than absorb it passively. But in many other contexts, for example television comedy or commercials, news and current affairs programmes, direct address is the accepted convention, although not everyone has the right to address the viewer directly. Anchorpersons and on-camera reporters may look at the camera but interviewers may not. In chat shows, hosts may use direct address but guests may not. In other words, direct address is a privilege which the media profession has by and large reserved for itself.

## The modality of motion

Discussions of modality are also fully applicable to moving images, but, again, in the case of moving images a further factor needs to be added and that is, of course, movement. Like visual detail, background, depth, light and shade, colour, etc., this can be represented to different *degrees*. The representation of walking, for example, could range from an animation in which a simple stick figure raises and lowers legs without any articulation of the joints or any movement of the rest of the body, to super-detailed representations showing the rippling of every muscle involved.

Most moving images invite us to use the naturalistic criterion (although this may change as the use of animation increases and the empirical criterion of faithfulness to reality loses its hold and authority). Such films and television programmes can then create contrasts in modality between, for instance, the present (high modality, realized by, for example, colour) and the past (lower modality, realized by, for example, black and white), or between 'reality' ('real' modality) and 'fantasy' or 'dream' ('more than real' and hence lower modality, realized by, for example, slow motion, more saturated colour, etc.). Because so many modality configurations are possible, modality is a never-ending source of creativity in the visual arts. In a dream sequence in the film *Wild Strawberries* (1957) the Swedish director Bergman not only used surreal events and objects (a man seeing himself dead in a coffin, a clock without hands), but also altered modality. All shades between black and white disappeared to create a very high contrast image. This not only reduced everything to the two basic forces of black and white (and all the symbolic meanings that might be attached to this contrast) but also, because he used such dazzling whites and such deep blacks, enormously enhanced the sensory, emotive impact of the scene.

In many animated cartoons, the background has higher (naturalistic) modality than the foreground (a reversal of what normally happens in 'live action' films). There is a technical explanation for this. As backgrounds do not have to be animated, they can be painted in more detail. But there is also a semiotic effect: the film presents us with fantasy characters in a real setting. In other words, the world is real, the people in it, and their actions, are less real, more stereotyped or abstract. Yet, in one aspect, these characters are 'more than real', due to the high saturation of their colours. This results in a modality configuration not unlike that of toys for very young children, where the shape of toy telephones, locomotives, etc. is highly simplified and abstracted, but the colour exaggerated (more than real). Thus the modality of such toys involves both 'cognitive', 'educational' aspects (learning the generalized, basic shapes of things) and 'emotive' aspects (so that children will be attracted to these key technologies and form an emotive bond with them).

## Spatial and temporal textuality

Halliday's notion of 'textual metafunction' refers to the combination and integration of ideational and interpersonal elements, of bits of representation and interaction, into a coherent whole, the kind of whole we call 'text' or 'communicative episode'. This function is therefore realized by what we usually call 'composition' and in the case of moving images this involves composition in space as well as composition in time.

### Composition in space

**Information value**

Like many film or television shots, the drawing in Figure 1 contains two participants, the hearse and the child. This is an artist's impression of a photograph by Robert Frank (entitled *Hearse*, 1951). Unfortunately we were not given permission to reproduce the original photograph. The two participants are connected by a vector, formed by the open door of the hearse, and clearly 'emanating' from the hearse, so that the hearse is actor. In other words, it is, ideationally, a transitive structure: the hearse (symbolizing, perhaps, 'Death') does something to the child (who, perhaps, symbolizes 'Life').

But there is another aspect to be considered. The photographer has placed the child on the left and the hearse on the right. This is not part of the ideational meaning. Reversing left and right would not affect the transitive structure. Yet it would change the meaning of the picture. Placing an element on the right or on the left (or at the top, or the bottom, or in the centre or the margin) gives the element a particular *information value* which is attached to the particular zone in which it is placed. As discussed earlier in this chapter, if something is placed on the left, it is thereby presented as 'given', as something which is already familiar to the viewer, and should therefore be taken for granted. What is placed on the right is the 'new' and thereby presented as not yet familiar, as something to which the viewer should pay particular attention, as the crux of the message. In Figure 1, Death is new. We are invited to a 'memento mori', a meditation about the ever-present threat of death.

In moving images, the given–new relation may be realized either spatially, as in Figure 1, or temporally, for the camera can pan from a given to a new element, and so show the given element *before* showing the new. In an ABC (Australian Broadcasting Commission) current affairs item about a 'Muslim Community School' in Perth, a shot opened on an Arabic sign on the wall, and then panned to a child's drawing of a clown, also pinned on the wall. This reflected the tenor of the item as a whole; its given was the 'strangeness' (the 'otherness' in dress, language, religion) of the staff and the children of this school. The new, the ultimate message, was that the children were, after all, just like other children: playful, spontaneous, expressive and so on. An Anglo-Australian teacher who had adopted the Islamic religion played a key role as 'mediator' between 'them' and 'us' – she sometimes had her hair covered with a scarf (like 'them') and sometimes wore it loose (like 'us'). It was as if only her presence, her mediating role, could make the school acceptable to the 'Australian viewer', to whom the item was addressed. Such assumptions ignore the fact that many Australians are Muslims, and that 'national' programmes should also be for Muslims. They force these Australians to regard their own language, culture and religion from the point of view of the dominant language and culture, i.e. as 'strange', 'foreign', 'different', etc.

Tilting the camera up or down may similarly connect the top and bottom elements of a pictorial proposition. The top element is the 'ideal', the most generalized or idealized essence of the message. The bottom element, the 'real', contrasts with it by being more 'down to earth', for instance more factual or more particular, or more practically oriented. In a Dutch television documentary about Christian art, a sequence showing statues of emaciated Christ figures ended by tilting down from such a statue, positioned on the top of a hill, to the busy highway at the bottom – as the highway came into view, the traffic noise drowned the ethereal music which had accompanied the earlier part of the scene.

### Salience

A second element of spatial composition is salience, which causes the elements of composition to stand out to different degrees. In Figure 1 the hearse is by far the most salient element, because of its size, its position in the foreground and because of the contrast between its deep black colour and the much lighter background. The girl, though small, also stands out, because her silhouetted figure forms a strong tonal contrast with the very light pavement.

Salience results from the interaction of a number of factors: size, sharpness of focus, or more generally the amount of detail and texture shown; tonal contrasts (areas of high tonal contrasts, such as borders between black and white, have high

Figure 1   Hearse, 1951

salience); colour contrasts (for instance the contrast between highly saturated and 'soft' colour, or the contrasts between red and blue); placement in the visual field; perspective (foreground objects are more salient than background objects, and elements that overlap other elements are more salient than the elements they overlap); and also quite specific cultural factors, such as the appearance of the human figure or a potent cultural symbol. This is not unlike salience ('stress') in speech, which also results from the interplay of a number of factors – pitch, loudness, duration and/or any other speech characteristics which can make a syllable stand out from the syllables that surround it.

Moving images make it possible for an element to 'become' or 'cease to be' salient in front of our eyes, as the shot proceeds. This can be subject-initiated, or camera-initiated. A subject can initiate the change by walking into the foreground, or from the shadows into a more or less brightly lit area. The camera can initiate the change, for instance by shifting focus from one object to another.

### Framing

A third aspect of spatial composition is framing. In Figure 1 the line formed by the edge of the footpath divides the image into two sections, one containing the girl and one containing the hearse. This can be seen as signifying that life and death, the girl and the hearse, are disconnected, and form two separate realities.

Framing disconnects elements of the composition from each other, signifying that they are to be seen as, in some sense, separate and independent, perhaps even contrasting items of information. It can be realized by framelines, which may either be abstract, graphic elements, or form part of some depicted element (window frames, columns, etc.) as in Figure 1. The thickness or, more generally, salience of the framelines can then indicate the degree of disconnection. Framing may also be realized by empty space between the elements, or by discontinuities of colour or tone. Connective devices, on the other hand, for instance vectors between elements, or repetitions of shapes or colours (visual rhymes), have the opposite effect. They express that the connected elements are to be interpreted as belonging together in some sense, as continuous and complementary, for instance. Again a comparison can be made with spoken English. Speech is segmented into 'rhythm groups', groups of words spoken without interruption, and carrying a distinct information contour. Such groups are separated by short pauses, or by other framing devices: a change of pace, long, drawn-out final syllables, etc., and each group then forms a distinct unit of information.

Framing, too, can be dynamicized in moving images, whether subject-initiated (the girl in Figure 1 could cross the line formed by the edge of the footpath), or camera-initiated (the camera could move down to a lower angle which would not allow the footpath to be seen and so place the girl and the hearse in the same space).

## Composition in time

Information value, salience and framing result from two factors: first the positioning and movement of people and things in the picture space; and second the positioning and movement of the camera in front of these people and things. In film theory the term *mise-en-scène* is often used to refer to these two together. But mise-en-scène mainly pertains to the composition of shots. We now need to move up a level and look at the way in which actions, transactions and events are sequenced, be it through the creation of complex shots or through editing.

Earlier we discussed how participants and processes combine to form actions, transactions and events, in other words, units comparable to clauses in verbal English. But in the film sequence, or the film as a whole, how are these 'clauses' combined, how are they made into a larger whole? One way of looking at this is to consider the *conjunctive relations* between them: how does the content of *this* clause logically relate to the content of the previous clause? Does it, for example, tell of an event that happened after an event narrated in the previous clause, or does it perhaps present a *reason* for what was stated in the previous clause, or a *contrast* to what was stated in the previous clause? Exactly the same questions can be asked about images: does this shot show us something that happened after what we saw in the previous shot, something that contrasts with what we saw in the previous shot, and so on? Such questions were in fact asked by the Russian film theorists of the 1920s (e.g. Eisenstein, 1943, 1963; Pudovkin, 1926) and later by the French film theorist Metz (1974). Here, however, as also in earlier work (van Leeuwen, 1991), they will be linked explicitly to a theory of linguistic conjunction (Halliday and Hasan, 1976).

### Temporal conjunction

One of the most common ways in which actions, transactions and events can be linked is by 'temporal sequentiality'. The first shot (or the first part of a complex shot) shows one action or transaction or event, and the next shot shows the next action or transaction or event, the one happening *after* the first one.

**Shot 1**

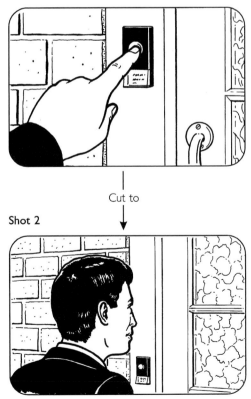

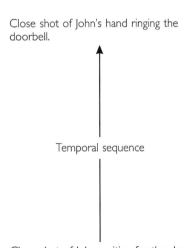

Close shot of John's hand ringing the doorbell.

Temporal sequence

**Cut to**

**Shot 2**

Close shot of John waiting for the door to be opened.

A verbal English equivalent could be: *He rang the bell. Then he stood there for a few seconds, waiting.*

The same thing is possible in one complex shot:

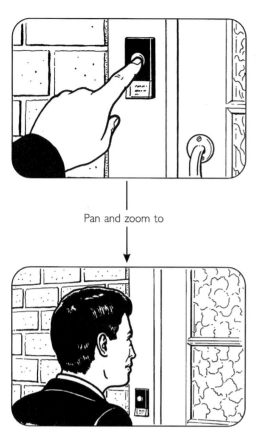

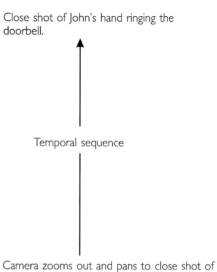

Close shot of John's hand ringing the doorbell.

Temporal sequence

Pan and zoom to

Camera zooms out and pans to close shot of John waiting for the door to be opened.

Another temporal connection is simultaneity: the first shot shows one action, transaction or event, the next shot shows another one, understood as happening at the same time, for example:

**Shot 1**

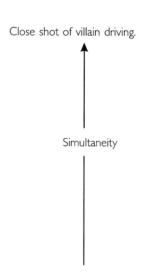

Close shot of villain driving.

Simultaneity

Cut to

**Shot 2**

Medium close shot of police car, in hot pursuit.

A verbal English equivalent could be: *He drove as fast as he could. Meanwhile the police were hot on his trail.*

A third temporal conjunction is the flashback, in which the first shot shows one action or transaction or event, the next shot another one, which is understood as having happened *before* it.

These conjunctive links (as well as the ones I will discuss below) can also exist between whole *scenes*, rather than between shots or parts of complex shots. And as already indicated, they are just as possible between the clauses (or paragraphs, or chapters) of an English text, as in these examples from *Animal Farm* (by George Orwell [1945] 1987):

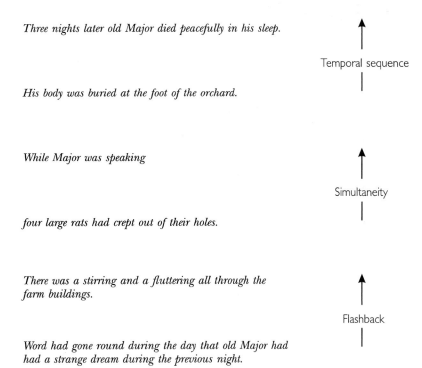

*Three nights later old Major died peacefully in his sleep.*

Temporal sequence

*His body was buried at the foot of the orchard.*

*While Major was speaking*

Simultaneity

*four large rats had crept out of their holes.*

*There was a stirring and a fluttering all through the farm buildings.*

Flashback

*Word had gone round during the day that old Major had had a strange dream during the previous night.*

## Spatial conjunction

Sometimes films 'describe' a place by showing different parts, different 'details' of
it one after the other. A sequence introducing the city of London might have:

**Shot 1**

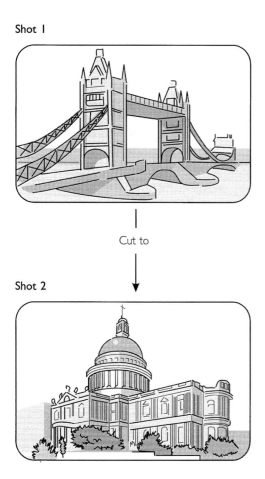

Cut to

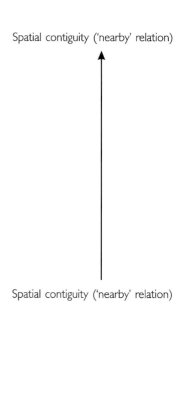

Spatial contiguity ('nearby' relation)

Spatial contiguity ('nearby' relation)

**Shot 2**

According to Eisenstein (1963) the descriptive methods of Charles Dickens
inspired the film pioneer D.W. Griffith to 'describe' locations in this way, rather
than through one long shot (such as an aerial view of London). This kind of
sequence often occurs in news. It is, for instance, impossible to show images of a
crime that has already taken place, but possible to show the authentic *location*
where the crime took place, and even to turn this into a whole sequence, to
accompany (and 'authenticate') the verbally told story of the crime.

Another spatial relation is more specific – the relation between one shot which shows the whole of something ('overview') and another which shows a part ('detail'). This link can also exist between the parts of a complex shot (e.g. through the zoom out or zoom in, or through dollying in or dollying out). A move from 'overview' to 'detail' can be shown by this arrangement of shots:

**Shot 1**

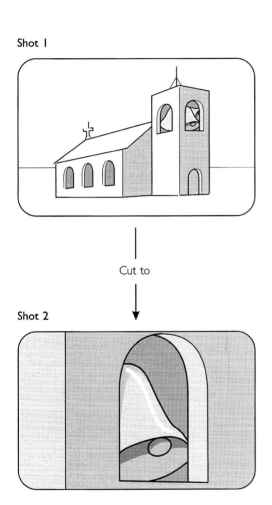

Cut to

**Shot 2**

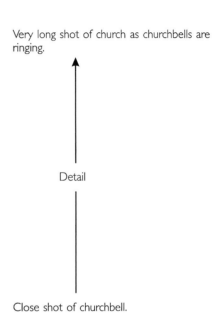

Very long shot of church as churchbells are ringing.

Detail

Close shot of churchbell.

Or a move from 'detail' to 'overview' could be shown like this:

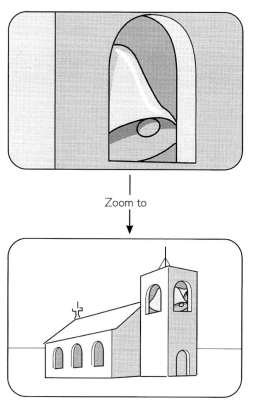

Zoom to

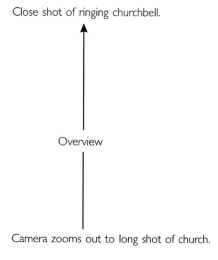

Close shot of ringing churchbell.

Overview

Camera zooms out to long shot of church.

For this kind of relation there is not, strictly speaking, an equivalent in verbal English, although linguistic texts can of course conjunctively relate the general and the specific, as in this quote from the narration of one of the first documentaries to use voice-over narration, *Industrial Britain* (Grierson, made in 1933; see Grierson, 1966):

> *Half the history of England lies behind these scenes of yesterday.*

Distillation ('to be more precise' relation)

> *The history of people who kept on through the centuries, growing things, making things, transporting things between the English villages and the English towns.*

The second sentence (the detail) gives a more precise version of the first (the overview).

## Comparative conjunction

In some sequences the shots are linked by relations of similarity or contrast. The example below is from the documentary already mentioned, *Industrial Britain*.

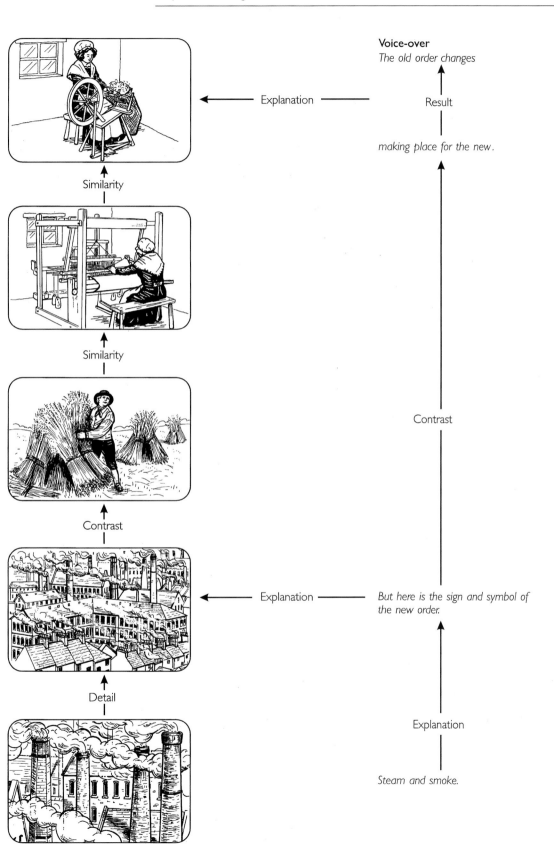

**Voice-over**
*The old order changes*

Explanation ← Result

*making place for the new.*

Similarity

Similarity

Contrast

Contrast

Explanation ← *But here is the sign and symbol of the new order.*

Detail

Explanation

*Steam and smoke.*

As we can see, the film opens with a series of shots showing disparate traditional rural activities: spinning, weaving, sheaving, etc. These we are to understand as all similar, all examples of the same overarching category ('traditional rural activities') and the voice-over confirms it: *The old order* ... says the disembodied voice. A little later there is a sudden *contrast* with a second series of shots, showing factory chimneys and grimy industrial cities, and this contrast, too, is reinforced by the voice: *But here is the sign and symbol of the new order. Steam and smoke* ... So there are conjunctive relations between the images (similarity and contrast), between the clauses (result, contrast, explanation) in the voice-over, *and* between the words and the pictures (the explanatory function of the voice-over). Language may be richer in logical conjunctions (such as 'because' relations and 'if' relations) and images may be richer in spatial relations (as mentioned before, there is not really a linguistic equivalent for the 'overview–detail' relation, for instance) but in both cases the logical coherence of the text is created by conjunction, by the sort of links and connections I have discussed in this section.

## Conclusion: 'interest'

I have described many of the options that the visual language of film offers to film makers. They can portray something from close up or far away, and from above or below. They can relate the things they 'say' with film chronologically or they can juxtapose them to one another, and so on. Of course, they may be limited by a lack of awareness of the options available, or by lack of *access* to a particular option. We can only choose from the semiotic means we have available. Our grasp of a foreign language may not be adequate for us to be able to choose the right level of formality with which to address people. In making a movie we may not have the right zoom lens to move closer to our subject. In each case, however, we will do our best to say what we want to say, with the semiotic means we have available.

The option we then choose will be determined by our 'interest', to use the term Kress (1993) employs in this connection – what we are interested in focusing on, the communicative aims we are interested in achieving, and so on. This interest may be very much our own, arising from our own particular biography, but it may also be an interest we share with some group to which we belong and to which we have to conform to a greater or lesser degree, be it voluntarily or out of economic necessity. British propaganda documentaries of the 1930s often used a disembodied narrator who not only explained the images but also addressed the viewers directly, by using the second person pronoun *you*, as in this example, again taken from *Industrial Britain* (all emphases are mine):

> This is the world that coal has created: black countries of belching furnaces and humming machinery, industrial towns of grimy surroundings and bewildering acres of streets. But if *you* look closely enough *you* will find the spirit of craftsmanship has not disappeared.

Direct address by a disembodied voice can be a powerfully impressive mode. Not for nothing has it often been called the 'voice of God' narration. Grierson quite consciously pioneered its use to give a sense of authority to a propagandistic message, a message which sought to 'light up every individual's life with a sense of active citizenship and pride in national achievements' (Grierson, 1966, p. 247) – this in a time of economic depression and mass unemployment. Later, however, the 'voice of God' commentary became a film language convention to which many documentarists unthinkingly conformed – and against which others rebelled.

This is just one example of the way in which 'interest' determines how the visual language of film is used. Languages (the language of film included) are made to be *used*. They come to life only when people use them to communicate specific messages to specific others for specific purposes, and in the context of a specific social and cultural setting. The study of those languages, too, will come to life only when it includes the study of how they are used, and when combined with the study of the relevant social realities and cultural histories.

## References

BAZIN, A. (1967) *What is Cinema*, vol. 1, Berkeley and Los Angeles, University of California Press.

EISENSTEIN, S. (1943) *The Film Sense*, London, Faber.

EISENSTEIN, S. (1963) *Film Form*, London, Dennis Dobson.

GRIERSON, J. (1966) *Grierson on Documentary*, edited F. Hardy, London, Faber.

HALLIDAY, M.A.K. (1978) *Language as Social Semiotic*, London, Edward Arnold.

HALLIDAY, M.A.K. (1985) *An Introduction to Functional Grammar*, London, Edward Arnold.

HALLIDAY, M.A.K. and HASAN, R. (1976) *Cohesion in English*, London, Longman.

KRESS, G. (1993) 'Against arbitrariness: the social production of the sign as a foundational issue in critical discourse analysis', *Discourse and Society*, vol. 4, no. 2, pp. 169–93.

KRESS, G. and VAN LEEUWEN, T. (1990) *Reading Images*, Geelong, Deakin University Press.

KRESS, G. and VAN LEEUWEN, T. (1996) *Reading Images: the grammar of visual design*, London, Routledge.

METZ, C. (1974) *Film Language*, New York, Oxford University Press.

ORWELL, G. ([1945] 1987) *Animal Farm*, London, Secker & Warburg.

PUDOVKIN, V. (1926) *Film Technique and Film Acting*, New York, Bonanza.

VAN LEEUWEN, T. (1991) 'Conjunctive structure in documentary film and television', *Continuum*, vol. 5, no. 1, pp. 76–114.

This reading was specially commissioned for this book.

# 3 ENGLISH IN CYBERSPACE

Simeon Yates

## 3.1 INTRODUCTION

According to many social scientists and technologists, we live in a world that is radically different from that experienced by our ancestors. This 'new world' is due in part to the rapid growth of communication technologies such as cable and satellite television, fax machines and multimedia computers, and the growing data networks sometimes called the 'information superhighway'. The ease of communication between different parts of the world and different parts of society afforded by such technology is leading, some social scientists claim, to changed social relationships, to new social groupings and dispersed communities, and to altered perceptions of time and space. The world is increasingly experienced (at least by those with access to the new technology) as a smaller, more compressed place – a kind of 'global village', as the visionary 1960s' writer Marshall McLuhan (1962) put it.

The **Internet**, which permits people in distant parts of the world to communicate via electronic mail ('e-mail') and other means without regard to distance or social position, has emerged at the end of the twentieth century as one of the key communications technologies. The imaginary space created by the Internet in which people interact and form social relationships has become known as **cyberspace**. In this chapter we examine the role of English in cyberspace, looking at some of the novel ways in which the language is used on the Internet, and at some of the new social groups and social relationships created through Internet communication.

## 3.2 WHAT IS THE INTERNET?

The Internet is both a technological and a social phenomenon; we need to understand something of both these dimensions to evaluate its impact on the English language.

### The Internet technology

The **Internet** is the largest and most expansive system of data links; it connects both large commercial computer-communications services and tens of thousands of smaller university, government and corporate networks. In some senses the Internet combines aspects of telephone communication and broadcasting. Like the international telephone system which makes possible conversations between individuals almost anywhere in the world, the Internet makes it possible for computers (and the people who operate them) to exchange messages and information. But like broadcasting, a message on the Internet from a single source can reach millions of people.

Though the Internet may appear to be a huge single network, it is actually an intricate series of smaller networks. The origins of the Internet help explain some of its distinctive characteristics. It grew out of a US government-funded research programme that began in the late 1960s. During the 'Cold War' which followed World War Two, the US Department of Defense was worried about the security and survivability of the network of defence command and control centres. It was feared, for example, that the entire system would collapse if just one part was subjected to disruption from a nuclear attack. To find a solution to this dilemma, the Department of Defense's Advanced Research Projects Agency (ARPA) began to examine the best way to interconnect widely dispersed computer systems at universities, laboratories and other research centres.

The solution that they developed enabled data to be transmitted from one site to another by chopping it up into small 'packets', each of which was tagged with the 'address' of its final destination. Because all the computers were connected, there was potentially a large number of routes by which a packet of data could be sent. The network could thus resist large-scale destruction; if one route was damaged, packets would simply travel along another that remained intact. This flexible routing system, first developed in 1970, was called ARPAnet and connected the University of California at Los Angeles and Santa Barbara, Stanford University and the University of Utah in Salt Lake City. By 1972 there were about 40 different sites connected to ARPAnet using **electronic mail** (e-mail), accessing each other's computers and communicating via electronic **bulletin boards** which have become known today as 'Usenet' **newsgroups**. It is estimated that there are now over 16,000 newsgroups accessible to the international community. Contributions ('postings') can be made to most newsgroups by anyone with access to the Internet and these gradually propagate around the world to other host computers. In this way, the Usenet now provides a global forum for announcements, advice and debate and brings together people with shared interests who are geographically dispersed.

In the mid 1970s, the software which controls the flow of data between computers on the ARPAnet – known as the Transmission Control Protocol (TCP) and the Internet Protocol (IP) – was made publicly available. The free distribution of the TCP/IP protocols caused a massive increase in the use of computer networks in the USA. In the late 1980s these protocols began to be used on computer networks based in other countries, eventually allowing computers in different parts of the world to communicate directly with one another. As personal computers became more widely connected in Local Area Networks (LANs) in offices and educational institutions, and as those local networks became connected to national networks, it became possible by the mid 1990s for one person's personal computer to establish a direct connection to another person's personal computer on the other side of the world. Such connections can be used to exchange various kinds of data, including images (both moving and still), sound and text in any combination.

Most people connect to the Internet either from their place of work or from home using a *modem* (a device which enables them to connect their home personal computer via an ordinary telephone line to a larger computer system which is connected to the Internet). Communications on the Internet take a variety of forms. Two of the most popular formats are **electronic mail** (which allows a text message to be sent from one user to another person anywhere in the world) and **World Wide Web** pages (which allow anyone with an Internet connection to browse through multimedia texts provided by other users). These and other forms of Internet communication are examined in this chapter.

# The social implications of the Internet

The Internet is playing a major part in the massive expansion in global communications which began in the 1970s and which now makes it far easier, and more affordable, for individuals to communicate with others in any part of the world. Such a transformation in patterns of communication has the potential to transform with it the quality of human relationships. It also has wider and as yet unclear political and cultural implications. As has been the case with earlier popular communications technologies (such as television), the popularizing of the Internet gives rise to many anxieties: its social impact has often been regarded as a negative one.

For example, people who devote large portions of their lives to communication over the Internet are often caricatured as male, social inadequates. Indeed, a new, denigrating vocabulary has emerged to describe such people ('anoraks', 'geeks', 'nerds', etc.). Like earlier groups of enthusiasts based around technology (radio amateurs or train-spotters, for instance), such people are sometimes suspected of having difficulty in managing their social relationships. This view undervalues the extent to which some people have found that the Internet helps them deal with interpersonal problems which cannot be managed face to face, or enables them to communicate with people who would otherwise be unreachable.

**Activity 3.1**   *(Reading A)*

Read 'I fell into the safety net' by Stephen Fry (Reading A), an account by a British actor of a difficult moment in his life during which the Internet allowed him to reconstruct 'normal' social relationships. What special virtues does Fry claim for text-based communication on the Internet? What do you think are the negative aspects of using such a medium of communication?

**Comment**

Stephen Fry seems to take an ambivalent, but generally positive, view of the potential of Internet communication to transcend the limitations of conventional communication. In particular, he suggests that there may be something empowering about electronic communication for some people:

> Put the average geek on the telephone and he or she will not be up to much. Put them behind a keyboard, however, and the act of literary composition forces a wit, an integrity, an insight, an emotional and moral honesty that would amaze even an optimist.

The idea that Internet communication allows people to construct and project different social identities for themselves – freeing them from the 'tyrannies' of face-to-face communication in which their personality and social status will be signalled through physical attributes such as body shape, skin colour and interactional style, accent, and clothing – is a recurrent theme in debates about the Internet. Later in this chapter we examine more closely how such new identities are constructed through Internet texts.

The idea that the Internet supports a distinctively *male* culture is also increasingly being challenged. At the beginning of the expansion of Internet usage in the UK, in the mid 1990s a survey by National Opinion Polls found that one third of Internet users were women (NOP, 1995). Surveys of Internet users in the USA have found a similar proportion. One survey claimed that by 1996 the gender balance among regular Internet users was equal. As Internet usage continues to expand and diversify, it will make no sense to regard it as a distinctive culture in itself: rather it will be a medium for engaging in a wide range of diverse cultural practices, including those that arise from women's interests or which support minority cultures and languages.

**Activity 3.2   Minorities on the Internet**   *(Allow about 10 minutes)*

The transcript below is an extract from an interview on British radio with two women ('R' and 'N') from the British Asian community (note that in the UK the term 'Asian' is commonly used to refer specifically to families with ancestral links with the Indian subcontinent). One of the speakers is setting up an Internet service for the Asian community in the UK.  Read the transcript now and note what social benefits and dangers they seem to be concerned about.

| | |
|---|---|
| Presenter | But how specifically can you see the Internet being used? Housewives, for instance: how would you envisage them using it? |
| R | Well, I think it's a fact that women from our background – especially the older generation – tend to be housebound, so here is a way where they can get easy access to information from all over the world, and in particular to do with their own country back home. Getting on to the Internet you can get immediate access of information to everything that's happening currently in India, whether it's in business, arts, politics, entertainment. So I think it's a good way, to begin with, of keeping in touch with your own country. |
| Presenter | But might it not be a negative influence … N., in that sense? Because one of the problems for older Asian women has always been isolation, partly because of the language barrier, partly because of lack of freedom to move around. Can this lead to more isolation if they're just stuck at home behind a computer screen? |
| N | Well, if they're just stuck at home then why not use the Internet to get connectivity with people across the world? Talking to people from different backgrounds etc. will only enhance their own knowledge and understanding of things which are happening out there. They have 24 hour access to the Internet. They can log in whenever they wish to. So not necessarily, no. If anything, it will only help to enhance their lifestyle to a certain extent. And going back to the point of housebound women – the Internet can also provide an access for women to possibly start up providing their own services – maybe hobbies that they're interested in or businesses that they have a keen eye on. For |

example, if they have a hobby in maybe cooking, or, you know, they've collected a series of recipes over the years – they could then use those recipes – publish them on the Net and start some sort of business up. There have been a number of cases in the past where women have actually started a business up using the Internet.

Presenter    It costs money though, doesn't it, to buy the equipment? It's a very expensive thing just to buy the computer, to have the modem and to then have all the stuff that goes with it. Is it going to be easily available to women because of its cost?

R            Well, I agree with you that the initial cost is there – it's an initial outlay but after that it's a cost of the phone call to hook into the Internet. It's the cost of a phone call, so in the long run it actually works out much more economical. But I'd like to come back to your point about creating isolation which you just mentioned … I don't think it's the older housewives whose lifestyle is going to change substantially because they're isolated anyway. But my fear is that for the younger generation – yes, there is a potential that it would create more isolation among the younger genera- tion. Because I've seen, for example, with my own son who is a computer whizz kid – he's sixteen years old, he's very much into the Internet when actually I would prefer to see him going out and interacting more with people of his own age or going out and doing things.

Presenter    So … do you accept there can be a negative impact on a culture that has always been family-centred, communal in its activities?

R            Yes.

N            If you take a look at technologies which have come along in the past, from the telephone through to the TV, through to satellite etc., there's always been that question it might isolate people further but it's up to the individual to what extent they wish to use this facility that's available to them. Having access to infor- mation around the globe is a very powerful thing and if an individual can use that then you know it's only going to enhance their lifestyle.

…

Presenter    Now one of the things I know you're going to be offering is a dating agency. I wonder if the proponents of traditional ar- ranged marriage will be throwing up their hands in horror at this?

N            Well, it's going to follow the traditional style of arranged marri- age where, you know, the listings – certain criteria about people are listed etc. But what we're hoping to do is bring a slightly modern approach to it whereby individuals within the Asian community – if they wish to – can put up pictures about them- selves, any sort of weird and wacky ideas they have about them- selves, hobbies they're in to.

R            My fear is, you see, the difference between a dating agency
             where you go to a company and use the services – as opposed to
             on the Internet – is that with a regular, normal style of dating
             agency there would be a certain process of screening whereas on
             the Internet, I mean, anyone can just put themselves on the
             Internet and it could, you know, be a serial killer who presents
             himself as someone very respectable. I think there is an inherent
             danger with the Internet because there is no regulatory control.

(*Woman's Hour*, BBC Radio 4, 27 November 1995)

## Comment

It seems to me that these women felt generally optimistic about the potential of
the Internet for supporting their own community, though aware of many dangers.
In fact, the 'agenda' which underlies much of their conversation seems to be
similar to one which has emerged more widely around Internet communication.
I noted the following issues:

*   What will be the impact on personal relationships?

*   Will it support or weaken traditional culture and minority communities?

*   Will the inequalities of access to the Internet magnify existing social and
    economic inequality?

*   Will our traditional ways of establishing social identities on the Internet be
    undermined? Will this be a good thing or a bad thing?

*   Should there be greater regulation over Internet use?

The discussion by these Asian women demonstrates how the Internet is raising
anxieties and aspirations not just about individuals' personal relationships, but
also about culture. In many countries around the world, people are debating the
impact of this new communications technology, its dangers and benefits.

## Activity 3.3    *(Reading B)*

Now read 'All the news that fits on screen' (Reading B), in which Jon Snow, a
British news journalist, discusses some political and cultural consequences of the
Internet. What are his main concerns? Do you share his anxieties?

## Comment

Jon Snow presents a much more negative view of the relationship between the
users, technology and information available on the Internet. He points out that
although the technology seems to bring with it new freedoms, it is not free of
existing systems of inequality, be they economical, political, or social. Another of
Snow's concerns is the freedom with which individuals may 'opt out' of a moral
and social responsibility to remain informed about the world. This raises issues
not only about democracy, but also, more broadly, about shared cultural experience. We discuss such issues in more detail later in the chapter.

The shared experience of traditional mass communications (such as television and newspapers) may have an important effect in constructing shared national culture and awareness of the world. The increasing use of the Internet to provide news coverage, information and entertainment services at times and in formats determined by individual users may have an individualizing, fragmenting effect on culture and society: there is so much information 'out there' in cyberspace that no two people will have the same experience of it. Individuals will, it is suggested, use 'intelligent agents' (special computer programs) to sift through the mass of available data and let through only those which fit personal needs and preferences.

Just as in the discussion of personal relationships, not everyone is as gloomy as Snow about the implications of this. Where Snow is concerned about the cultural and political consequences of permitting individuals to create newspapers tailored to their own interests, the feminist writer Dale Spender looks forward to the prospect:

> Take newspapers, for example. An agent will let me read exactly what I want. It will mean an end to all those football grunts and jerks: an end to any violent sport (such as boxing); indeed, an end to any game that I might find offensive. I could even request my intelligent agent to transmit to me only women's sport, or any good news of the day.
>
> If the agent resides at the *Courier Mail* office, this will be like having my own staff reporters. I will get on my screen each morning (and I can download if I wish), a newspaper which has been custom-made for me. This is one of the ironies of the so-called new *mass* media: the audience may often be just *one* person!
>
> If, however, the agent lives at my place, it could be that during the night a number of different newspapers send out their information, and my agent samples all of them, looking for anything I might like. Then it provides me with a personalised coverage from this wide range of sources. Oh what joy to be able to manage my own news. And what implications it will have for newspapers. Not only could women's newspapers be constructed for the first time, but newspaper editors might start to see the potential of such a niche market, and set about making news which is of greater concern to women. Good news for all.
>
> (Spender, 1995, p. xviii)

The views of Jon Snow and Dale Spender help to illustrate that the Internet is a complex technological innovation which may lead to wide social and political change. In the following sections we focus on those issues surrounding the Internet which are related to language: how it is used and what it is used for. This discussion will necessarily focus on the English language because it seems to have become the Internet lingua franca.

## 3.3   ENGLISH AND THE INTERNET

Three main issues have arisen around the English language and the Internet. The first is the extent to which the technology of the Internet supports and encourages the use of English more than other languages. The second is a concern about the political and cultural dominance by English-speaking countries of a key global communications technology. The third issue is the extent to which English is itself changing as a result of its use on the Internet.

## English language and new communications technologies

The brief history of the Internet's development given in section 3.2 shows how the Internet relies on standardized software protocols. Such standards are not always decided in open, free and fair ways: they reflect the needs of the dominant users and the developers of the technology.

When computers were first developed, a standard (similar to the Internet's IP/TCP standards) had to be set for the representation of letters as digital or binary data – the series of ones and zeros which computers require. This was to allow standard ways for people to instruct the computer, for the computer to provide information to the users on screens or print-outs and for computers to be able to pass data between each other. To represent something such as a letter in the computer the letter has to be given a 'code number', which can then be turned into a binary version of the number. The standard that was agreed upon was the American Standard Committee for Information Interchange (ASCII) code, though more recently the American National Standards Institute Character Set has become the actual standard. Originally, the technology permitted only 7-bit binary numbers to be used, which limited the number of available characters to 128. Some of the codes, the first 32, had to be used for controlling output to the screen or printer, such as creating a new line or positioning the text. The codes for actual characters are given in Table 1.

**Table 1**   ASCII codes for the English alphabet (omitting control codes)

| Code No | Letter | Code No | Letter | Code No | Letter | Code No | Letter | Code No | Letter |
|---|---|---|---|---|---|---|---|---|---|
| 32 | (spc) | 51 | 3 | 70 | F | 89 | Y | 108 | l |
| 33 | ! | 52 | 4 | 71 | G | 90 | Z | 109 | m |
| 34 | " | 53 | 5 | 72 | H | 91 | [ | 110 | n |
| 35 | # | 54 | 6 | 73 | I | 92 | \ | 111 | o |
| 36 | $ | 55 | 7 | 74 | J | 93 | ] | 112 | p |
| 37 | % | 56 | 8 | 75 | K | 94 | ^ | 113 | q |
| 38 | & | 57 | 9 | 76 | L | 95 | _ | 114 | r |
| 39 | ' | 58 | : | 77 | M | 96 | ` | 115 | s |
| 40 | ( | 59 | ; | 78 | N | 97 | a | 116 | t |
| 41 | ) | 60 | < | 79 | O | 98 | b | 117 | u |
| 42 | * | 61 | = | 80 | P | 99 | c | 118 | v |
| 43 | + | 62 | > | 81 | Q | 100 | d | 119 | w |
| 44 | , | 63 | ? | 82 | R | 101 | e | 120 | x |
| 45 | - | 64 | @ | 83 | S | 102 | f | 121 | y |
| 46 | . | 65 | A | 84 | T | 103 | g | 122 | z |
| 47 | / | 66 | B | 85 | U | 104 | h | 123 | { |
| 48 | 0 | 67 | C | 86 | V | 105 | i | 124 | | |
| 49 | 1 | 68 | D | 87 | W | 106 | j | 125 | } |
| 50 | 2 | 69 | E | 88 | X | 107 | k | 126 | ~ |

Such codes are fine if you are working only in the English language. In fact, they are even further limited to US English – notice that there is no pound sign, only a dollar sign! If you were working in French you would find there were no characters with accents (for example, ê, à). Those working with non-roman characters, such as those in the Greek or Russian alphabets, have to 'romanize' their words (i.e. find a way of representing the sounds of their language using only the Roman alphabet), or write special software to match ASCII codes to characters in their own alphabet. The situation improved through the development of 8-bit ASCII, which allowed 256 characters. Characters with accents and those alphabets with more than 24 characters could now be accommodated. Eight-bit ASCII establishes a 'common core' of 128 characters required by US English and a separate, nonstandard 'upper set' (of codes in the range 128–255) which are customized for different countries. The lack of standardization for these 'extra' characters means that the exchange of electronic documents between European countries or even between software systems is still notoriously problematic.

Eight-bit ASCII makes document-processing technology more accessible to other western countries and those areas of the world using roman-based alphabets but still fails to provide for many other parts of the world where other forms of writing system are used. The writing systems used for some major world languages, such as Arabic, Chinese, Japanese and Hindi, were not initially supported by computer technology. Only in the second half of the 1990s did standards which permitted other languages to be transmitted by e-mail (such as MIME and Unicode, a 16-bit method of representing characters in many languages) become reasonably widespread.

The history of the ASCII code thus represents a wider problem in relation to leading edge communications technology. The idea of representing characters of the English alphabet by means of numerical codes is derived from the tradition of the telegraph and telex, and earlier systems of digital representation such as the Morse Code. The telegraph (as we see in Chapter 5) was invented and controlled for many decades by English-speaking countries. This has been a recurrent experience: leading edge communications technology is designed first for the predominantly English-speaking markets in which it is first developed. Support for other languages comes later and often requires additional complexity, 'work-arounds' and reversioning, which may produce software which is slower and more prone to error. English-speaking countries may thus always maintain a competitive edge: they have more advanced and more reliable computer software. One of the rare exceptions to this rule is the fax machine, which was developed in Japan as a communications technology better suited to handwritten documents.

The development of ASCII provides an example of how the development of a communications technology within one or a group of nation states can encourage the spread of the national language. In this way, the dominance of the USA in computer hardware and software development generally, and in the creation of the Internet in particular, has undoubtedly helped the global expansion of English into cyberspace.

## The dominance of English on the Internet

The *Linguist* list is one of many electronic discussion groups ('listservs') which enable one person to broadcast an e-mail message to many other people (in this case about 7,000) around the world who have registered their interest in the topic of the list. Figure 3.1 shows one message on *Linguist* which described a survey of linguistic diversity on the Internet. It reported that no more than 20 languages were used as the 'primary medium of posting' even within discussions of ethnicity and culture.

```
Date: Tue, 14 Nov 1995 16:55:39 PST
From: Benjamin Ao <bao@firstbyte.davd.com>
Subject:inguistic Diversity on the Internet

            Linguistic Diversity on the Internet

    The rapid expansion of the Internet has many social ramifications.
One of them is its impact on the linguistic diversity among different
ethnic groups. I recently conducted a survey of postings in the 116
culturally diverse discussion groups under the Usenet news.soc.culture
node, and found that no more than 20 languages are used as the primary
medium of message posting. The results are as follows:

        82          English
        11          Spanish
        3           Serbo-Croatian
        2           French
        2           German
        2           Portuguese
        1           Africaans
        1           Albanian
        1           Bulgarian
        1           Czech
        1           Dutch
        1           Esperanto
        1           Estonian
        1           Flemish
        1           Indonesian
        1           Italian
        1           Polish
        1           Russian
        1           Turkish
        1           Vietnamese
        ---------------------
        116         Total
```

From these numbers, we can make the following observations.

1. The linguistic diversity is greatly reduced on the Internet.

2. All but two (Russian and Bulgarian) posting languages have writing
   systems based on the Roman alphabet.

3. Speakers of languages that do not have Roman alphabet based writing
   systems don't bother with transliteration (with the exception of
   Russian and Bulgarian speakers). They simply adopt English.

4. English is by far the most popular language on the Internet, even
   if the subject matter is highly culturally and ethnically oriented.

It will be interesting to see how the current linguistic diversity
on the Internet will develop in the future.

```
Benjamin Ao
First Byte
A speech technology company
in California
```

*Figure 3.1   A posting on* Linguist *list*

John Paolillo (1995) carried out research into the interactions of one such group on the Internet whose interest topic was that of the Punjabi language and culture. He discovered that only 15 per cent of the words used in the e-mail messages passed were in Punjabi. Much of this communication also required the romanization of the language and clever use of ASCII codes to build larger representations of letters.

   When Benjamin Ao's message was posed on the *Linguist* list, it provoked a couple of respondents to query how representative the Usenet groups were of

Internet culture as a whole. Although the Usenet groups were available world-wide, they are, it is claimed, dominated by North Americans or other nationals working in North America (see Figure 3.2).

```
Date: Sun, 19 Nov 1995 16:32:45 +0100
From: KNAPPEN@VKPMZD.kph.Uni-Mainz.DE
<KNAPPEN@VKPMZD.kph.Uni-Mainz.DE>
Subject:Linguistic Diversity on the Internet
```

The recent posting is a nice example, how the method of a survey determines quite well the outcome. At least here in germany, the so-called `big 8' newsgroups are seen as mainly US-american ones, including soc.culture.german.

There is an own german language top level hierarchie, de.all, with lots of traffic (readers of this mailing list may be interested in reading de.etc.sprache.deutsch). Another interesting group is alt.letzeburger, where letzebuergisch is the predominant language.

For smaller language communities, a mailing list on a given topic is often more appropriate than a newsgroup, and I know of mailing lists for many languages not mentioned in the above list.

So what else to expect, than a vast english dominance?

--J"org Knappen.


```
Date: Tue, 21 Nov 1995 12:24:34
From: Narahiko INOUE <Narahiko INOUE>
Subject: Re: 6.1629 Linguistic Diversity on Internet
```

About "Linguistic Diversity on the Internet" posted by bao@firstbyte.davd.com (Benjamin Ao):

>2. All but two (Russian and Bulgarian) posting languages have writing
>    systems based on the Roman alphabet.
>
>3. Speakers of languages that do not have Roman alphabet based writing
>    systems don't bother with transliteration (with the exception of
>    Russian and Bulgarian speakers). They simply adopt English.


If we consider messages exchanged on the Internet WITHIN a country (ethnic group, etc.), a different picture may emerge. In Japan, the majority of messages (at least in my impression) are written in Japanese with the Japanese writing system (a combination of Chinese characters and syllabic characters both using two-byte codes). Most e-mail messages sent to addresses within Japan and news group postings in Japan are written in the Japanese writing system. WWW home pages often have two versions in Japanese and in English with links to each other.

Use of English or transliteration in Japan is probably considered impolite to Japanese readers. Of course,messages across borders or to and from sites which cannot deal with the Japanese two-byte codes are written in either in English or transliteration (Romanization). Again, I do not have any statistical data but the transliteration is not uncommon. Sometimes, the transliteration carries more personalized or affectionate overtones. It is also intended for Japanese computer users who do not necessarily understand English except for very simple expressions.


Narahiko INOUE, Ph.D.
Institute of Languages & Cultures
Graduate School of Social and Cultural Studies
Kyushu University, JAPAN

*Figure 3.2  Two responses to the posting shown in Figure 3.1*

Both these responses suggest that the Internet *does* support communication in languages other than English and that even if the technology is unfriendly towards non-roman scripts, it is not impossible to use the Internet to communicate in languages such as Japanese. The exchanges demonstrate several features of Internet communication, however: first, that US users (mainly because of their sheer numbers) dominate many parts of the Internet; secondly, that communication *across* national groups tends to be in English; and thirdly, that the Internet can support communities wishing to use languages other than English. Furthermore, the discussion in these 'minority' language groups is, in principle, available to anyone in the world who is sufficiently interested to investigate.

## Who experiences the global village?

The dominance of the Internet by the USA is demonstrated by statistics of data flows. From Table 2 we can see the extent to which the use of the Internet is biased in favour of the developed world (and the USA in particular).

**Table 2**   Global distribution of Internet data traffic by region: year ending 1994

| Area | Number of networks | Data into area (MB) | Data out of area (MB) |
| --- | --- | --- | --- |
| North Americas | 8569 | 8646736 | 8123284 |
| Europe | 3210 | 536451 | 832772 |
| Asia Pacific | 977 | 190846 | 373504 |
| South America | 146 | 6262 | 25325 |
| Middle East | 89 | 7609 | 24038 |
| Africa | 68 | 2073 | 9032 |
| Central America | 5 | 1931 | 3951 |

(Internet Society, on-line data services)

Within Europe, the country with the highest data traffic is the UK.

The fact that the USA has dominated computer and software development in the second half of the twentieth century means that the *discourse* of computing and computer science is also English-based. Most technical terms, both formal and informal, connected with computing derive from US English. Even texts printed in British English will use US spellings for some computer terminology: for example a computer 'program' is spelled the US way in British English, but a television 'programme' is not. Most of the world's programming languages and operating systems are also based on US English. Although it is a relatively trivial matter to 'translate' such software into local languages, this has occurred only in some countries. Locally versioned software, with menus and instructions in languages other than English, also typically lag behind the latest versions available in the USA.

The language most affected by English dominance on the Internet is probably French, which is the most widely used international lingua franca after English. France has maintained a progressive public policy towards new communications technology, establishing a national data network (Minitel) which reached into almost every home and business in France by the 1980s. The existence of this national network, combined with a more centralized telecommunications policy than existed in English-speaking countries, greatly inhibited the development of Internet connections in France. In mid 1995, the cost of Internet connections in France dropped considerably and public policy began to change, as Brent Gregston (1996) reported:

> despite the sudden enthusiasm, a nationalistic attitude still pervades much of the discussion about public investment in the Internet – why build an electronic pipeline to funnel American products into France? Some officials are asking for cultural safeguards that look suspiciously like a preservation of their entrenched power over telecommunications.
>
> Others have floated the idea of a quota system for content on the Net, like the one for French movies on television and in cinemas. But at least one thing has changed – the French now realise that, if the Internet is spreading Anglophile culture all over the planet, it could do the same for French culture as well.
>
> (Gregston, 1996, p. 48)

The French government has itself established a World Wide Web site (see later sections) which is intended to encourage the use of French on the Internet, and which provides suggested translations for US terminology.

It should be clear from this discussion that the effects of the economic and technological dominance of English-speaking nations on the development of global communications technologies are not simply those of cultural imperialism through their content; the effect of this dominance is also found on the technological functioning of global communications. Technological standards such as ASCII, which are based on the English language, have helped tie the new communications media to the English language, making it harder for non-English speakers to exploit the opportunities provided by new media. Later developments may not be so constraining, though; indeed, it is doubtful whether the hegemony of English on the Internet will continue to be so strong. Many more languages are being used on the Internet, particularly in the new publishing medium offered by the World Wide Web, which is described more fully later.


## 3.4   NEW TEXTS, NEW GENRES

The way people communicate over the Internet has itself been the subject of research. Although much Internet communication (such as e-mail) is text based, the texts which circulate do not display the characteristics of traditional print genres. Indeed, they often show the spontaneity and informality of spoken, rather than written language.

Many new forms of text have arisen which both exploit the potential of electronic media to construct more fluid and dynamic texts and reflect the new social relationships which often obtain between participants in Internet communication. In this section we examine some of the features of electronic texts on the Internet; and in the following section, we explore some of the implications they may have for participants' social identities.

The hybrid nature of computer-mediated communication is explored in Chapter 2 Reading C in the second book in this series, *Using English: from conversation to canon* (Maybin and Mercer (eds), 1996).


## Word processors and the electronic text

The one common aspect of all new computer-based media is their reliance upon the '**electronic text**'. The encoding of a communication, such as a picture, speech

## How to use the new logo

There are only two permitted versions of the logo—either with the title on the right of the shield or underneath it (as illustrated).

OU yellow PMS 123

OU blue PMS 300

Lettering specially drawn — not typeset

*The two permitted versions of the logo*

---

Here are some of the main rules for using it.

### Logo on the front
All public documents prepared by the OU should carry the logo on the front cover.

### Colours
Two colours are specified for formal applications such as high-quality stationery and degree certificates— blue (reference PMS 300) for the shield and lettering, and yellow (PMS 123) for the circular inset. Single-colour stationery should be in blue (PMS 300) if possible, otherwise in black.

For publicity material, covers, packaging and similar purposes, other colours may be used. However, the shield and title must never be in different colours from each other; the circular inset must be the same colour as the overall background. The logo may be used in positive or negative form as illustrated.

### Approved sizes
For printed items up to A4, the logo should appear in one of the sizes shown.

### Watch the space
A clear area must be left around the logo according to the measurements shown. No other graphics or lettering may intrude within this space.

*Permitted sizes with clear area required (box does not print)*

*Logo in positive form*

*Logo in negative form*

*Colour examples of positive and negative use*

### Supporting typeface
For departmental names on stationery and for signs and other formal items, the Linotype Palatino typeface is to be used (as in the text of this broadsheet).

## Palatino
## Palatino bold

*Supporting typeface in medium and bold*

### Use with other logos
Where the OU logo is used with the logos of outside bodies, the two must be placed adjacent to each other, either side by side or one above the other so that the boundaries of each are in alignment.

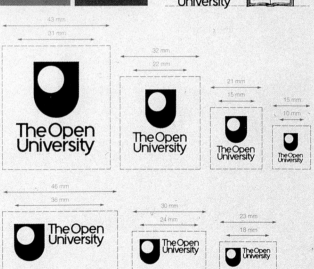

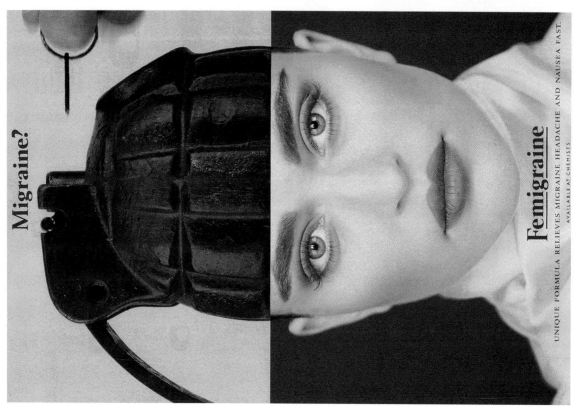

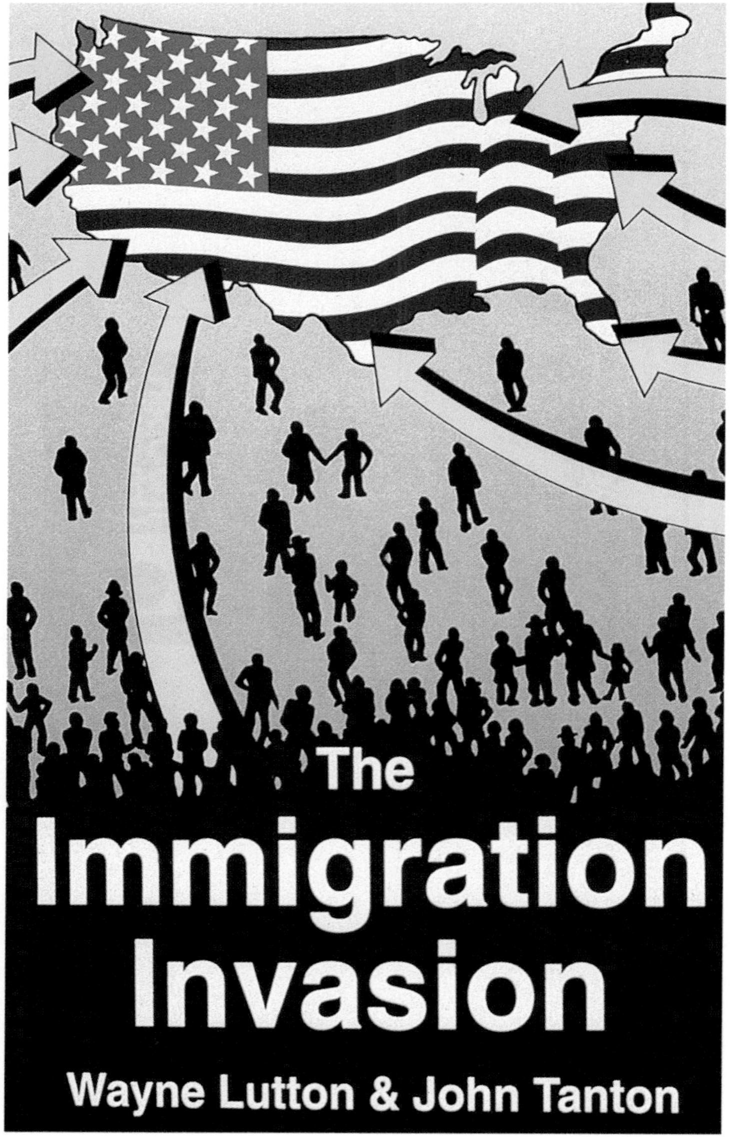

Plate 3    Book cover (Chapter 2)

Plate 2    Advertisement for migraine tablets (Chapter 2)

*Plate 4   Page from* The Adventures of Mighty Max *(Chapter 2)*

# THE Sun 25p

Friday, January 1, 1993  **25p**    Today's TV: Pages 24 and 25    Audited daily sale for November 3,515,236

Picture: PHIL HANNAFORD

## Bikini Di strips to defy Palace

**DEFIANT DI** stages a paradise-island peepshow — in a bikini parade to snub Palace protocol yesterday.

She wore her skimpy blue and green swimsuit in full view of photographers at the start of her

Continued on Page 13

# HUMAN PREY...
## Man feeds himself to lion

*Savaged . . wounded Silcott lies moaning in agony in the lions' enclosure yesterday as Arfur prepares to attack again*

A LION stands over a screaming man yesterday after savaging him in front of horrified zoo trippers.

Victim Ben Silcott had his chest ripped open when he climbed into the beast's den.

The rare Asiatic lion, named Arfur, pounced as 27-year-old Silcott stood feeding it with oven-ready chickens.

**BY NICK PARKER and TONY SNOW**

Families on a day out at London Zoo watched helplessly as the 24-stone jungle king tore at its victim. Brave keepers saved the man's life by dashing into the den, firing a shot over the animal's head and driving it off with fire extinguishers.

Last night, Mr Silcott was fighting for life. Doctors said he had a "better than

50-50" chance of survival. Arfur — who got the name after he lost "arf" an ear in a fight — was sharing the open-air compound with two lionesses when ponytailed Mr Silcott, dressed in jeans and leather jacket, shinned up a 20ft metal fence and leapt among them.

One witness claimed he shouted: "These animals should be set free." Housewife

Continued on Centre Pages

*Plate 5    Newspaper front page (Chapter 2)*

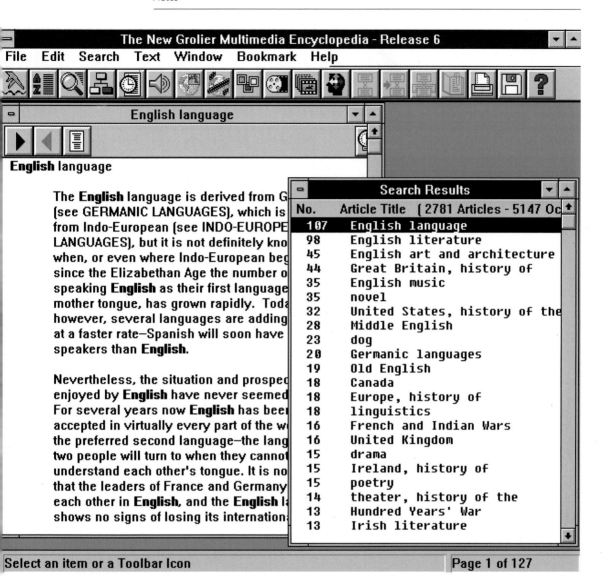

*Plate 6   Extract from a multimedia encyclopaedia (Chapter 3)*

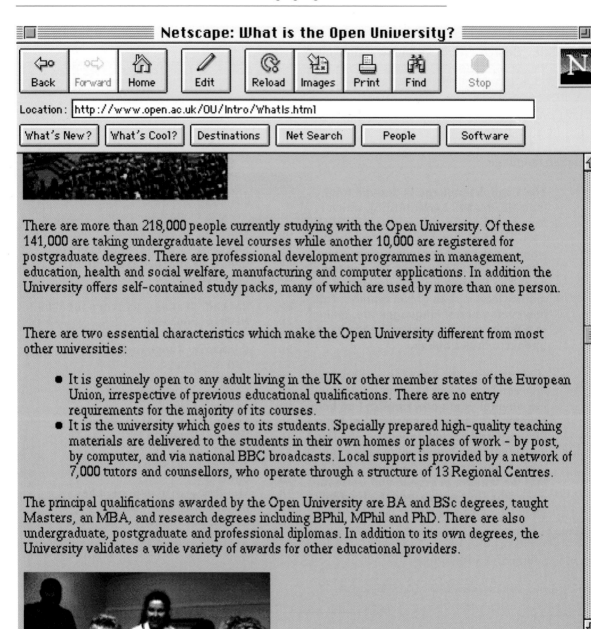

There are more than 218,000 people currently studying with the Open University. Of these 141,000 are taking undergraduate level courses while another 10,000 are registered for postgraduate degrees. There are professional development programmes in management, education, health and social welfare, manufacturing and computer applications. In addition the University offers self-contained study packs, many of which are used by more than one person.

There are two essential characteristics which make the Open University different from most other universities:

- It is genuinely open to any adult living in the UK or other member states of the European Union, irrespective of previous educational qualifications. There are no entry requirements for the majority of its courses.
- It is the university which goes to its students. Specially prepared high-quality teaching materials are delivered to the students in their own homes or places of work - by post, by computer, and via national BBC broadcasts. Local support is provided by a network of 7,000 tutors and counsellors, who operate through a structure of 13 Regional Centres.

The principal qualifications awarded by the Open University are BA and BSc degrees, taught Masters, an MBA, and research degrees including BPhil, MPhil and PhD. There are also undergraduate, postgraduate and professional diplomas. In addition to its own degrees, the University validates a wide variety of awards for other educational providers.

Plate 7   *Hypertext links across the world: a World Wide Web page (Chapter 3)*

# QUEUES *cutting*

## Nobody wants to wait a long time to be served.

Hardly surprising, then, we have set ourselves the key target of reducing waiting time. Exactly how though?

Few organisations put as much effort into understanding and improving waiting times as we do. To give an example, we set targets and continually monitor performance. In some Post Offices there are very high points on Thursday mornings when pensions are paid out. In others, the greatest demand may be at the end of the month when there are bills to pay.

The changes are already showing. For example, a recent survey published in the *Sunday Times* reported that our queueing times are better than banks, building societies, DIY stores and supermarkets.

Good news. But, even so, we believe we can do better, and have set ourselves the following target:

*to ensure that at least 95% of customers in this Post Office never have to queue for more than five minutes.*

*page four*

Plate 8   *Page from UK Post Office Charter (Chapter 4)*

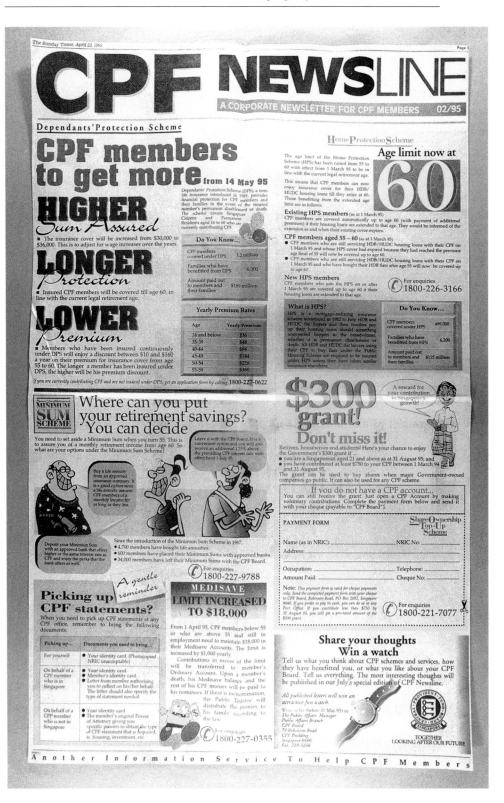

*Plate 9    Singapore government newsletter (Chapter 4)*

or a document, into an electronic form allows the material to be transmitted to another part of the world and then decoded. It also allows the encoded communication to be manipulated in ways not possible previously, with the help of computers and digital technology.

### Activity 3.4   Working with the electronic text   *(Allow about 10 minutes)*

Many people at some time in their lives have used a computer to produce some kind of document. Even if you have never used a computer, try to list the types of new writing, or rather text production, abilities that are enabled by computer-based technologies. Think about how you might draft and produce a handwritten letter by comparison. Consider also this chapter and the material within it. How might the 'new abilities' change the manner in which people write and communicate?

### Comment

Word processors and computer-based text production facilities bring many new possibilities. At one level there is the ability to include pictures and graphics more easily in the text, whether you are a publishing house or a person working at home. It is also easier to set out the page typographically and in many different ways. While still in electronic form, the text can be changed and changed again very quickly and without leaving any indication of these changes. In writing this paragraph for the first time I deleted and rewrote sections of every sentence. Think of the number of crossings out that would adorn a written page with that number of changes. Later, one of the academic editors of this book made further alterations to the text (including the addition of this sentence). Yet further changes were then made by the publishing editor. These are processes which hitherto took much time and effort (and paper!).

**Computer conferencing** is a text-based electronic group communication system. The Open University uses computer conferencing systems in its distance teaching on some courses.

Word processors may then have altered the manner in which we conduct the practice of writing itself. This point has not been lost on the users of the technology, as demonstrated by the messages in Figure 3.3, from a discussion of this issue on a computer conferencing system.

In exploring the effects of word processors on the activity of writing Bolter (1991) has argued:

> in the case of writing as elsewhere, it is not possible to put away the technology. Writing with pen and paper is no more natural, no less technological than writing at the computer screen. It is true that the computer is a more complicated and fragile device than a pen. But we cannot isolate ourselves from the technology by reverting to older forms of writing. The production of today's pens and paper also requires a sophisticated manufacture.
>
> (Bolter, 1991, p. 37)

```
============================
dt200-forum/turing #209, [discussant1], 573 chars,   6-Apr-93 08:51
This is a comment to message 208
There is/are comment(s) on this message
There are additional comments to message 208
--------------------------
I recently had to compse a short concise text (an
abstract) on paper withou access to my machine.  It
was almost impossible.  With paper you get commited
to versions of your sentences and can only change
them with scriblings out etc.  But it was more than
this.  I type what I think and revise it as I go
often going over sentences again and again, crafting
them and redrafting them interactively.  These
abilities that the Word Processor provides are now
central aspects of my 'literacy practices'.  That
is how I write, pen and paper are now the more alien
medium.
[discussant1]
============================
dt200-forum/turing #226,[discussant3], 1487 chars,   7-Apr-93 15:51
This is a comment to message 219
There is/are comment(s) on this message
--------------------------
I was thinking again about your word-processor example, and though my
first reaction was that using one doesn't change /what/ I write, I now
think that I was wrong.  There are certainly technological jokes and
technological analogies which one can use now and which would have
been gibberish to most readers a few years ago

You'll know better than I what we're trying to do in this discussion:
are we trying simply to discover what the changes in our habits are,
or are we also trying to put a value judgement on them? [...]
============================
dt200-forum/turing #231, [discussant4], 1299 chars,   9-Apr-93 11:30
This is a comment to message 226
--------------------------
[...] IT has, however, changed the way I write.

When I had to do it on paper, I almost never changed anything.  I
suppose it looked like one of [discussant5]'s messages :-). Now, as
[discussant3]
said, I update constantly as I go along. My spellings and grammar are
not much now, but they used to be far worse when the effort to make
changes seemed greater than the gain. Now I percieve that balance has
shifted in favour of it always being worth putting right any errors
that I notice
The CMC smiley is something that I miss in spoken conversations
(especially on the phone) now that I have got used to it.
An interesting corollery  to this is that I now prefer to write a wp
letter than to make a phone call.  It used to be categorically the
other way around.
[discussant4]
```

*Figure 3.3   A computer conferencing discussion*


Bolter sees the relationships between writers and the texts they produce as social
ones, describing them as '**economies of writing**' and claiming that:

> Each culture and each age has its own economy of writing. There is
> a dynamic relationship between the materials and the techniques of
> writing and a less obvious but no less important relationship between
> materials and techniques on the one hand and the genres and usage of
> writing on the other.
>
> (Bolter, 1991, p. 37)

Bolter does not confine the concept of technology simply to the objects or tools
(e.g. clay, paper and floppy disks or wooden markers, pens and computers) but

considers it to be a set of skills and practices around these tools (Bolter, 1991, pp. 35–6).

For Bolter then, the electronic production of text represents a new economy of writing, one that alters the relationship between writer, reader and text. Bolter argues that the encoding of text into electronic digital form and its storage in computer media (magnetic disks, computer memory, etc.) distance both the reader and writer from the text. Further technology (screens, printers, etc.) is required to make the text once more accessible to the human reader or writer (Bolter, 1991, pp. 41–3). Though the electronic medium creates this distance, it also makes the text more easily copied and transmitted. Bolter sees this as a continuation and expansion of the effects of the printing press. On the other hand, the malleability of electronic texts creates a new role for the reader, who is no longer the passive recipient of fixed and preserved texts. This issue of the proactive reader is central to some contemporary social scientists' and philosophers' interpretations of texts and is returned to in later sections.

Such issues might seem to be about the impact of new communications technologies on general language practices; however, you only have to look back at the previous sections to see how they are directly pertinent to the English language. The dual combination of technological bias in production and distribution to western, especially English-speaking, nations ensures that one of the first languages that will go through these processes of change is the English language. As we saw in Figure 3.3, an example of a computer conferencing interaction, it is clear that individuals are finding that their productions of and interactions with electronic versions of English are different from those with written and spoken English texts.

Bolter's definition of 'economies of writing' is rather limited given the plethora of media which now exist. A model concerned with '**economies of communication**' might be more useful. These new economies of communication, based upon the use of various forms of electronic text, are now central to many of the linguistic interactions taking place within contemporary societies and produce many new forms of 'text'.

## The hypertext – making English texts dynamic

One of the major new textual forms brought about by digital media is the **hypertext**, in which 'active' connections are provided between different parts of the text and with other texts. By clicking on such a link with a pointing device such as a mouse, it is possible for a reader to jump between text segments and on to other texts. Rather than reading the text in a linear way or in an order predetermined by the author, each reader constructs a different pathway through the textual resources which reflects their own interests and decisions. Many hypertexts take the form of 'interactive books' especially complex reference books such as encyclopaedias.

Individual texts in an interactive book are connected to each other through a database of links. Plate 6 in the colour section of this book is from *The New Grolier Multimedia Encyclopedia*. A text describing the English language has been called up via a link in another text; the word *language* has then been accessed to produce the list of further texts relating to language. The term '**intertextuality**' has been used by a number of writers in the field of discourse and textual analysis to describe the manner in which any individual text relies for its meaning upon overt and latent references to other texts. Hypertexts turn these potential connections into actual ones, allowing readers immediate access to associated texts. Documents are no longer linear and fixed but multidimensional and dynamic.

In the above example, it is very easy for readers to collect large amounts of texts and, by cutting and pasting both words and pictures, create texts for themselves that the authors of the encyclopaedia did not conceive of. This is nothing new; we could all do this with the books in our houses. It is the ease with which this can be done, and the fact that the process does not destroy the original, which are seen as defining features of electronic texts.

## The World Wide Web

An encyclopaedia on a CD-ROM may contain a bewildering range of resources in comparison with a conventional printed book. Similar interactive texts, however, are available on the Internet, making available to readers an indefinitely large and constantly growing range of information resources. This possibility has been created by the rise of World Wide Web (sometimes identified as WWW or Web for short) technologies. When you interact with a textual link on a World Wide Web page you are not simply connecting to data on the computer in front of you but to information that might be stored on the other side of the world.

Plate 7 in the colour section shows part of a Web 'page' taken from the Open University's World Wide Web site. Each of the underlined or emboldened pieces of text mark a link to another Web page, which could be anywhere else around the world on the Internet. These pages range from actual computer-based infor-mation, to lists of other useful pages, to personal and group 'home' pages where people place a public description of themselves, their group or organization. Such home pages usually then provide links with other pages and also to pages of related interest at other, remote sites.

Most people access the World Wide Web through the home page of a particular institution, company or 'Internet service provider'. Such a home page will provide access to the services and information available from that institution but they are also, as with personal home pages, expressions of the identity of the institution. **Web pages** are a complex interplay of self and group presentations, information access structures, personal and group communications, and specific stopping-off points along one individual's interaction with the Web at large.

Though many languages can be presented on the World Wide Web because of its ability to deal with both graphical and textual data, the majority of Web usage and Web sites are in the USA and Europe. Once again, it is the English language that is being used to juggle these multiple tasks of representation.

Writers of World Wide Web pages have limited control over the manner in which the texts they produce are viewed. Different access software will display the page differently in terms of typeface and structure. Even people using the same software can alter the settings to their own preferences. Web pages are written in a standardized language called **HTML (Hyper Text Mark-up Language)**, which sets out which sections of the text are headings, which are links to other pages and so forth. Figure 3.4 shows part of the HTML code for the World Wide Web page shown in Plate 7.

```
<HTML>
<HEAD>
<!-- This document was created from RTF source by rtftohtml version 2.7.5 -->
<TITLE>What is the Open University?</TITLE>
<!--OWNER_NAME="Les Holloway, Public Relations" -->
<LINK REV="made" HREF="mailto:WebMaster@open.ac.uk">
<!--OWNER_INFO="Open University, Milton Keynes, UK" -->
</HEAD>


<BODY>
<iMG SRC="/OU/Images/LogoLS4.gif" ALT="The Open University">
<H1>The Open University: an introduction</H1>
The Open University is Britain's largest and most innovative university.
Founded by Royal Charter in 1969, it has grown rapidly both in student numbers
and range of courses.<P>
<iMG SRC="/OU/Images/DerbyGroup.gif" ALT=""><P>
At present there are more than 200,000 people studying with the Open
University. Of these 132,000 are taking
<A HREF="/OU/Studying/StudyProgs.html#UGCourses">undergraduate
level courses</A> while another 10,000 are registered for
<A HREF="/OU/Studying/StudyProgs.html#PGCourses">postgraduate
degrees</A>.  There are professional development programmes in
<A HREF="/OU/Studying/Courses/Manage.html">management</A>,
<A HREF="/OU/Studying/Courses/Ed.html">education</A>,
<A HREF="/OU/Studying/Courses/HSW.html">health
and social welfare</A>,
<A HREF="/OU/Studying/Courses/PGCM.html">manufacturing</A>
and
<A HREF="/OU/Studying/Courses/PGCM.html">computer
applications</A>. In addition the University offers self-contained
<A HREF="/OU/Studying/StudyProgs.html#StudyPacks">study
packs</A>, many of which are used by more than one person.<P>
<iMG SRC="/OU/Images/CourseUnits.gif" ALT=""><P>
```

Figure 3.4   *HTML source code for World Wide Web page shown in Plate 7*

At first there seems little to connect the complex set of codes to the readable example of a World Wide Web page. The author of the page probably had little to do with the creation of these codes, as many World Wide Web authoring tools are variations on word processors. The author creates the text and images to go into the page, arranges them using a word processor, providing extra information for the links to other pages and sites, and then saves the document in a specific format. A specially designed program then converts this file into HTML code. The HTML code itself indicates this has happened:

```
<!-- This document was created from RTF source by rtftohtml version 2.7.5 -->
```

Within the code are markers to indicate the purpose of the following text:

```
<TITLE>
```
(Indicates the title of the page)

```
<H1>
```
(Indicates a 'level 1' heading)

```
<iMG SRC="/OU/Images/DerbyGroup.gif" ALT="">
```
(Indicates a picture)

```
<P>
```
(Indicates a new paragraph)

```
<A HREF="/OU/Studying/Courses/PGCM.html">
```
(Indicates a link to another WWW page)

One theme that runs through discussions of language change is the tension between **unification** and **diversification**. At any one time, social, economic, political and technological structures can create greater or lesser tendencies towards unification or diversification. Bakhtin (1986, 1981) calls these **centripetal** (unifying) and **centrifugal** (diversifying) forces. One clear example of a technology that has helped to unify aspects of language use, and which itself has been assisted by specific social and political factors, is that of print and writing. Written language provides what Bolter (1989, 1991) describes as 'fixivity' (and Anderson, 1991, as '**fixity**') – the ability to ensure that the content does not change over time.

Anderson (1991), writing on the relationship between language literacy and nationality, argues that languages themselves become constrained and limited in their ability to change once they are fixed in a permanent medium such as print. For the linguist Michael Halliday, the 'fixity' of written English is reflected in its very clause structure (Halliday and Hasan, 1989; Halliday, 1987). Halliday sees the embedded and lexically dense structure of written language as reflecting its social role as the fixed legitimate bearer of historical and contemporary knowledge. This contrasts with spoken language, whose more open-ended, less information-dense, clause structure reflects the active and dynamic social roles to which it is put.

Electronic communication can thus be said to threaten the fixity of print in two ways: firstly, because electronic texts take such a transient and changing form; second, because for a variety of reasons, electronic communication appears to be more like speech in its clause structure.

We have, then, in a World Wide Web page both constraining forces – those defining the use of HTML – and diversifying forces, in that users can set their own software to interpret the HTML in certain ways. Therefore, underlying the diversity in the presentation of an English text is a set of rules constraining the structure of that presentation. The reader is the person who defines the presentation of these elements. Users of hypertext and the World Wide Web are being asked to engage in new English language practices and to construct the language in new ways for new contexts and new technologies of communication.

## 3.5   NEW TEXTS, NEW SUBJECTIVITY

We have seen how new communications technologies are leading to new relationships between author and reader and within the text itself. The importance of our interactions with texts and the way they encourage us to see ourselves, other people, and the world in particular ways, has become central to contemporary social theory and philosophy. Jacques Derrida, an influential writer on this issue, argues:

> The end of linear writing is indeed the end of the book, even if, even today, it is within the form of a book that new writings – literary or theoretical – allow themselves to be, for better or worse, encased ... That is why, beginning to write without the line, one begins also to reread past writing according to a different organization of space. If today the problem of reading occupies the forefront of science, it is because of this suspense between two ages of writing. Because we are beginning to write, to write differently, we must reread differently.
> (Derrida, 1976, pp. 86–7)

For some social theorists, Derrida's writing indicates a philosophical acceptance of the effects of the electronic text and new communications technologies on language use (Ulmer, 1985, p. 303). If some of the complex dressing around Derrida's arguments is removed, it can be seen that questions are being raised on two key issues: first, the effects of electronic communication upon language use, especially 'fixity' in communications media; and secondly, the relationship between the people who are communicating and the actual texts or utterances they produce. In this section we explore more carefully some of the issues around electronic texts, social identity and agency. Who is speaking in an electronic text? Who takes responsibility for what elements of the text?

**Activity 3.5**   *(Reading C)*

Now read 'Communication and new subjects' by Mark Poster (Reading C). Poster uses the term '**subjectivity**' to describe a person's sense of self and perception of relationships to others and refers to the 'subject' when writing about the 'self'. As you read, note the various forms of computer-mediated interaction which Poster describes. Drawing on your own experience (or lack of it!), do you agree with the author's claim that new communications media will have such a huge effect on our presentation of self and perception of others? Do you think that everyone is likely to experience new communication technologies in this way?

**Comment**

Poster suggests that new forms of English language are coming into being which allow individuals to construct new subjectivities, identities, through new media. One of the key aspects of this new form of interaction is the lack of physical location and presence. Poster notes that this may have direct effects upon the way in which people communicating in such media perceive themselves. 'Electronic writing ... disperses the subject so that it no longer functions as a centre in the way it did in pre-electronic writing' (Poster, 1990, p. 100).

   For Poster, the manner in which centred conceptions of ourselves, other people and language are challenged comes through the way in which electronic texts are malleable. That is, they are much more easily altered than texts produced with a pen or a typewriter. This is again the issue of **fixity**, in which the fixed written object becomes, like spoken texts, a fluid and dynamic object. The fluidity of electronic texts destabilizes the subject through blurring the distinction between the writer and the text.

Let us now examine some examples of electronic communication in order to see what visible evidence we can find for Poster's ideas.

## Electronic mail

Electronic mail is one of the most extensively used facilities on the Internet, but like the World Wide Web page, e-mail messages frequently transgress our usual conception of authorship. For example, an e-mail message can frequently constitute a collage of other electronic texts.

**Activity 3.6**   *(Allow about 10 minutes)*

Look at the e-mail message in Figure 3.5. Which parts of the text do you think are products of the writer, which parts come from other texts, and which are produced by the technology itself?

```
Date sent:        Fri, 24 Feb 1995 20:56:16 +0200
To:               foucault@jefferson.village.virginia.edu
From:             [discussant 6]
Subject:          Re: "local" vs "universal"
Send reply to:    foucault@jefferson.village.virginia.edu

[discussant 5] wrote:

>I tend to see what [discussant 6] is saying about Foucault's version of
>modernism as inclusive of a strand of postmodernism-- although I'm
>nervous about the claim that relying on reason vs authority to free
>ourselves isn't one of those metanarratives.  The Enlightenment project
>is afterall the exemplary metanarrative that post-modernists point to as
>having lost its legitimacy.
>
>Foucault's response, and again this is where he leans toward the "local,"
>was several times to refuse to found anything on a unitary Reason
>(opposed to madness, the irrational, etc.),   but instead to reason within
>relatively specific situations, beginning with the diverse discourses of
>reason applicable (e.g., "reasons of state," medical reason, economic
>reasons, etc.).

It is true that the Enlightenment is the project post-modernists have said
as having lost it's credibility, but that is not the point I tried to say.
What I meant was that in his late writings Foucault tried to find a
_positive_ way to think about Enligtenment and modernity.

In his reading of Kant's "Was ist Aufkl{rung" Foucault found that in the
Enligtenment there is a new way to understand reason in a self-reflexive
manner. By that he meant that reason thought itself in it's own
historicity. This, I feel, is by no way a unitary Reason but a reason that
understands itself in local terms; a critical reason that posits itself a
task to investigate "the events that have led us to constitute ourselves
and to recognize ourselves as subjects of what we are doing, thinking,
saying," as Foucault put it.

Of course everything can be thougt at least in two different ways. I'm sure
that it is not a coincidence that at the same historical era there emerged
another reason too. And it was also historical. Foucault calls this reason
bio-power, as you know. - There is always two sides in modernity, as
Baudelaire said.

[discussant 6]

**********************************************************************************
[discussant 6]
University of Jyvaskyla
Department of Literature
P.O. Box 35
SF-40351 Jyvaskyla
FINLAND
**********************************************************************************
```

*Figure 3.5   An electronic mail message*

## Comment

The example in Figure 3.5 is an e-mail message from a group interaction. Note that much of the message is not actually generated by the person who ostensibly wrote it. The only part of the text to have come directly from the author is the last three paragraphs of the main text. The lines preceded by the '>' symbol are copied from an earlier message. The copying of parts of one message into another is an automatic facility in many e-mail software systems. The '>' character which marks the embedded text has been generated by the software rather than by the writer. The final 'signature' area was probably, though not necessarily, designed by the author at some point in the past but is appended by their electronic mail software automatically to every outgoing message. The remainder of the text is generated by the various computer systems which carried the message around the world to its recipient. Less than half (936 characters from 2,028) were input by the signatory to the message.

# Synchronous Internet communication

Electronic mail is only one of the established genres used in communication across the Internet. Like computer conferencing, e-mail is an asynchronous mode of communication. There are also several ways of interacting synchronously across the Internet – in 'real time'. One such is known as **MUD** (**Multi User Dimensions**), another is known as IRC (Internet Relay Chat).

**MUDs** were originally designed as multi-player text-based interactive games, similar to the text-based adventure games available for personal computers. When someone first connects to the MUD, they are asked to create the 'character' which they will control in the game. The genre of the game will establish what kinds of characters are available and what powers and characteristics they will have in the game. For example, a game might include Wizards, Dragons or Swordsmen. The MUD will include many 'virtual places' such as rooms, roads and countryside and there are many 'virtual objects' within these spaces. None of these exist in any real sense: they are fictional environments in which players can carry out certain actions, limited by the characters they are playing and by the actions of other players.

Although MUDs arose first in game-playing, the software is now often used as a kind of 'virtual social space' where people from either one self-defined group or from all over the Internet can interact via their MUD 'characters'. There are, for example, MUDs designed to support language learning, as well as for ordinary chat.

**Activity 3.7   Life in the MUD**   *(Allow about 10 minutes)*

Figure 3.6 shows a transcript from a MUD interaction. Note down your reactions to this text. Can you understand the text as a whole and can you work out the relationships between the individual utterances?

```
1     Ray  laughs
2     Tom  watches Ray document his laughter
3     Tom  says, "mudding with people in the same room is weird"
4     Ray  laughed before typing :laughs
5     Tom  nods
6     Ray  thought he did
7     Ray  says "wait, now I'm confused"
8     Tom  eyes Ray warily
9     Ray  says, "which world is the real world?"
10    Ray  eyes himself warily
```

*Figure 3.6   A MUD interaction*

## Comment

You may not be able to make much sense of this text at first glance. It is not the transcript of a spoken conversation; rather it is the output from a computer-based interaction and is essentially in the same form as it appeared on the screen. It is the final record of the exchanges; participants, however, experienced the exchanges in real time, like a spoken conversation.

The MUD creates an environment where identities and agency are often problematic. Is a character talking in his or her 'real' voice or as an imaginary character? Is the person you are interacting with a real person at all, or a software 'robot' ('bot') programmed to behave like a human being? Has the text which has just appeared on your screen been produced by the software or by a human participant?

For example, to make the text 'Ray laughs' requires the user controlling 'Ray' to type the command 'laughs'. In other words, as with the e-mail message, pieces of English text are being produced by a computer system in response to actions and commands, often themselves in English (note the metacommunication discussion of this in line 4, indicating that the user laughed in person in the real room before indicating this in the MUD interaction).

Some of the features of MUD interactions have been taken up elsewhere in Internet communication, in electronic mail and conferencing. It is quite common, for example, for writers to describe their reaction to another posting using the third person. Some participants even employ acronyms such as ROFL (rolls on floor laughing). This loosening of the tie between the identity of the writer and the authorial character projected by the text is thus reflected in the use of language. As Cherney's (1995) work (from which the example is taken) indicates, this complex relationship of real and virtual identities mediated by a computer requires the final text to engage in unusual uses of person and tense in order to be coherent at all.

Levinson (1988) makes a similar argument to Poster, commenting upon the manner in which, at all stages, digital technology speeds up the production of texts, be they written texts, video games or television programmes. Beyond this, the electronic text allows for the almost instant transmission of information, text and knowledge around the world (Levinson, 1988, pp. 135–6). Others too have become concerned over the definition of the literate text. Crane (1991) considers the implications of setting up a multimedia database, and highlights many of the issues raised above. Crane takes a deliberate step further by considering the role of the reader or consumer of electronic texts, and argues in conclusion that:

> The electronic environment subverts the technological foundation on
> which the author–reader relationship is erected. We can expect a vigor-
> ous but fruitful period in which authors, readers, and the ever-present
> third party, publishers, negotiate anew what is and is not a text.
> (Crane, 1991, p. 302).

There is indeed an increasing concern raised by publishers and authors over the
status of texts on the Internet and the intellectual property rights associated with
them. The existing, territorially based, legal frameworks which govern the
creation, circulation and consumption of texts are visibly failing to cope with the
new forms of communication which the Internet provides. Some governments
are claiming the right to control Internet access by its citizens; others are experiencing difficulties in establishing legal jurisdiction, in cases ranging from the
distribution of pornographic pictures to libel.

## 3.6   'IMAGINED COMMUNITIES'

Though such discussions can often seem a long way from the practical day-to-day
uses of the English language, there is one concrete area where these issues of
subjectivity, of the perception of texts, others and ourselves, have a direct connection to English – nationality. The question to be considered here is not what
nationality 'is' but rather the role of language play in maintaining nationality, and
vice-versa. We are also concerned with the effects that changes in communications media might have upon national communities. Goody and Watt (1963)
link the development of many aspects of western and European society with the
development of a specific form of western alphabetic literacy. At the centre of
their argument is the claim that democracy and individual rationality are the
products of literacy:

> To begin with, the case of alphabetic reading and writing was probably an
> important consideration in the development of political democracy in
> Greece: in the fifth century a majority of the free citizens could appar-
> ently read the laws and take an active part in elections and legislation.
> Democracy as we know it, then, is from the beginning associated with
> wide spread literacy …
> (Goody and Watt, 1963, p. 332)

They also claim that literacy aids the development of 'organic solidarity', a term
used by one of the first sociolinguists, Emile Durkheim, to describe modern
industrialized society (Durkheim, 1964). Though there are many problems with
Goody and Watts's argument, especially its clear Eurocentrism, there is an important underlying claim for all forms of literate practice, where the medium of
writing supports specific kinds of social relation. Following their model, as we
have noted already (Bolter, 1989, 1991; Anderson, 1991), writing in any form
provides fixity, that is, the content does not change over time, which allows both
the past history and separated geographic and cultural areas of a society to be
experienced by all who are literate. This kind of argument also reflects the central
role which the industrially developed nations, and especially Europe, have attributed to written language. The role of written, or rather printed, language in
industrially developed societies has become so central that some contemporary
social theorists and philosophers, for example Derrida (1976), claim that writing,
rather than speech, must be considered as being the 'primary' medium of

social communication. Reducing these developments simply to the effects of one communication technology, that of writing, is of course far too simple a model. There are many other historical, social and economic factors to be taken into account.

Indeed any theory of literacy itself, let alone the development of modern societies, needs to take into account the effects of literacy upon individuals' perception of the world and of themselves. Street (1984) has argued vehemently that we must take account of the 'ideological' role of literacy, and, along with others such as Heath (1983) and Levine (1986), has also asserted that literacy is not a single phenomenon, but consists of a set of 'literacies', each with a specific social role, position in the social structure and so on. The question that needs to be asked is: how can the technologies of writing and reading affect our perceptions of the world and of ourselves? There is strong evidence that the printed word has played, and still plays, a major part in the construction of national discourse communities and therefore in defining the concept of nation-hood and nationality.

## Mediating nationality

Today, when we think of English as a language we may not think of England, the country where it first developed. We may be from the USA or from Singapore and speak an English whose features are part of our nationality. There are also many speakers of English as a foreign language for whom the language does not play an important role in their sense of national identity. When we attempt to define nationality, we obviously cannot use language as a definition; one is not English because one speaks English. Defining nationality. is not easy; other definitions based upon geography, politics or culture similarly face problems. As Anderson notes:

> Nation, nationality, nationalism – all have proved notoriously difficult to define, let alone analyse. In contrast to the immense influence that nationalism has exerted on the modern world, plausible theory about it is conspicuously meagre.
> (Anderson, 1991, p. 3)

Anderson's solution is to re-examine the role of language, concentrating on media and what can best be described as the constraining or unifying forces at play. For Anderson (1991, pp. 9–36) three social factors had to lose their influence in order for modern European nations to be conceivable to their members. These were:

Chapter 4 in the first book in this series *English: history, diversity and change* (Graddol et al. (eds), 1996) discusses the rise of English as a national language in the 1500s.

- the tying of truth solely to one particular written language (e.g. Latin);
- the belief that monarchs or hierarchical leaders ruled through divine right;
- the belief that the development of human history was tied to the develop-ment of divine intention.

When such factors were still accepted, it was possible for European people to believe that they were part of religious communities spread across large geo-graphic areas. Anderson himself talks of the imagined community of Christendom. For Anderson, the technology which helped most in the change from belief in religious community to a national community was the printed text (Anderson, 1991, pp. 37–46). Through the use of the printed text, it became possible for knowledge and ideas to be communicated in vernacular languages such as French and English rather than the religious forms of Latin. Anderson notes that it was not the association of a particular language with a particular geographic area that formed the concept of nationality, but rather the interplay between the diversity within languages such as the Spanish or English of the 1500s or 1600s, new technologies and the development of capitalism (Anderson, 1991, p. 43). For Anderson, print vernaculars allowed European national consciousness to develop in the 1600s and onwards for three reasons. First:

> they created unified fields of exchange and communication below Latin and above the spoken vernaculars. Speakers of the huge variety of Frenches, Englishes or Spanishes, who might find it difficult or even impossible to understand each other in conversation, became capable of comprehending one another via print and paper. In the process, they gradually became aware of the hundreds of thousands, even millions, of people in their particular language-field, and at the same time that *only those* hundreds of thousands, or millions, so belonged.
>
> (Anderson, 1991, p. 44)

This is an example of the kind of unifying or constraining force described earlier, placing bounds upon the development of language. Indeed this is Anderson's second factor:

> print-capitalism gave a new fixity to language, which in the long run helped to build that image of antiquity so central to the subjective idea of nation ... to put it another way, for three centuries now these stabilised print languages have been gathering a darkening varnish; the words of our seventeenth-century forebears are accessible to us in a way that ... twelfth-century ancestors [are] not.
>
> (Anderson, 1991, pp. 44–5)

Anderson's third factor concerns the power structures that this fixity also ossified. The vernaculars which became fixed were those of the dominant classes: the King's English, a specific regional vernacular of English, became the 'language-of-power' (Anderson, 1991, p. 45). What is important to note about Anderson's work is that he does not see this process as creating nationalities around specific languages, but rather as allowing groups, especially those in power, to conceive of nationality, of the nation state, of its history, and of its 'natural' existence. Nationality is to imagine oneself as part of a community and one can only imagine this if the language and the media of power, and, in Anderson's argument, print, provide a fixed linguistic and ideological basis.

## Doing nationality on-line

We have noted that at the end of the twentieth century new communication technologies such as the Internet are not equally available to members of different nations around the world. There has also been much argument as to how the technology of the Internet may be limiting its interactions to the English language. But even if Internet communication does encourage the use of English, the technology does not seem to limit people's ability to express nationality, even when communicating mostly in English.

## Chatting about nationality

**IRC** (**Internet Relay Chat**) is a highly interactive medium consisting of one-line utterances preceded by an identifier indicating the user who typed the utterances, rather similar to the format of MUDs. Participants can be situated anywhere on the Internet. Research by Hock (1995) into IRC found that in chat lines devoted to countries where English was the national language (for example, UK, USA, Australia) or where it had a key role as a second major language in one form or another (for example, India, Singapore, Philippines) then English was the major language used by participants. Hock also found forms of codeswitching taking place between English and the language or languages of the nation to which the chat line was devoted.

One of the important findings in Hock's work is the concentration of messages from countries where English is the national language. Even when looking at electronic conversations devoted to the discussion of specific nations where English is an important second language, the majority of the postings came from elsewhere around the world, such as the USA. Thus, although IRC enables people to discuss shared national and linguistic interests, the majority of participants are expatriates from the country concerned.

Hock looked at chat lines devoted to India, the Philippines and Singapore. Only Singapore had messages posted from within the country and then they only counted for 22.5 per cent of postings (Hock, 1995, p. 40). The majority of the postings came from the USA in all three cases. Such a finding clearly reflects the unequal global distribution of access to the technology.

Hock explored how users indicated their national identity through IRC and noted several practices that either directly or indirectly indicate users' national origins. Some of these practices may seem 'stereotypical' but the examples are drawn from actual data. One area where those using the English language mark their identity is in various informal greetings. Hock gives the following examples taken from different interactions:

&lt;Icpic&gt; – g'day all [Australian]

&lt;Barnsley&gt; – cheers all! [British]

&lt;MelGibson&gt; – hiya kara!!! [American (US)]

(Hock, 1995, pp. 30–34)

For those IRC lines where the interactants used English but were from nations where English was an important second language (what Hock describes, following Kachru (1991), as 'outer circle' countries), other nationality markers also come through. In the case of the IRC line devoted to India (though none of the postings by Indian nationals were made in India itself) Hock notes that identity is expressed through codeswitching as indicated in the following examples taken from Hock (1995, p.41):

&lt;rini&gt; stop ignoring me

&lt;limka&gt; rini: <sup>Hindi</sup> **ghar jake so jaaaa**!!!!
            *go home and sleep*

&lt;rini&gt; limka: I am bengali.<sup>Hindi</sup> **mai hindi nahin bolti hoo**
              *I do not speak Hindi*

The text in bold type indicates utterances in Hindi; the italics indicate Hock's translation of these.

In this example not only national but regional identities are being expressed both directly and indirectly. There are two interesting points to note: in the first place, as Hock also indicates (Hock, 1995, p. 41), the user <rini> uses Hindi to empha-size their Bengali identity! The second issue is the re-use of identifiers to ensure that the utterance is directed towards a specific recipient.

Another example provided by Hock concerns the use of nonstandard English language practices. In examining the English used on the IRC line devoted to Singaporean issues, Hock noted that Singaporean users indirectly indicated their identity through the use of informal Singaporean English practices. Hock noted the use of sentence end particles (marked in bold) considered characteristic of Singaporean English (see Hock, 1995, p. 44, for example):

gimme his acct **lorr**

u dating larry **ah**

huh din see her **leh**

work got money **wat**

Thus, though the technology of the Internet may favour the use of the English language, its users, through various textual practices, are able to express their national identities.


## 3.7   CONCLUSION

At the end of the twentieth century, print is no longer so clearly the main medium of power, and its role in defining communication and power is changing. In this chapter we have examined a key change in the properties of media, namely its lack of fixity. Some of the new types of text, electronic texts, that exploit this lack of fixity have been explored and the new types of English language use which are taking place are examined.

This lack of fixity combined with global reach, which many new media possess, may also have direct effects upon the English language. If Anderson is correct to argue that the fixing of language, in a medium such as print, provides the basis for that language's longevity, how can the English language survive the pressures of both its universal and particular global roles? Unlike printing, which, according to Anderson, allowed specific social groups to put in place conceptions of nationhood, these media could play the role of removing the 'imagined community' of nationalism, in favour of other communities based either upon global economic ideologies or patterns of personal interest and opinion. It remains to be seen if new communications media can provide the basis for 'imagined communities' on a global scale.

## Reading A

## 'I FELL INTO THE SAFETY NET'

*Stephen Fry*

... Mad as it sounds, it had never occurred to me that there would be much fuss caused by my flight, outside the world of the play I had abandoned, that is, and my own circle of family and friends. I pictured a line or two in an Arts Diary page and a few (rightly) cross actors saying some terse things about professionalism and the need for shows to go on.

What I was not prepared for was the sight that met my eyes in the station books stall in Hanover four days into my journey: ranks of English newspapers bearing photographs under which ran phrases like 'fears were growing last night ... ' 'sources close to the missing actor said ...'.

A fraught three hours later I had managed to track down a vital piece of cabling that enabled the modem in my Powerbook to connect to the German telephone system ...

Now, you may be asking why the knowledge that Britain had gone all of a doo-dah about my disappearance should have led me to reach for a modem. What's wrong with the good old-fashioned telephone? Well, there's something even more old-fashioned than a telephone and that is a letter.

It may be, if we are lucky, that we shall look back on the last 80 years or so as constituting a blip in human communications, during which mankind lost the art of letter-writing and fell in love with the phone. Consider (especially, I would contend, if you are British) how dreadful the telephone is as a means of communication.

It operates in real time ('live' in other words) and carries the human voice. Which is to say all the embarrassments of accent, gender, articulacy, shyness, class and age are brought into play whenever you speak through it. I was not in a state where I could trust my voice to carry my meaning without it cracking or failing or succumbing to pressure. I felt an urgent need to get across a message which neither revealed my whereabouts nor forced me to speak in real time.

Letters take an age to arrive, but e-mail is more or less instantaneous; moreover on the Internet it is also possible to *fax* the unconnected, such faxes being free of tell-tale phone numbers running along the top of each sheet.

Once armed with the paraphernalia of German telephone socketry, I moved to Hamburg (someone had seen me at the station in Hanover and I wasn't brave enough to risk being found by the press) and went on-line to tell my agent that I was more or less all right and hoped I might be left alone to wrestle with my demons before coming to some conclusion about what I was up to and what I should do. It was then I checked my digital doormat and saw the vast heap of e-mail awaiting me.

There was mail from friends and from family that communicated more than a telephone conversation ever could have done. There were letters by the hundreds from complete strangers; letters that joked, coaxed, chivvied, wheedled, hugged, clucked, reproved, wondered, wailed, applauded, doubted, damned, supported and forgave. Alone and fretful in a hotel room overlooking the Alster I could read them slowly, without the need for an instant response. A few hours later I swallowed my pride and a bockwurst, pointed the car towards Holland and drove home to family, friends and help.

If the majority of 'netizens' are really still nerds, geeks, dweebs, anoraks, phreaks and hackers, as we like to think, the 'Net' is living proof of the superiority of the written word. Put the average geek on the telephone and he or she will not be up to much. Put them behind a keyboard, however, and the act of literary composition forces a wit, an integrity, an insight, an emotional and moral honesty that would amaze even an optimist ...

Source: Fry, 1995

# Reading B
# ALL THE NEWS THAT FITS ON SCREEN

*Jon Snow*

The Internet is a male world, a lone male world. It is self-seeking, self-serving and self-fulfilling. Surfing shuts out all other physical and environmental contact and takes the user deeper into a world of 'me', 'my choice' and 'fuck you'. Not for nothing is the Net peppered with porn; not for nothing do the statistics show that most surfers are men and that the Internet holds less attraction for women.

Early in my first voyage through the Internet, the instructor told me about the Daily Me, the brave new organ that will enable the surfer to construct a newspaper or television news designed solely for him. He will be able to establish precisely what he is interested in and exclude the things that bore him ...

The Internet is nevertheless a beguiling world, its potential not in replacing conventional news sources but in improving them. Some surfers will naturally abandon conventional information-providers to play the Internet ...

The real questions about the Internet are – how many people will allow it to become a permanent part of their life, and how many professionals will use it to supply the information for their work. Knowing how little the existing products, Nexus, Lexus and the rest, are used by journalists, I wonder at the fuss surfers make of the news potential. Currently the Internet is slow. Retrieving information, or adding to it, is relatively laborious. The thrill is in tumbling into the front page of the Buenos Aires Herald or the St Petersburg Press. But when did our interest in Argentina or Leningrad demand such pampering? How often will we want to do it?

The Internet's fans preach that it will expand the sum total of human understanding. I suspect it will do the opposite. The more time the surfer spends on the Internet, the less time he spends relating to other people in anything other than a fantasy capacity. Many argued that ham radio would produce the great global communications revolution. Yet hams represent the same kind of orderly minority as Freemasons. There are plenty of them, but not enough to dominate the information we receive.

And the same unreal, unlived relationships that radio hams establish with callers in New Zealand exist for the surfer. The posted message, photograph, the snatched conversation and even the pop jam session, are all conducted through a machine that boasts virtual reality but offers few clues as to how to improve on reality itself. Who are the Internet's most fervent bedfellows? The United States Government, and a cluster of multi-nationals and big businesses. Their message-posting on the Internet is fast outstripping all others. They don't miss a trick. Even the surfers' paradise can be turned to good works.

The implications for news and current affairs are far from being all good. The Internet takes us further down the disastrous road of ratings related news. Already the appalling practice of observing electronically which television news items viewers channel-hop away from shapes news choice. 'No more Bosnia, please God' goes the programme editor's cry – 'the viewer simply doesn't want to know'. Here is a medium that enables the viewer/surfer to exclude Bosnia from his information menu for all time. As the surfer's temporal troubles build up around him, his intellectual being is hoisted on to the Internet – too busy surfing into the ever-evolving games, fantasy play, disc talk, shopping-crazed world.

The origins of news are the eye-witness accounts shared with a public that was never able to travel to the event. William Russell of the Times in the Crimea looked at what he saw and then wrote about it for those back home to read. One man's eyes changed the perceptions of a nation. Potentially the Internet offers many pairs of eyes and an interactive opportunity for those back home to input their offerings besides. People in Sarajevo post notices on the Internet, but they appear to be opinions about the conflict rather than eye-witness accounts. And while the obsessed surfer and the journalist may trawl for them, it is hard to imagine that Joe Public will be patient or interested enough to do the same.

The Internet offers an adjunct, not a replacement for television news. History offers little evidence that Everyman has either the desire or the capacity to replace the journalist. But the Internet does threaten unsuspecting TV moguls with competition or alternatives. If they trivialise and debase their products, the individual will search for other options that the Internet may provide …

The Internet is new, packed with potential, prey to pollution, and more vulnerable for being the creature of unreality than for being the creator of virtual reality.

Television's power is the capacity to produce depth and quality. The temptation is to disregard both in the interests of profit. So long as television news invests in reality, eye-witness, and avoids second-hand information dubbed on to fifth-hand pictures taken from the networks of the global village, it need not fear the Internet.

Source: Snow, 1995

## Reading C
# COMMUNICATION AND NEW SUBJECTS

*Mark Poster*

Electronic message services and computer conferencing substitute (computer-ized) writing for spoken conversations. In this sense they extend the domain of writing to cover areas of communication that previously were limited to face-to-face interactions, mail and the telephone. These forms of computer writing appear to have definite effects on the subject:

1   they introduce new possibilities for playing with identities;

2   they degender communications by removing gender cues;

3   they destabilize existing hierarchies in relationships and re-hierarchize com-munications according to criteria that were previously irrelevant; and above all

4   they disperse the subject, dislocating it temporally and spatially

...

## [Electronic message services]

Message services are commonly found on computerized bulletin boards. Major cities in the United States each have hundreds of them. Bulletin boards are set up by individuals on their phone lines, sometimes in association with a computer club or other special interest group. They are usually free to the caller and offer public domain software files, games and a message service. Messages most often concern questions about computers or about the software available on the bulletin board. Some friendships get started by the exchange of messages and some messages are sent between people who have prior, non-electronic knowl-edge of each other. One bulletin board in Orange County, California, 'the French Connection,' is intended to stimulate and simulate a singles bar or dating service. One may participate in private communications with a 'lover,' 'locker room' chats with other men and 'powder room' chats with women, or a 'public' area where one 'meets' other participants...

An individual may leave a message for any other user whether or not that user is known. What is so new about message services is that the only identity an individual user has in many of them is a name or 'handle', which may be, and most often is expected to be, fictional. The telephone may also be used to contact any number, anyone connected to the network. But conversations with individuals selected by this method are unusual, normally considered intrusive, in bad taste, and practised mostly as pranks by teenagers. By contrast, participants in message services are normally eager to 'talk'. In addition, phone conversations preserve the signature of the individual in voice and tone so that conversers feel that their 'true' identities are being revealed along with their mood. In message services no such traces of identity are preserved. Anonymity is complete. Identity is fictional in the structure of the communication.

Conversationalists on message services assume that their partners are not 'real' people, even if they are using their actual names, normally considered inappropriate, or if they are expressing themselves as they would in face-to-face conversations. The subject is thus in question in a historically new sense. In the small communities of tribal society, individuals are 'known' from birth, enmeshed in extensive kinship structures that reproduce identity in daily experience. In this context the subject is social, constructed and reproduced as a relational self. In cities, by contrast, the individual is extracted from such identity reproduction, but here conversations … required face-to-face positioning and therefore bodily 'signatures' which specified the individual so that, if necessary, actual identities could later be recalled. With writing and print, identity is further removed from communication, but authorship even under assumed names, serves to fix identity, With computer message services, language use is radically separated from bio-graphical identity. Identity is dispersed in the electronic network of communi-cations and computer storage systems.

For the first time individuals engage in telecommunications with other individuals, often on an enduring basis, without considerations that derive from the presence to the partner of their body, their voice, their sex, many of the markings of their personal history. Conversationalists are in the position of fiction writers who compose themselves as characters in the process of writing, inventing themselves from their feelings, their needs, their ideas, their desires, their social position, their political views, their economic circumstances, their family situ-ation – their entire humanity …

While the anonymity of the computer message may be experienced by the computer conversationalist as a liberation from social constraint, I am not arguing that such is at all the case. The computer conversationalist is not 'free' at all but bounded in many ways: first, to the new, computerized system of positioning subjects in symbolic exchanges; second, by the prior constituting of the self, typically the experience of that self as restricting, evoking the sense of trans-gression when that self may be concealed or suspended; finally, to the language used in the conversation, with all its semantic, ideological and cultural specificity which does not diminish when converted into ASCII codes. I suspect that com-puter messages may strengthen certain aspects of the subject that were consti-tuted in daily life in a denegated form. I am not claiming that in fact electronic messages enable some 'total' or 'true' act of self-constitution, but instead that a reconfiguration of the self-constitution process, one with a new set of constraints and possibilities, is in the making.

## Electronic communities

In their important book on computer conferencing, Hiltz and Turoff cheerfully propose that

> We will become the Network Nation, exchanging vast amounts of both information and social-emotional communications with colleagues, friends, and 'strangers' who share similar interests … we will become a global village …An individual will, literally, be able to work, shop, or be educated by or with persons anywhere in the nation or in the world.

[Hiltz and Turoff, 1978, p.xxiv]

It is doubtful that computer conferencing will alter the world in all the ways and to the extent alleged by its proponents ... A computer conference is like electronic mail, except that any number of participants (though usually no more than about 50) may be included in the 'discussion'. Messages are transmitted to a central computer which sorts and stores them, instantaneously making them available for other participants. The order of retrieval is entirely up to the reader, thereby diminishing significantly the role of authorship. To the contrary, the entire conference becomes a single text without an author in the traditional sense of the term.

The process of the discussion is alien and disorienting to those accustomed to synchronous meetings. In ordinary conferences, so much depends not on what is said but on who says it, how they make their intervention, what clothes they wear, their body language, facial and oral expressions. All of this is absent in computer conferencing, as a result of which the subject is placed in a substantially new situation. New conversationalist protocols to guide the dispersed participants in computer conferences remain to be invented, though some conventions and terms have begun to take shape. 'Lurkers', for example, are those who read conference messages but do not contribute to the discussion. And 'whispering' means private asides, messages restricted to one or a few of the participants. New 'social pathologies' have also emerged. In place of the little fears people experience in face-to-face speech, computer conferencers suffer the anxiety that their messages will elicit no response and in fact participants are in a significant number of cases quite casual about reacting to the communications of others.

Without the normal cues and routines of face-to-face speech to guide the conference, simple procedural issues may raise fundamental difficulties. Problems arise over matters like taking turns and keeping the discussion going. Certain types of statements, those of expository style and logical rigor, tend to stifle discussion, while open-ended statements invite responses and further the work of the conference. Even more importantly, participants continuously must be as explicit as possible about what they are saying, and frequently clarify their statements by the use of metastatements. A good portion of the discussion must be devoted to messages about messages, supplementary information to supply what is ordinarily embedded in the context of speech. Unlike synchronous speech acts, computer conferencing messages reflect on their own linguistic practice to an unprecedented degree. Because the conventions of speech are so drastically upset, computer conferencing easily becomes talk about talk.

In addition to authorlessness and self-reflexivity, computer conferences upset the power relations, both economic and gendered, that govern synchronous speech. Factors such as institutional status, personal charisma, rhetorical skills, gender, and race – all of which may deeply influence the way an utterance is received – have little effect in computer conferences. Equality of participation is thereby encouraged. New, serendipitous considerations, like typing speed, determine who 'speaks' most often. In problem-solving situations at synchronous conferences, pressures are great to conform to existing paradigms or to an emerging consensus. By contrast, computer conferences, with the veil of anonymity and the temporal/spatial distance they provide, encourage open criticism and the presentation of unpopular or eccentric points of view.

Computer conferences also promote the decentralization of power by the simple fact that meetings no longer require expensive and cumbersome spatial synchronization. Advanced telephone technologies, such as communications satellites, permit world-wide participation in conference. Conference scheduling becomes infinitely more flexible and inclusive. The ideal of participatory democracy of the Greek *agora* and the Colonial New England town meeting becomes technically feasible in advanced industrial society. Hiltz and Turoff foresee the best: 'The fundamental effect of computerized conferencing, we believe, will be to produce new kinds of and more numerous social networks than ever before possible. Along with this will come massive shifts in the nature of the values and institutions that characterize the society'. In their futurist vision, Hiltz and Turoff are not always attentive to the political process of such institutional change. They assume that the democratic tendencies of this computer technology will be realized by open, free access and wide distribution of skills. Computer conferencing, with its obvious advantages of economy – move words, not people – may become widespread. If so it will introduce a communication form in everyday life that upsets the positioning of subjects in their acts of enunciation …

The decentering effects of computer writing on the subject are not, of course, entirely unanticipated. The industrial revolution inaugurated transport systems – railroad, automobile, airplane, spaceship – that progressively increase the speed with which bodies move in space. By doing so these technologies may be said to disperse the self in the world. The practice of masked balls, personal ads and clothing styles provide opportunities for playing with identities. But computer writing, as it is being inscribed in our culture, intensifies and radicalizes these earlier forms. To what degree this is achieved will depend upon the extent to which computer writing is disseminated in the future. Only empirical studies of the phenomena can determine their true social and cultural impact. Yet computer writing is the quintessential postmodern linguistic activity. With its dispersal of the subject in nonlinear spatio-temporality, its immateriality, its disruption of stable identity, computer writing institutes a factory of postmodern subjectivity, a machine for constituting non-identical subjects, an inscription of an other of Western culture into its most cherished manifestation. One might call it a monstrosity.

## References

HILTZ, S.R. and TUROFF, M. (1978) *Network Nation: human communication and the computer*, London, Addison-Wesley.

Source: Poster, 1990, pp. 117–27

# 4 MARKET FORCES SPEAK ENGLISH

*Sharon Goodman*

## 4.1 INTRODUCTION

This chapter examines the concept of 'border crossing' as it relates to forms and uses of English. **Border crossing** is the term used by several linguists and sociologists (for example the British discourse analyst Norman Fairclough) to describe what they identify as a phenomenon of postindustrialized societies: that a complex range of new social relationships is developing, and that behaviour (including linguistic behaviour) is changing as a result (Fairclough, 1996). Forms of English associated with one situation are crossing the borders into new ones: informal English, for example, is said to be crossing into professional relationships, and 'advertising English' migrating into public information campaigns.

Working practices worldwide are changing to suit the needs of a 'global economy', and changes in the various relationships that English speakers have with other speakers are said to be bringing about these new uses of the English language. A decline in manufacturing and heavy industry in many countries has engendered the rise of the service sector, so the language forms used at work are different, as are people's relationships inside and outside the workplace. Fairclough, for example, believes that traditional, hierarchical social structures are becoming far more fluid and precarious than they once were. Relationships based automatically on authority, as well as personal relationships based on family duties and obligations, are in decline: 'people's self-identity, rather than being a feature of given positions and roles, is reflexively built up through a process of negotiation' (Fairclough, 1993, p. 140).

Analysts working in this area locate English language border crossings, then, in the context of wider social, political and economic changes. These changes have consequences for the forms of English that speakers use, and the range of contexts in which they use them. This chapter looks at the phenomenon of border crossing in English. In order to judge the extent to which English forms are migrating into new contexts, the chapter considers aspects of verbal (and visual) language in some detail, focusing particularly on informalization and marketization.

- **Informalization**. Is the English language becoming increasingly informal? The argument put forward by some linguists (such as Fairclough) is that the boundaries between language forms traditionally reserved for intimate relationships and those reserved for more formal situations are becoming blurred. Professional encounters, for example, are increasingly likely to contain informal forms of English: they are becoming, in his term, 'conversationalized' (Fairclough, 1994). Institutions, too, such as the state, commerce and the media, are increasingly using less formal, more conversational styles. In many contexts, then, the public and professional sphere is said to be becoming infused with 'private' discourse.

    This issue can be considered from two points of view. On the one hand, it could be argued that using more conversational, 'everyday' English in a widening range of contexts is a good thing, because it allows people to understand and participate in interactions more easily – for example when talking to a solicitor, or listening to a political interview on the radio. The counter-argument would be that using 'the language of the people' allows those in positions of power, such as government officials or politicians, to imply the existence of a friendly relationship between themselves and 'the public' where no such relationship actually exists. It could therefore be seen as manipulative.

- **Marketization**. A related issue is that 'advertising language' is seen to be crossing over into the domain of 'information'. Government documents and information leaflets, for example, may use styles of verbal English and visual presentation more commonly found in commercial advertising. English texts are therefore becoming increasingly 'market-oriented', or marketized, subject to political expediency and/or commercial pressures. The chapter considers examples of 'real' advertising and selling techniques, and then goes on to look at some institutional texts, drawn mainly from Singapore and Britain, that use similar devices. How do these texts use English to 'sell', and what are they selling? How do they attempt to position their readers in certain ways, and what strategies do people develop in order to resist this positioning?

If the processes of informalization and marketization are indeed becoming increasingly widespread, then this implies that there is a requirement for English speakers generally not only to deal with, and respond to, this increasingly marketized and informal English, but also to become *involved* in the process. For example, people may feel that they need to use English in new ways to 'sell themselves' in order to gain employment. Or they may need to learn new linguistic strategies to keep the jobs they already have – to talk to 'the public', for instance. In other words, they have to become *producers of promotional texts*. This can have consequences for the ways in which people see themselves. What happens to a person's 'sense of self' in an environment in which certain forms of English have to be used, and other forms are discouraged or banned altogether?

In this chapter I first consider some of the forms that informal and marketized English can take. I then look at how such linguistic forms can be used – and resisted – in a world that is becoming increasingly complex and where a multitude of new types of social relationship is developing. The focal point throughout is border crossing between forms of English that traditionally have been seen as distinct – although in practice they probably weren't – between formal and informal; public and private; informative and promotional.

## 4.2   INFORMALIZATION

To examine the claim that English is becoming increasingly informalized, it is necessary to look at some of the markers of informal English, and at how these might be crossing into situations more traditionally associated with formal English forms.

### Some markers of informal English

One marker of informal English can be the term of address used. Different countries and cultures around the world that use English have different conventions for addressing people in a variety of situations. Susan Ervin-Tripp suggested in 1969 that speakers of a language share a set of 'rules of address' – which may not be consciously known or rigidly adhered to, but which may be inferred as appropriate in specific situations (see Ervin-Tripp, 1969). In Britain, for example, in a formal encounter you might have used someone's title and surname, instead of their first name, as well as perhaps avoiding more colloquial words. When talking to close friends or family members, you would probably be more intimate

Informal conversation, and terms of address, are discussed in Chapter 1 of the second book in this series, *Using English: from conversation to canon* (Maybin and Mercer (eds), 1996).

and informal. It is these sorts of division that some believe are changing and breaking down. It may no longer take months or even years of familiarity for speakers to address each other by their first name – people seem likely to use each other's first name at a first meeting, and rarely ask permission to do so. Do you think this matters? How would you (or do you) feel about being on first-name terms with your doctor, parliamentary representative, tax collector or clients?

We can view this issue from two sides. On the one hand, relationships built and conducted on an informal basis can be beneficial to both parties. Seeing yourself as a 'friend' – with the rights that the status of 'friend' affords you – can be an empowering experience. On the other hand, the speedy establishment of this kind of informal relationship can have disadvantages. In cases where a degree of distance is subsequently required (for example if you need to make a complaint) it may be much harder to make the required shift – to put things back on a professional footing.

Another aspect of address is the use of pronouns. Pronouns have particular implications for social relationships. Many languages employ different pronouns for intimate and for formal interactions (see Brown and Gilman, 1972, pp. 252–82). In French, for example, you might use *tu* to address friends and relatives, *vous* to address your elders and 'superiors', and those you wish to keep at a distance. Speakers of these languages are acutely aware of the significance of using one pronoun rather than another, and will often ask permission (when unsure) before using the more familiar form. In languages that have this pronominal distinction, there seems to be an increasing tendency to use the more informal pronoun in a wider range of contexts.

Standard English no longer has this specific resource, although it used to have familiar and polite forms. The familiar form *thou* still survives in several British regional dialects, and in certain liturgical texts. Informality in Standard English, however, can be established and negotiated in other ways. Names themselves can be shortened (*Richard* becomes *Rich* or *Ric*), or replaced by nicknames. Diminutive suffixes (such as *-ie* or *-y*) can be used (*James* becomes *Jamie*, *Deborah* becomes *Debby*, and so on). As these are associated with childhood names, they convey an impression of intimacy and familiarity. Salespeople have realized this and often attempt to turn it to their advantage: many now use the shorter version of their name when introducing themselves to customers.

Here are some other informal markers in English:

- Contractions of negatives (*wouldn't*) or auxiliary verbs (*he'll*): associated with less formal, often spoken English, these are increasingly likely to occur in writing.

- An increased use of more informal vocabulary, such as colloquialisms and slang forms: *this guy comes up to me and he says…* These seem to be increasingly common in professional encounters.

- The use of active rather than passive verbs: the active voice is more common in spoken (usually more informal) English than written. *We carried out an experiment* is more informal than *An experiment was carried out.*

- Intonation, too, can be used to signify informality – think about how you answer the telephone in different situations. Do you use different 'voices' to talk to friends, and to colleagues or officials?

**Activity 4.1**   *(Allow about 10 minutes)*

Think of some of the people you have spoken to in the last day or two. How did you address them, and how did they address you? To whom did you use, or avoid using, colloquial language or slang? Why? Can you identify any changes in your use of different styles of English, by thinking back to ten, or perhaps twenty, years ago?

❖ ❖ ❖ ❖ ❖

There may be many different reasons for adopting an informal or conversational style of English. Between intimates, or 'equals', informal English can serve to build and maintain social bonds. It can also be used deliberately to make writing or speech more accessible to an audience. The writers of Open University course materials, for example, try to write as accessibly as possible, avoiding more formal, 'academic' English. In this chapter I sometimes use the contractions *doesn't* and *weren't* rather than *does not* and *were not*, and the second-person pronoun *you* to address the reader. Here is an extract from the introduction to an Open University study guide:

> If you go into any large bookshop you'll see bits of the English language dotted around the 'language' shelves: grammars, dictionaries, perhaps phrase books and courses for foreign learners. Maybe you learned English yourself initially from these sorts of books.
>
> (Open University, 1996, p. 3)

There are many informal markers in this text, as the author wants to welcome students to the course and put them at their ease; this is particularly important for Open University students, as they are learning at a distance.

Formality, on the other hand, can be used as a resource to create and maintain professional relationships, or to keep people at a distance. What happens, though, when institutions, or those in authority, use informal language to speak to those who are not on an equal basis with them? Some aspects of this are not new: the use of first names by managers when addressing their 'subordinates', for example. But there are other informal English forms that seem to be increasingly common in a widening range of contexts.

## Informal English in the public and professional domain

Official or institutional English is generally associated with a formal, impersonal style. An impersonal style is significant as it establishes a 'top-down' relationship of power, in which the 'official' is addressed as, and perceived as, being in control of the exchange. Thus an impersonal, formal style of English can be instrumental in creating and maintaining hierarchical relationships (see Fowler, 1991, p. 128).

Government officials, lawyers and public broadcasters are just a few of those who traditionally have been associated with this style of English. In recent years there have been attempts to simplify the language of institutions with a view to making it more straightforward and comprehensible to 'the public'. Ernest Gowers's attack on what he saw as the incomprehensible 'bureaucratese' or 'officialese' he encountered while working in the British Civil Service, resulted in the publication of his book *Plain Words* in 1948. There have since been many revised editions, and the book is still widely consulted by officials, journalists and others who wish to write as clearly and as concisely as possible. 'Plain English' does not necessarily entail informality, but there are links, which will be explored below. The sort of 'officialese' Gowers sought to erase from government and commercial language is shown below; this example is taken from the revised edition of *The Complete Plain Words*, published in 1973:

> I regret however that the Survey Officer who is responsible for the preliminary investigation as to the technical possibility of installing a telephone at the address quoted by any applicant has reported that owing to a shortage of a spare pair of wires to the underground cable (a

**Plain English** is a term associated with a movement towards making formal documents more comprehensible through the use of plain language. It is discussed in Chapter 2 of the second book in this series, *Using English: from conversation to canon* (Maybin and Mercer (eds), 1996).

pair of wires leading from the point near your house right back to the local exchange and thus a pair of wires essential for the provision of telephone service for you) is lacking and that therefore it is a technical impossibility to install a telephone for you at …

Gowers's advice to this writer is:

> Do not say more than is necessary … This explanation is obscure partly because the sentence is too long, partly because the long parenthesis has thrown the grammar out of gear, and partly because the writer, with the best intentions, says far more than is necessary even for a thoroughly polite and convincing explanation. It might run thus:
>
> > I am sorry to have to tell you that we have found that there is no spare pair of wires on the cable that would have to be used to connect your house with the exchange. I fear therefore that it is impossible to install a telephone for you.
>
> (Gowers, 1973, p. 32)

This sort of clarity is obviously an advantage to the recipient of such letters. However, 'plain English' has not been uncontroversial.

### Activity 4.2   *(Reading A)*

Notions of 'good' and 'bad' English are discussed in Chapter 9 of the first book in this series, *English: history, diversity and change* (Graddol et al. (eds), 1996).

Read Deborah Cameron's discussion in Reading A of the tension between the two sides of the 'plain English' debate. This is an extract from Cameron's book *Verbal Hygiene*, a term she uses to describe the ways in which speakers try to keep a language 'clean' and free from corruption. She notes that the debate over style has been going on for centuries, and that modern technology is also being harnessed in the quest for good English prose, with the wide availability of computer programs that check style and grammar. She questions the assumptions underlying these software programs, pointing out that there are often moral and 'class' issues behind movements for changes in English style.

The 'plain English' debate has been influential in making the English of official documents and newspapers more comprehensible to the public and nonspecialist audience. A parallel tendency is the increasing use of informal forms of English in the public domain, whether in letters from government departments, in telephone calls between professionals or in political speeches. Official or 'public' English is increasingly using the linguistic resources of informal or 'private' discourse. Look back through the list of informal markers in the previous section – how many of these would really seem out of place now in a professional encounter, or a public speech? Some of these informal markers seem relatively insignificant. (Does it really matter, for example, if a politician says *he'll* rather than *he will*?) However, the increasing occurrence of informal English *itself* in these situations can mean that an overall impression of informality can be built up over time, and can leave you with the feeling that you have just been listening to a friend.

It is not necessary for an entire exchange, or speech, to be presented in an informal style for this impression to be conveyed. Textual cues can function to **foreground** the impression of informality: a small segment of informal English in an otherwise formal document or speech can be sufficient to convey an overall impression of informality.

Deborah Tannen (1992, p. 32) observes that conversation (ordinary talk) can 'create interpersonal involvement and meaning'. Because informal language forms are traditionally reserved for, and associated with, more intimate relationships, they can be seen as implying a social solidarity with listeners, a claim to share their point of view and concerns. If, as Fairclough suggests, traditional hierarchical relationships are in decline (that is, people no longer automatically respect others simply because they hold a government post, or other official position) then the use of a conversational style could be seen as significant. A general distrust of those in authority could mean that people are more likely to pay attention to the opinions of friends and close acquaintances than to what particular authority figures are saying. Consequently, those in authority might use more informal English in an attempt to regain the public's trust.

The use of an informal style is not necessarily a practice to be regarded with suspicion. New journalists at the BBC, for example, are encouraged to write their stories in an informal and friendly way: 'Write a story as you would tell it to a friend – but without the ums and ers' (said by a trainer to a group of journalist trainees at the BBC, in the author's hearing). The aim throughout their training is to develop 'good, spoken English' – language that is clear, informative and accessible. Norman Fairclough analysed the script of a BBC radio interview in some detail (Fairclough, 1995, pp. 142–9). He looked at a section of the *Today* programme, which is broadcast in Britain every morning during the week on BBC Radio 4, focusing on the language of the presenters during a political interview. He noted many instances of colloquial English, as well as inclusive pronouns such as *we* and *our* (which imply that the presenter shares the same world and culture as the listeners) and a general informality of style. The presenters used discourse markers associated with conversation, such as *oh, well* and *right*, and shortened words such as *because* to *coz*. Fairclough sees the BBC presenters as aiming to create a sense of linguistic (and, by extension, social) solidarity with the listening public. By using informal language in a radio interview – as well as by explicitly claiming to put forward the views and concerns of the listeners – the interviewer is creating a sense of 'community'. It may also be significant that the activity the presenter is using the language *for* – giving politicians a hard time – means that audience approval is even more likely.

Fairclough's analysis demonstrates the *tension* between the standpoints reflected in both formal and informal discourse. As he puts it elsewhere:

> [this illustrates] an important contemporary tendency: for the informal, conversational language associated with face-to-face interaction and group interaction in more private spheres of life to shift into public and institutional spheres ... There is a deep ambivalence about the contemporary 'conversationalisation' of language, as we might call it, in its implications for power: on the one hand, it goes along with a genuine opening up and democratisation of professional domains, a shift in power towards the client and the consumer. But on the other hand, conversational style provides a strategy for exercising power in more subtle and implicit ways, and many professionals are now trained in such strategies.
>
> (Fairclough (ed.), 1992, pp. 4–5)

A related issue concerns the reception of the discourse. Who is the real addressee in such broadcasts? A radio interview, of course, means that the politician is not the real addressee, even though he or she is being directly addressed by the presenter. There are many other people listening. There may be other interviewees present in the recording studio awaiting their turn. Often, in both radio and television broadcasts, a studio audience is present. Then there is the listening audience at home. This is a wide, fragmented audience, which can be local and international simultaneously. Who, then, is speaking to whom? Is the interviewer addressing the politician? Are 'we' (the public) addressing them? And is there any way of knowing who is listening?

**Activity 4.3**   *(Allow about 20 minutes)*

Try to listen to a radio or television interview. How do the interviewer and interviewee address each other? Are any abbreviated names, or nicknames, used? What markers of formal and informal English are there? Are there any colloquial words, or slang? What signs are there in the language that this is a conversation designed to be overheard (by the audience)?

The following section looks at another example of border crossing. To what extent is the language of advertising being used in spheres associated with information or politics?

## 4.3   THE MARKETIZATION OF ENGLISH

Many of the forms of informal English discussed in section 4.2 are widely used in the discourse of sales. This is because the seller hopes that being friendly to the customer will mean a greater chance of a sale. In 'sales English' there are also linguistic devices designed to persuade customers to buy the product – to convince them that a particular need will be fulfilled by purchasing it. These can range from the use of slogans in advertisements, which may be alliterative or 'catchy' and thereby stick in the customer's mind, to ways of speaking to customers face to face to convince them to buy.

Sales personnel are often trained by their employers to speak effectively to their customers. It is worth looking at a few aspects of this, before turning to look at how these same strategies can be used by institutions not explicitly aiming to sell, such as public-information campaigns or government documents.

### The English of sales

Sales interactions often take place on the basis of scripts, which employees are expected to follow as closely as possible when they speak to customers. Below is an example of one of these sales scripts, which covers the initial telephone call from a financial services sales consultant to a prospective client (the 'prospect'). The script is given to employees by a firm of insurance and pensions consultants operating in English, worldwide.

**First telephone call: how to approach your prospect**

| | |
|---|---|
| Consultant | Mr Brown? |
| [Prospect | Yes?] |
| Consultant | Good morning, sir. |
| [Prospect | Good morning.] |
| Consultant | My name is [employee's name] from [company name]. You may have heard of us? |
| [*Wait for reply*] | |
| | [*Softly*] Would you allow me to explain why I'm calling you this morning? |
| [Prospect | Yes.] |
| Consultant | We are a company of international insurance and pensions consultants. I live and work here in [prospect's town/city]. |
| [*Pause*] | |
| | Within [company name] my job is to advise people on investing for their future … |

This is an example of a 'cold-call' script (where the salesperson telephones the prospective client, often at home during the evening or weekend, without prior arrangement). The interaction above is intended to lead to the client agreeing to an appointment to discuss things further. You can see that the employee is explicitly told, step by step:

1    *what* to say;

2    *how* to say it ('Softly');

3    *when* to say it ('Pause'); and

4    how the prospective client is likely to react.

There are linguistic strategies for personalizing the encounter, too: 'I live and work here in …'. The place-name is always the town or city where the client lives, and the deictic word *here* functions as a claim to proximity. Claims to a shared world are an important means of establishing personal links between client and salesperson, so deictic markers are widely used in sales English.

> Deixis is discussed in Chapters 1 and 2 of this book.

Cold calling (or cold faxing, increasingly) in order to sell products or services is still one of the most common forms of sales approach. The problems facing people on the receiving end of this approach are twofold. One problem is that they may not be aware of some of the persuasive techniques being used; the second is that the sheer speed of these sales interactions – face to face or by telephone – means that the time for reflection is minimized. It is very difficult to deflect persuasive sales techniques on the spot. (This is why many countries now make it a legal obligation for a company to provide a 'cooling-off period' before such a sale is confirmed, to allow consumers to reflect on their decision to purchase.)

Although these persuasive techniques are still used, the 'hard sell' is becoming dated and increasingly ineffectual. This is largely because consumers have become so accustomed to it that they have developed strategies for deflecting it, and for checking the attempts of salespersons to make them part with their money. Another reason for the increasing wariness of the consumer is the harsh economic climate worldwide – people need to be very convinced about the benefits of a deal or purchase. Later in this section I will be looking at some of the strategies people develop to resist this sort of sales approach.

The next stage in the sales encounter that we are looking at is the first meeting. The client is again referred to in the company literature as a 'prospect', and the salesperson is told that the purpose of this meeting is to 'educate the prospect about the necessary process'. There are three words here that may jump out at you: *educate, prospect* and *necessary*. There are interesting assumptions behind the use of these terms. Who 'educates' whom, and for whose benefit is this 'education' given? What does it mean for the client to be seen as a 'prospect', with all the implications contained in that somewhat impersonal word? And 'necessary' for whom?

Again, the entire conversation is scripted:

Consultant      Is all that clear to you, Mr Brown?
[*Wait for him to reply*]
                Are you happy so far?
[Prospect       Yes.]
Consultant      Good.
[*Remember to smile*]

One significant element of this type of discourse is that the script prescribes turn-taking. Employees are told, for example: 'Don't thank him and he'll thank you!'

Throughout, it is the salesperson who is supposed to be in charge of *who* speaks, and *when*. Questions are, furthermore, put to the client in ways that prescribe a certain response (usually positive). Questions can even be designed so that the customer grants permission for a further sales pitch:

> Consultant    May I just explain what our Special Care policy covers?
> [Prospect     Yes.]

By the time of the second meeting between the client and the consultant, first-name terms are to be used. The pronouns have also shifted in this second meeting, client and salesperson now being presented as partners in a joint endeavour:

> Consultant    Fine, John, well *we've* actually got an agenda for today's meeting. If you recall, John, when *we* finished last time *we'd* worked out that your most important concern was ... [my italics].

As I noted earlier, pronouns can be highly significant because they can be used to signify, or imply, intimate relationships. Goodin describes the use of inclusive pronominal forms such as *we* and *our* as 'hidden co-optation'. Here he is talking about the linguistic strategies employed in political speeches:

> An important aspect of appealing to audience prejudices is the orator's claim to share their perspective ... The 'language of participation' in general, and the word 'we' in particular, figure importantly in this process. Use of the first person plural implies a unity between the speaker and his audience that is typically a fraud.
> (Goodin, 1980, p. 105)

## Activity 4.4   *(Allow about 15 minutes)*

Political speechmaking, and other forms of persuasive language, are discussed further in Chapter 4 of the second book in this series, *Using English: from conversation to canon* (Maybin and Mercer (eds), 1996).

Here is a section of a speech from *Animal Farm*, George Orwell's satirical novel criticizing the Stalinist regime in the USSR. At this point one of the leaders, a pig named Major, is trying to rouse the other animals to rebel against the authority of humans. He uses many linguistic strategies common to political speeches and other types of discourse where the aim is to persuade the audience of a certain point of view. As you read, note carefully Major's use of pronouns and other inclusive devices.

> Now, comrades, what is the nature of this life of ours? Let us face it, our lives are miserable, laborious and short. We are born, we are given just so much food as will keep the breath in our bodies, and those of us who are capable of it are forced to work to the last atom of our strength; and the very instant that our usefulness has come to an end we are slaughtered with hideous cruelty. No animal in England knows the meaning of happiness or leisure after he is a year old. No animal in England is free. The life of an animal is misery and slavery: that is the plain truth.
> (Orwell, 1987, p. 3)

Modality is discussed in Chapter 2 of this book and Chapter 2 of the second book in this series, *Using English: from conversation to canon* (Maybin and Mercer (eds), 1996).

## Comment

There are many claims to solidarity in this speech, which is not surprising as Major is trying to convince his audience that he shares their concerns. Words such as *comrades*, as well as pronouns such as *we* and *our* are used. Note also the high **modality** in the above extract from the speech. There are generic statements (statements that make a claim to a universal truth) such as *The life of an animal is* *misery and slavery*. The use of the present tense aims to tell the animals in the audience how the world *is*, rather than how it might be, or might appear. This speech is therefore highly **monologic** – that is, it attempts to suppress any interpretation of events or the world, other than the one given.

It is not only spoken discourse that uses these techniques. Newspapers, particularly in editorial comment, frequently use generic statements:

> The outcome of the battle against age is predetermined.
> (*Indian Express*, 8 November 1994)

In addition the pronoun *we* and other inclusive devices can be employed:

> We are still far from the classless society which John Major claimed he wanted to see in Britain. But all Mirror readers know from their own lives how this country has changed.
> (*Daily Mirror*, 5 December 1994)

Phrases such as *all Mirror readers know* function to imply high modality for a proposition – that is, high truth value. This is also a device for assuming a shared point of view, and for speaking on behalf of the newspaper readers, as it appeals to notions of 'common sense'. Deictic markers such as *this* also point to participation in a collective world.

## Multimodal sales techniques

I noted in Chapter 2 that written and electronic texts are becoming increasingly **multimodal** – that is, they use devices from more than one semiotic mode in a single text (words and pictures, or pictures and sound, for example). Many written texts also incorporate visual or verbal elements that suggest speech, rather than writing. Speech is generally more informal than writing, so devices used in print to imply speech can be seen as another aspect of informalization. They are also part of increasing multimodality: the two modes (or channels of communication) – speech and writing – appear in the same text.

Written texts can use a variety of visual elements to imply spoken English. These can include the following.

- Typographical devices, such as changes of case, size and emphasis, can be significant. The headmaster–pupil poem in Chapter 2 uses a bold typeface for the headmaster's words, while the pupil's speech is set in a lighter typeface. Typeface *change* can also be used to imply contrastive stress in the clause.
- Speech bubbles can be used to suggest people, or characters, actually speaking.
- Punctuation: parentheses in a printed text can suggest that the 'speaker' is thinking on his or her feet; exclamation marks and question marks can imply speakers interjecting or disagreeing with one another.
- Triadic structures (presenting a proposition in three parts, as in *our lives are miserable, laborious and short* in the extract above from *Animal Farm*) are a rhetorical device traditionally associated with public oratory, and therefore reminiscent of speech.
- Semi-phonetic representations of nonstandard English (*wot, yer*, etc.) are widely used in popular newspapers and comics, and give a strong impression of speech styles, and of social values associated with those styles.

**Monologic** is a term associated with the Russian theorist Bakhtin. It refers to 'single-voiced' dialogue, where the author's voice is dominant (see Bakhtin, 1981).

Three-part lists are discussed in Chapter 4 of the second book in this series, *Using English: from conversation to canon* (Maybin and Mercer (eds), 1996).

- Intonation can be implied visually, by, for example, repetition of letters (*b-b-but*) or changes in font size. Suspension points (…) can imply a speaker's voice trailing off.

Markers of spoken English in written texts will be revisited in examples later in this chapter.

Advertising in all media has long been using multimodal strategies. Figure 4.1 shows an advertisement that dropped through my letterbox in 1995, which uses many visual and verbal strategies in order to persuade me to respond to it.

It contains examples of border crossing between spoken and written English, formal and informal styles, and printed and electronic communication. It is printed on glossy paper, but is made to look like a computer printout, presumably to imply and emphasize how urgent it is – they haven't had time to print it on company letterhead! In case I missed the visual 'hole marks' printed down both sides of the paper, the company has added COMPUTER PRINT OUT in words at the top of the page, and informed me that the *Data run commenced 8.05 am*. The omission of *at* implies haste, and is potentially intertextual with newspaper headlines, which routinely omit prepositions and auxiliaries. Is the customer intended to be impressed by this evidence of such early working hours? Does *8.05* imply that I was almost at the top of the list that day, and therefore a priority?

I am then told that I have been allocated an award, a stereo hi-fi, but the exact description of my prize is crossed out with a line of Xs, and the words

La Redoute would prefer to surprise you!

printed as if handwritten below. There are several double bluffs here, typical of a more aware, knowing relationship between companies and consumers in the (post)modern world. I know, and the company knows that I know, that it wants me to buy something. All parties also know that if the company had really wanted to cross something out, it would simply have erased it from the advertisement during the printing process and left no trace. But the company wants the connotation of urgency, so has *added* something to make it look *deleted*. This also creates the impression of additional agency: it looks, visually, as if a harried supervisor has rushed over and corrected the work of a careless employee, who is obviously unaware of my importance as a customer.

The 'data run' apparently finished at 8.15 a.m. – rather a long time, on reflection, for such a short printout – but of course that is not the point. To validate the fact that I have been allocated an award, a company stamp has been applied (very carefully positioned so as to appear rushed and smudged). High modality is therefore portrayed visually. The designing of this advertisement as a computer printout carries with it all the connotations of speed and urgency that are presumably meant to imply, by extension, the efficiency with which the company will treat me as a customer.

Experienced consumers are generally aware of most of these sales techniques, and recognize them for what they are. But what happens when government circulars, public-information leaflets and even tax forms use the same devices? The use of a conversational style and 'advertising techniques' in these texts are becoming increasingly widespread. In a sense the Campaign for Plain English, by encouraging official institutions and companies to put documents into forms of English that all citizens can readily understand, together with the growth of mass-media advertising, has opened up new possibilities for persuasion. Is an informal style of presentation to be welcomed because it makes the text more readable, lively and accessible? Or is it to be regarded with suspicion, because it aims to create a 'friendly' basis from which to convince us of the need to part with our money or to espouse a political viewpoint?

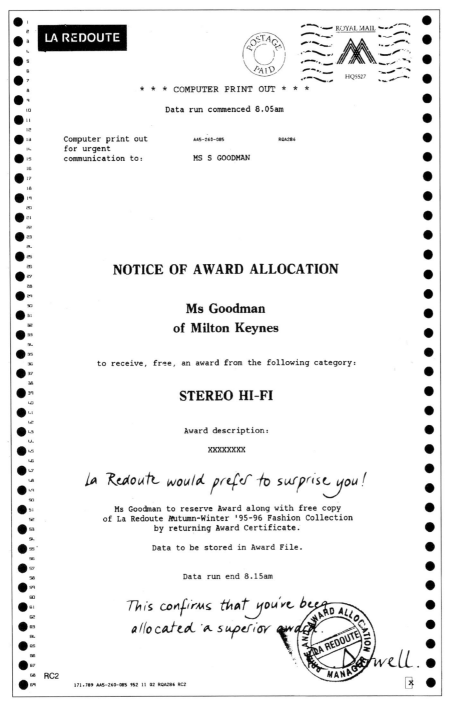

Figure 4.1    *An advertisement from a clothing company*

# The marketization of official English

That political speeches are often infused with the language of selling has been noted by many analysts (for example, Atkinson, 1984; Goodin, 1980). Modern electoral campaigns often make use of commercial advertising agencies (the Conservative Party in Britain, for example, used the services of a London company, Saatchi and Saatchi, and Margaret Thatcher was completely 'repackaged' during her term of office as prime minister). Wernick notes, in fact, that elections in the USA and western Europe are commonly described as 'a battle between rival advertising campaigns' (Wernick, 1991, p. 140).

What has been less widely noted, at least until recently, is the use of the strategies of promotional discourse to 'sell' government policy. Deductions from citizens' earnings to pay for public services such as road-building programmes or hospitals are not, of course, voluntary. Increasingly, however, the decisions made by institutions responsible for these policies are 'advertised' – that is, they are put into the public domain in the format of advertising, rather than as information. The function of 'advertising' them, therefore, has more to do with winning the public's approval than with selling in the traditional sense. Look at these examples:

> HIGHER Sum Assured … LONGER Protection … LOWER Premium …

> TRIPLE cover from one plan … vital protection for you and your family

These are taken from printed newspaper advertisements, from two different organizations. Both appear to be selling insurance. One, however, is from a government scheme in Singapore, whereby taxpayers compulsorily contribute from their earnings on a regular basis to pay for the public health service. The other is from a private British insurance company. Which is which?

We will return to the first of these two (the government one) later, where the complete text will be considered as a multimodal example of border crossing between 'advertising' and 'information'.

Plate 8 in the colour section shows a page from a British government leaflet, the Post Office Charter. This is one of a number of charters produced by the British government, usually prior to the privatization of a public-service utility, setting out what the public could expect by way of standards of service. British citizens have had a Passenger's Charter for the train service, a Patient's Charter for the health service, and a Post Office Charter. There was even a Citizen's Charter, a more general document dealing with the rights – and duties – of the citizen. Analysts have commented at some length on the verbal language of these charters, noting that they use many rhetorical techniques common to other persuasive discourse, and that power relationships are usually still portrayed as 'top-down' in the language used. The hospital patients in the Patient's Charter, for example, are usually in object position in the clause, the doctors and managers being in subject position (Department of Health, 1991). This can be seen as a reflection of the power balance in doctor–patient relationships themselves: doctors and managers are still represented as 'acting upon' or 'doing things to' the patients. 'Who gets the verb' is often significant in these texts.

Visually, too, the charters have taken on board many of the tenets of commercial advertising: they make full use of colour, they include devices such as 'bullets' to set out points, and there are usually logos as well. Logos are a strong clue to marketization in many written texts produced by institutions. Unremarkable in advertising, where brands need to be instantly recognizable, nearly all government departments and public service utilities worldwide now have them.

Striking examples of border crossing between advertising and information are shown in the two texts in Figures 4.2 and 4.3.

Figure 4.2 is part of an advertisement for a new shopping complex in Singapore. The advertisement shows a streetscape, in full colour, with speech bubbles emanating from various parts of the shopping centre. We therefore have crossovers here between visual and verbal, and spoken and written, English. There is much that one could say about the positioning of the reader here: who is actually supposed to be speaking? Note that there are no people actually depicted, only their speech. It could be argued that the readers are supposed to

JT IT.

Figure 4.2    *Extract from a shopping centre advertisement*

'fill in the gaps' and imagine the voices of excited people exploring their new shopping centre – or even to 'become' those people themselves in their imagination. It can therefore be seen as a device for *involving* the readers in the text.

Figure 4.3 Part of a public-information notice issued by the Singapore government

Speech, and particularly informal speech as we have seen, plays an important role in constructing a sense of personal involvement. Here speech is not only implied, it is visually depicted. The text's cartoon-like presentation provides another clue to informality: cartoons are associated with childhood and leisure time, rather than the adult world of work. They are therefore familiar and reassuring.

Now look at Figure 4.3, where you will find what appears to be a very similar advertisement.

The same device of speech bubbles is used, and this time we see both people and cartoon characters interacting with each other. This, however, is not a normal advertisement. It is a notice from a Singapore government department that takes contributions from citizens' earnings for its state savings scheme. Citizens cannot *choose* whether to contribute to the Minimum Sum Scheme (as they can to visit the new shopping centre). This, then, has more to do with explaining government policy and setting out the new regulations than with advertising in the more usual sense. Its layout, and visual and verbal use of language, can be seen to cue the reader's background knowledge of advertisements and advertising genres. The reader may therefore bring very different assumptions to this text than to a plain, official-looking document.

**Activity 4.5**   *(Allow about 20 minutes)*

Turn to Plate 9 in the colour section. The text here looks even more like an advertisement. Issued by the same government department in Singapore that issued the notice in Figure 4.3, it has the layout of a company newsletter. Consider the visual layout as well as the linguistic forms. What advertising strategies, or forms of marketized discourse, can you find in this text?

**Comment**

Some of the most striking elements are the triadic structure, *HIGHER ... LONGER ... LOWER*, and the use of cartoon characters to 'sell' this savings scheme. In addition, there is the promise of a prize in the bottom right-hand corner.

We can view the use of this style of presentation positively or negatively. On the one hand, it makes the information clearer, less intimidating and easier to read. On the other, readers may feel that the production of expensive 'advertisements' to disseminate public information is not something to be welcomed.

**Activity 4.6**   *(Reading B)*

Read Anthea Fraser Gupta's 'Selling in Singapore' (Reading B), where she provides a practical analysis of marketized texts in Singapore. The reading discusses the stylistic devices used by the producers of two Singaporean texts, one promoting a government housing scheme, the other a private shopping centre. Both texts draw on styles found in other texts, and have certain similarities such as the use of a cartoon format and of ethnic and gender stereotypes. In addition, Gupta notes that each text has influenced the other in its style of presentation. The process is therefore two-way: each has an effect on the other.

You may also like to consider these texts in the light of the discussion of multimodality in Chapter 2.

We have been looking in this section at some of the strategies that can be employed by speakers and writers wishing either to persuade an audience of their point of view, or to sell them something, or both. We come now to the strategies that clients, readers and audiences use to reject these persuasive devices – to refuse their positioning in the discourse.

## Resisting the sales pitch

Some of the points made so far may seem to suggest a passive, 'acted upon' consumer (or reader, or viewer) who is being subjected to the malign influences of politics and industrial expediency. While there are many linguistic strategies for attempting to position readers in certain ways, the readers/receivers of a text are not so defenceless as they may appear at first sight. The increasing sophistication of consumers, in particular, means that many of the traditional or established sales pitches may not be as effective as they once were. A complex situation arises where consumers are no longer the 'dupes' of the persuasive devices of the professional seller. They develop skills to deal with unwanted salespersons. These may include subverting attempts to make the customer initiate the 'thank yous' in an exchange, or waiting on the telephone line until the seller is finally forced to say goodbye – contrary to all the rules of the training manual. Junk mail, too, seems to be almost universally regarded with suspicion. Certainly anything in my house that is printed with the words 'Urgent Communication' is immediately thrown away! Those who do actually order goods from these companies may deliberately misspell their name on the order form, so that when further unsolicited mail arrives its origin can be traced.

Here is the final part of the pension consultant's sales script that we were looking at earlier in this section. You may find that it raises some questions about the power of the client to subvert sales techniques.

| | |
|---|---|
| Consultant | I trust this meeting has been useful? |
| [Prospect | Yes.] |
| Consultant | Fine. Could I ask you for your help with something, John? |
| [Prospect | Yes, of course.] |

[*Remember: he can't refuse!*]

| | |
|---|---|
| Consultant | You realize that I can only help people by meeting them. You can help me to help more people by giving me the names and phone numbers of people you know – business partners or friends. OK? I'll just wait a few minutes while you fill this sheet in. |

[*Remember: you are in control. Let him thank you.*]

How effective do you think this strategy would be? How many people would happily give the names of their friends (more 'prospects'!) to this salesperson, even if the request were put in terms of a favour? It is highly likely that many people would resist. It also seems to me that the method of introducing this request to the client is likely to trigger resistance even before the favour is asked. Background knowledge on the part of the client, and awareness of the present situation, will inform the client immediately that doing a favour for the salesperson is likely to have financial implications. In this case there are social consequences, too – how many friends would the client still have after releasing their names and telephone numbers?

**Activity 4.7**   *(Allow about 15 minutes)*

Reread the above extract from the pension consultant's script, noting the use of conversational English, and the linguistic indications of the relationship between the participants.

If you were the salesperson in this extract, what could you do linguistically to ensure the success of your sales pitch – to get those telephone numbers?

If you were the client, how could you resist? Assume that you want to stay polite!

The client, then, is far from powerless. Wernick, too, notes a complexity in this type of interaction, saying that consumers have developed 'a hardened scepticism about every kind of communication in view of the selling job it is probably doing' (Wernick, 1991, p. 192). Just as television viewers often develop strategies for deflecting advertising – such as leaving the room to make a cup of tea – so those on the receiving end of promotionalized official discourse may also develop strategies for 'talking back'. Readers become sensitized to the 'buzz-words' of advertising and to lexical changes, especially as these issues are often discussed by the very media in which they occur. People quickly learn that when a company announces a decision to *downsize*, this means that it is going to make redundancies among its workforce. Those using the train service in the UK have been renamed as *customers* rather than *passengers*, and there has been widespread discussion in the media about this word and its implications. Those who want the railway company to be seen as a commercial business accept the new term *customer*, while those who want to emphasize the concept of a public service insist on calling themselves *passengers*.

Readers or audiences cannot, then, simply be manipulated by language designed to persuade, or which repositions them as consumers. Corner states that a theory of straightforward top-down manipulation is in any case unsustainable:

> any idea of influence as linear transmission, the direct reproduction (by manipulation, implantation etc.) in the viewer of certain attitudes, is radically put into question by a theory of meaning as contingent on interpretation. For a start, the very fact of *variation* works against the idea of any uniform influence, while the emphasis on 'activity' works against that characterisation of viewers and readers as essentially passive which has been a feature of theories of 'heavy influence' (including theories about ideology).
>
> (Corner, 1995, p. 137)

He notes, however, that producers of texts will *try* to create preferred meanings (to indicate the way in which the text is to be read) even though they cannot guarantee success. The extent to which they can hope to succeed depends on a variety of factors. Cameron believes that the inferential abilities of readers have been vastly underestimated. Here she is talking about proponents of 'good style' in English, but the analogy holds:

> The creative inferential powers of competent language-users are seldom acknowledged by those who write style books. On the contrary, such texts assume a world full of people whose literal-minded obtuseness borders on the ridiculous. For example, a much-cited illustration of the perils of ambiguity, quoted in Gowers, is 'if the baby does not thrive on raw milk, boil it'. Now, this sentence invites editing on the grounds that the

ambiguity makes it risible, but to say it requires editing to make the meaning clear strains credulity. What degree of idiocy would be needed to ponder the ambiguity and conclude, either that it was undecidable or that the writer recommended boiling the baby? Here the charge of unclarity is no more than a pretext for the critic to parade his or her superior linguistic sensibilities.

(Cameron, 1995, p. 71)

Cameron goes on to comment on the reaction to the vocabulary used in the press in the USA and Britain during the Gulf War in 1991, where phrases such as *collateral damage* were used instead of *civilian casualties*. Such euphemisms were intended to dehumanize the war and obscure the fact that many thousands of people had died. Cameron argues that when faced with a meaningless phrase such as *collateral damage* people will not simply dismiss it as meaningless. If they cannot see the meaning, they will infer one – and they will infer not only the meaning (that civilians have died) but also that *the phrase was intended to conceal this fact*. They will therefore be doubly angry, because they have discovered that a euphemism was used (Cameron, 1995, p. 73).

So far I have looked at some ways in which commercial enterprises and institutions address or position their customers and readers, and ways in which such positioning can be resisted. I now look at similar interactions from the point of view of the employees – those who use these forms of English at work. Many companies and service industries now have specific training in language or 'communication skills' for their workforce, and I will consider some aspects of this in the next section.

## 4.4   DESIGNING THE LANGUAGE OF EMPLOYEES: 'SPEAKING ANOTHER LANGUAGE' AT WORK

Commercial institutions of all sorts train their employees in how to talk to 'the public' or to their clients. The script in section 4.3, used to sell financial services, is one of these. Language training at work can also include such things as the type of greeting to be used:

Good morning, Jackie speaking, how may I help you?

Or repetition of the company name at the end of the encounter:

Thank you for calling [company name].

For further discussion of the use of English in the workplace, see Chapter 3 of the second book in this series, *Using English: from conversation to canon* (Maybin and Mercer (eds), 1996).

Service encounters, in particular, often proceed according to a script, which may in some instances be laid down word for word by the company. Hochschild (1983) cites one example where an American company ensures that its workers speak to customers according to company guidelines. Cashiers at a store in St Petersburg in 1982 were brought into a courtesy campaign: if the cashier didn't greet the customer in a friendly way and say *Thank You for Shopping Winn–Dixie* sincerely, the customer received a dollar (Hochschild, 1983, p. 149). Anyone who has ever been to a fast-food restaurant, or telephoned a mail-order company, will have heard an institutionalized script in some form. Furthermore, companies that trade world-wide, such as fast-food restaurants, often use the same scripts in all their outlets. This adds a global element to the scenario, as customers in Dubai, Hong Kong and the USA may be spoken to by employees in exactly the same way.

Hochschild studied working practices in a particular service industry, Delta Airlines, based in the USA. He looked closely at the work of Delta's flight attendants, at the language of their training programmes, and at the ways in which

the (largely female) workforce is trained to deal with difficult passengers. He
notes that the use of customers' names is a technique explicitly taught:

> Attendants were urged to 'work' the passenger's name, as in 'Yes, Mr
> Jones, it's true the flight is delayed.' This reminds the passenger that he is
> not anonymous, that there is at least some pretension to a personal
> relation.
> (Hochschild, 1983, p. 111)

This is an example of using a deliberate strategy, for the benefit of the employee as
well as the passenger. Other, broader, strategies for deflecting the anger (justified
or otherwise) of passengers were also noted. These largely took the form of claims
to solidarity, the phrase *I know just how you feel* being a particularly useful one.

In some cases, however, designing the language of employees can be seen as
depriving them of the right to express themselves in certain ways. There may be
rules established for lexical choices – the use of one word rather than another:

> Supervisors never speak officially of an *obnoxious* or *outrageous* passenger,
> only of an *uncontrolled* passenger. The term suggests that a fact has
> somehow attached itself to this passenger – not that the passenger has
> lost control or even had any control to lose. Again, the common phrase
> 'mishandled passenger' suggests a bungle somewhere up the line ... By
> linguistically avoiding any attribution of blame, the idea of a right to be
> angry at the passenger is smuggled out of the discourse.
> (Hochschild, 1983, pp. 111–12)

Fairclough refers to the deliberate design by institutions, whether in the public or
private sector, of employees' language as the 'technologization of discourse'
(1993, p. 141). He notes how widespread this practice has become, and that it is
occurring throughout the company structure, from top to bottom:

> There has been a large-scale restructuring of employment which has led
> to a larger service sector and a smaller manufacturing sector, and this in
> itself has major implications for the linguistic demands of work – many
> more people are having to communicate with 'clients' or 'publics', for
> example. The quality of the communication is coming to be seen as part
> of the quality of the service. Even within manufacturing, there is a shift
> away from isolated work on a production line to team work, and workers
> are seen as needing more complex 'communicative skills'. One interest-
> ing development is that discussions of such skills increasingly highlight
> abilities in face-to-face interaction, group discussion and decision-
> making, 'listening skills', and so forth – abilities which have previously
> been seen ... as general 'life skills' rather than vocational skills.
> (Fairclough (ed.), 1992, p. 4)

An example of the relevance of this can be seen in changes to recruitment
practices in Britain. Careers centres have in recent years become acutely aware,
for example, that employers seeking newly qualified staff are now less concerned
with qualifications or examination grades, and more concerned with evidence of
'communicative skills' and team-working abilities. Many job interviews, too, now
have a language element to them: candidates must demonstrate that they can
communicate effectively or persuasively with others.

Wernick puts this type of cultural and linguistic change into the context of an
increasingly sales-oriented social and political environment. For him, the rise of
commercial culture combined with mass-media advertising has led to 'culture'
itself becoming a commodity (Wernick, 1991, p. 185). The political arena has
provided the impetus for this change in the UK. An increasingly market-oriented

political agenda has meant that it is expedient to rename *students* and *passengers* as *customers* – particularly as budgetary changes have meant that, for example, an additional student per course is worth a certain sum of money to an educational institution. Walsh notes the following:

> The system that is emerging is based upon market principles and the idea of the citizen as consumer. Competition is to replace authority as the basis upon which decisions are made, and in ensuring that there is adaptation to changing circumstances.
>
> (Walsh, 1994, p. 201)

That institutions and governments have introduced lexical changes for financial or political reasons is one aspect of this scenario. The problem for those working in what used to be considered as public services (education, public transport, local administrative bodies) is that to some extent they eventually have to use this language themselves, and in some way that must imply taking on board the social values encoded within it. A few months ago I telephoned an organization listed under 'Educational Services' in the telephone book. Unsure whether I was speaking to a school or a related institution, I asked what they did. 'We are providers,' was the reply, 'and we have about 350 teaching units.' This apparently means that it is a school, with 350 pupils! Teachers increasingly report that they *need* to see their pupils as customers/consumers, in order to fulfil the responsibilities of their job.

If education becomes a 'product' that is sold to 'consumers', then teachers may come to see themselves as 'salespeople', needing to promote both their courses and their own expertise. To a greater or lesser extent, in fact, we are all somehow involved in selling. If you were responding to an advertisement for a job, or trying to persuade somebody that extra financing was needed for a project, the chances are that you would need to 'sell' yourself or your idea. Wernick believes that we must take this into account in understanding changes in society. It is not enough to consider the question only from the side of reception, the ways in which the public are addressed. We must also look at the ways in which people are all, increasingly, becoming involved in the *production* of promotional texts:

> from dating and clothes shopping to attending a job interview, virtually everyone is involved in the self-promotionalism which overlays such practices in … everyday life.
>
> At one level or another, then, and often at several levels at once, we are all promotional subjects.
>
> (Wernick, 1991, p. 192)

**Activity 4.8**   *(Reading C)*

Read Norman Fairclough's account, in Reading C, of the linguistic strategies he had to use in order to be promoted at work. As an academic in a British university, he analyses how marketization is becoming routine in the linguistic practices of British higher education.

**Comment**

Fairclough feels a deep ambivalence about the activity he had to become involved in: 'selling himself'. What other situations now require the use of the same promotional linguistic strategies? Is it a reasonable assertion that you must 'sell yourself' in an increasing range of contexts: in job interviews; when renting accommodation; when arranging a mortgage? Wernick believes that many social encounters now require people to behave (both socially and linguistically) in these ways, and voices his concern about the possible consequences. He refers to this phenomenon as producing a 'profound problem of authenticity' (1991, p. 193) – in other words, people don't know who they are any more:

> If social survival, let alone competitive success, depends on continual, audience-oriented, self-staging, what are we behind the mask?
>
> (Wernick, 1991, p. 193)

Do you agree that people increasingly need to become involved in self-promotion? If so, do you think this is a good or a bad thing?

We can link questions of 'self' in marketized English to questions of identity in globally structured industry. English is becoming increasingly important for all employees in transnational companies. English is now used not only by company executives, but also by administrators and clerks. In some companies, employees are permitted to speak only English at work. Tollefson (1991) believes that the imposition of English on employees in transnational companies, and a corresponding ban on the use of local languages, can have a fragmenting effect on employees' sense of identity:

> What we do is what we feel we are. Therefore when individuals are not permitted to use their own languages at work, they are alienated not only from their work and the workplace, but from themselves.
>
> (Tollefson, 1991, p. 207)

The use of English and other languages at work is discussed in Chapter 3 of the second book in this series, *Using English: from conversation to canon* (Maybin and Mercer (eds), 1996).

If this is true when different languages are at issue, it may be true, at least to some extent, in companies where there is a requirement to use marketized English at work, or to follow scripts laid down by company regulations.

Both informalized and marketized English can be seen to throw into the arena all sorts of issues about agency – about 'who does what to whom' – in these situations. It would be somewhat simplistic to assume that the sales techniques in the scripts given earlier simply aim to produce the desired response in the client, persuading him or her to buy the product. That is of course one function, but equally important is the positioning of the *employee* – the salesperson – by the discourse. The script is a complex interplay of instructions from the company to the employee, and from the employee to the client. There are unseen people involved in the immediate interaction between the 'prospect' and the salesperson (see Figure 4.4).

The 'prospect', too, of course, draws on his or her knowledge and experience of sales interactions in dealing with the current situation. Who, then, actually holds the cards? The answer seems to be that all the participants, whether present or implied, have a certain amount of power in this interaction. It is not simply a case of the seller 'acting upon' the buyer – even though this may seem at first to be the case. The salesperson, too, is subject to pressures, and needs to behave linguistically according to company guidelines, in order to do the job and achieve certain goals. And this involves not only *saying* certain things rather than others; it involves, to some extent at least, *believing* them. In order for the exchange to result in a successful conclusion, the salesperson, too, has to be convinced that the deal is a good one. Cold calling is a difficult and somewhat emotionally threatening task, and employees, once trained, are more or less left to their own devices. The job requires high levels of motivation and commitment, and employees who appear half-hearted are not going to succeed. The employee, therefore, is co-opted into the exchange, just as the customer is. The forms of English used are an

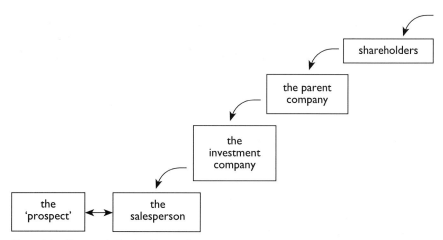

Figure 4.4   The people involved in a sales encounter

important element in the process: the pronouns *we* and *us*, the use of first-name terms, deictic markers – all these create an involvement between the customer and the salesperson, which can act upon the *salesperson's* sense of self, just as much as the customer's.

One of the most important points that emerged during Hochschild's study at Delta Airlines is that the workforce, dealing as it does with the public, and having to deflect anger and smile through sometimes very difficult situations, requires a large *emotional* investment in the job. He terms this 'emotional labor', saying that *'the emotional style of offering the service is part of the service itself'* (Hochschild, 1983, p. 5; original italics), and believes that an employee's sense of self can become fragmented when his or her private emotions are being 'sold' in the public sphere.

Some cases of institutional language design, then, can have consequences for the employee as well as for the customer. These come from being required (sometimes by contract) to speak in certain ways rather than others, to respond according to a script, and to use the same script as every other employee. Customers, too, may be left wondering whether they are dealing with an individual or an institution. They may, for example, get the same response, in the same *words*, from different company employees, in different branches, even in different countries.

## 4.5   CONCLUSION

In this chapter I have outlined some of the changes in English use that are occurring in increasingly postindustrialized societies. Informalization and marketization in English are the result of many interconnecting factors, some political, some social; some local, some international. These include the decline of industry-based employment and the rise of the service sector, the need for political and commercial institutions to gain public approval for policies and financial imperatives, and the need for many English speakers in general to adopt these changes in the language they use, in order to remain employed or to become employable. These factors are not clear-cut and distinct, and neither are the merging and emerging forms and uses of English: rather, they connect and intersect.

No one person or institution is in control of these types of English border crossing: they are neither completely top-down nor bottom-up. Informalization and marketization can be seen as good or bad, depending on your point of view. If a government circular or broadcast interview addresses readers or listeners in an informal, friendly way, this can be seen as a benefit if it allows them a greater degree of comprehension or involvement in the interaction. It can also, however, imply a basis of social solidarity with the audience, which may well be fraudulent in the wider context.

In addition, it may be that the sheer amount of informal and marketized English produced by institutions will have similarly fragmented effects: 'consumers' will become adept at decoding it and will therefore develop skills for deflecting its potential influence. They will also learn to adopt similar promo-tional or conversational strategies themselves when dealing with those insti-tutions. These same strategies can, after all, be adopted by the relatively power*less*, in their interactions with institutions – once people are aware of what those strategies are and how to use them. Furthermore, they will have to hand not only linguistic resources, but multimodal ones. It is not only institutions and commer-cial enterprises that have access to the increasingly sophisticated technology required for the production of glossy, professional-looking documents.

A final example of marketization is shown in the box below. Here, 'marketized English' has a double meaning: in this case English itself is being marketed (as a product or commodity).

---

**The marketization of the British Council**

*From the British Council's inaugural ceremony in 1935:*

> The basis for our work must be the English language ... (and) we are aiming at something more profound than just a smattering of our tongue. Our object is to assist the largest possible number to appreciate fully the glories of our literature, our contribution to the arts and sciences, and our pre-eminent contribution to political practice. This can best be achieved by promoting the study of our language abroad.

(Cited in Phillipson, 1992, p. 138)

*From the Aims and Objectives of the British Council's English 2000 campaign, 1995:*

To maintain and expand the role of English as the world language into the next century; to exploit the position of English to further British interests; and to ensure Britain's dominant role in the provision of English language goods and services.

To survey what competitor countries are doing in each market and assess where Britain's comparative advantage lies.

To identify specific needs and market opportunities.

To uphold standards and ensure British products offer quality and value for money.

To achieve better co-ordination between the various UK suppliers of English language goods and services.

To stimulate basic and applied research leading to the development of new products and services to meet identified future needs.

To bring British suppliers and overseas customers together to maximise British input to education and training overseas.

(British Council, press release, 23 March 1995)

---

# Reading A
# EXTRACT FROM *VERBAL HYGIENE*

*Deborah Cameron*

Postmodern societies are characterized economically by post-industrialism, consumerism and globalization. The reflexes of these characteristics in language management, according to [J.V.] Neustupný ['History of language planning: retrospect and future prospects', keynote address to the tenth AILA World Congress, Amsterdam, 13 August 1993], are on one hand a desire for rationalization (regulating language use to make production more efficient), but on the other hand a move towards diversity and democratization (maximizing markets by catering to various consumer reference groups with varying needs and tastes).

Geoffrey Nunberg's point about the new 'permissiveness' or 'pluralism' represents one side of the postmodern coin, the diversifying and democratizing side. Postmodern societies are often linguistically diverse, migration being one consequence of a globally organized economy, and linguistic diversity has long been felt to require management. Currently, however, there is a shift towards evaluating diversity more positively, and seeking to preserve rather than eliminate it – what Neustupný labels 'the variation ideology'. This finds expression in many contemporary verbal hygiene movements and practices: policies or campaigns promoting minority language rights, the maintenance of heritage languages and the preservation or revival of 'endangered' languages and dialects. Conversely, there are movements of resistance to diversity, of which 'US English'-style campaigns are the most visible examples.

Democratization, the principle of equal access to and participation in important linguistic practices, can also be seen at work in contemporary verbal hygiene movements. Apart from the 'variation ideology' which valorizes linguistic (and ethnic) diversity as a social good in itself, a further argument for accommodating diversity is that it enables minority participation in public discourse. But democratic ideals have other verbal hygiene reflexes too, many of them falling under the heading of anti-elitism. For example, Neustupný referred to 'plain language' movements whose aim is to force arcane professional registers to converge towards lay vernaculars. He also spoke in less specific terms of a general weakening of norms and a postmodern preference for innovation over conservatism (which in language will often entail a preference for vernacular over historically cultivated elite varieties).

Again, there are verbal hygiene movements of resistance to this development (e.g. the Queen's English Society); the tendency itself is more often observable in the weakening or abandonment of traditional practices such as the rigid policing of accent that used to be routine in broadcasting, or the lexicographical principle of illustrating usage only from the 'best writers'.
...
The most common reason editors give for their insistence on correct and consistent usage is that it makes the writer's meaning more directly accessible to the reader, without distracting attention from the content to the form.

Uniformity may be a necessary condition for transparency, but it is not a sufficient one. In addition to rules about the minutiae of grammar, spelling and punctuation, good writing requires a set of global stylistic maxims, too general to be formulated as specific rules of usage: injunctions to be clear, precise, definite, simple and brief, while avoiding obscurity, ambiguity, vagueness, abstraction, complication, prolixity, jargon and cliché. And whereas authorities acknowledge, however reluctantly, the natural mutability of grammar and vocabulary, they typically present clarity *et al.* as if they belonged to some pure and timeless realm of self-evidently desirable qualities. In fact these norms are neither universal nor neutral. They have a history and a politics.

The way of using language that I am calling 'transparent', after Orwell's memorable image of writing as a pane of glass, is more often referred to as Rees-Mogg refers to it [*The Times* 1970], using the term *plain*: plain style, plain language or plain English. Anyone familiar with the history of English will know that the merits of plainness have been much debated in the past five hundred years. Plainness was a key term, for example, in the so-called 'inkhorn controversy' of the sixteenth and seventeenth centuries, when the question at issue was whether to enrich English vocabulary by importing Latin loan-words or by coining alternatives. In this case the supporters of Latin 'eloquence' won. But only a little later the Enlightenment brought renewed emphasis on plainness, and a correspondingly strong distrust of rhetoric – criticized by Locke in *An Essay Concerning Human Understanding* (III:x, section 34) as 'that powerful instrument of error and deceit'.

In literary discourse there have been various moves to and from plain English (e.g. the rejection of the 'euphuistic' for the 'plain' style by prose writers in the seventeenth century, or the Romantics' reaction against 'polite' poetic diction at the end of the eighteenth); while in the sphere of religion, attitudes towards plain versus elevated language have been, and continue to be, a source of dispute among believers. During the last fifty years, the question of plain English has become particularly salient in the domain of 'official' communications addressed by the state to its citizens. Sir Ernest Gowers's classic *Plain Words* was written for British civil servants just after the Second World War as part of a deliberate effort to 'improve official English' (Gowers 1973: iii). A number of US states have 'plain language amendments' serving a similar purpose.

Examples such as these show that plainness is, if not timeless then at least a very old ideal (among those whom Gowers cites in support of it are Aristotle, St Paul, Roger Ascham, Cervantes, Defoe and Macaulay). Historically it has also however been a contested ideal, whose defenders have often felt the need to counter criticisms that plain language is flat, dull, commonplace, unrefined or vulgar. Today, though, the notion that anyone could reasonably be against plainness runs counter to common sense. In recent times it seems there has been less and less need to defend plain language, *per se*.

It is striking that the virtues of plainness are no longer presented as merely functional, but also as aesthetic. To judge from Gowers's disclaimers in *Plain Words*, where he emphasizes that he is not promoting 'fine writing' in the civil service, but only intelligible prose, he would be surprised to find himself cited by *The Times* style guide forty years later as one of 'the masters on style' (*The Times* 1992: 8). But the sentiment is endorsed by all kinds of contemporary commentators, in academe and even literary circles as well as in journalism and administration.

The dominance of the plain language ideal is particularly noticeable in guidance aimed at relatively unskilled writers, such as the handbooks used by American college students taking composition classes, or the style-checking software which has recently become available to users of personal computers. The compilers of such guidance ground their prescriptions in a set of general assumptions about good and bad writing, and overall these exhibit a remarkable unanimity.

A good illustration of the stylistic values that pervade guidance on how to write is provided by the manual that accompanies a piece of software entitled *Editor*, which is published and recommended for use with students by the US Modern Language Association (Thiesmeyer and Thiesmeyer 1990). *Editor* works by going through a text that the user has written and flagging usages that the program's authors have included in a large dictionary of problems and errors. The user must then consider how to eliminate the problem or correct the error.

Some of the problems *Editor* flags up are superficial errors of typography, spelling and punctuation, or else more serious cases of ungrammaticality. These will come to light when the user runs a dictionary called FIX; as the name implies, they are problems that require fixing if the finished product is to be in correct standard English. There are, however, three further dictionaries: TIGHTEN, POLISH and CONSIDER. These embody assumptions about good style rather than correct usage. In the manual, *Editor*'s authors explain what markers of poor style they have programmed the system to draw attention to.

TIGHTEN, for example, is 'based on a common stylistic assumption: shorter is better' (p. 38). It 'flags three kinds of phrases – redundant, wordy and tautological – to promote concise, forceful writing' (p. 38). The authors claim that 'repeated use of this dictionary and thoughtful attention to its messages constitute a tutorial in concise, vigorous style' (p. 38). POLISH embodies the stylistic assumption that 'fresher is better', and therefore checks for 'pretentious diction, clichés, trite expressions, and vague terms' (p. 38). 'This dictionary', the authors comment, 'has the goal of educating your taste' (p. 38). CONSIDER is somewhat less prescriptive than TIGHTEN or POLISH: it picks up such features as archaisms, jargon, colloquialisms and slang, sexist language and 'empty modifiers', and asks the user to consider whether he or she really wants to keep them.

*Editor* belongs to a well-established tradition of twentieth-century commentary on style; many readers will have noticed its very obvious debt to the rules for plain English formulated by George Orwell in 'Politics and the English language' … *Editor* is also typical of its genre in offering only the vaguest of justifications for its stylistic norms: reflecting 'common assumptions' (p. 38) and 'widely accepted principles of usage' (p. 12), they are presented as matters of consensus, not controversy. The program's authors are conscientious in spelling out exactly what assumptions and principles are embodied by its various dictionaries – 'shorter is better', 'fresher is better', good writing is 'concise', 'vigorous' and 'forceful', whereas bad writing is 'trite', 'pretentious' and 'wordy' – but they apparently consider these judgements so obvious as to require no further comment. Nor do they feel impelled to explain what they mean by asserting that 'x is *better*'. Better for what, and according to what criteria?

*Better* here is probably intended as both a functional and an aesthetic judgement: better for making your meaning clear, but also better in the sense of being more pleasing to read. *Editor* wants, among other things, to educate the developing writer's *taste*. This might suggest one reason why plainness has come to be so highly valued. Like many aesthetic norms, this one has a social dimension. The aesthetic of plainness is a class aesthetic, an affirmation of aristocratic and educated middle-class good taste, whereas 'pretentious' diction is the mark of the socially pretentious. It is notable for example how many of A.S.C. Ross's infamous distinctions between 'U' (upper class) and 'non-U' vocabulary are in effect distinctions between the plain and the more elaborate and/or 'refined' term (thus *wealthy* is 'non-U' for *rich*, *ill* in the sense of 'nauseated' is 'non-U' for *sick*, *home* is the 'non-U' for *house* (see Ross 1954 [extract reprinted in Crowley 1991])).

The supposed vulgarity of elaborate diction has also attracted correspondence in the letters column of *The Times*. In 1939, for instance, a Mr G.H. Palmer wrote enquiring why a railway menu promised diners 'a supplementary portion' instead of 'second helpings'. A.P. Herbert replied the next day by referring Mr Palmer to the railway's official reply, which asserted that 'for the few who do not understand the meaning of "supplementary" there would be many who would accuse us of uneducated crudity if we quoted the phrase in such plain verbiage as you suggest' (Gregory 1989: 193). Long and fancy words are preferred by the class of people who fear they might otherwise be suspected of 'uneducated crudity'; but as the use of such words becomes the mark of that class, the class above distances itself by deriding them as 'non-U' – or, in the more contemporary vocabulary of *Today* newspaper, as 'coy genteelisms'.

In order to understand fully the rise and rise of plainness, however, it is also necessary to consider the fact that arguments about plain versus more elaborate language have typically arisen in the context of broader moral, ideological and political debates. The inkhorn controversy was partly about national identity; other controversies have been about the proper relationship of humankind to God, or of citizens to the state. There is thus much more at stake than simply getting a message across intelligibly, or even tastefully. Obviously, the question whether to address the deity in everyday vernacular, in a special archaic or poetic register or in a sacred liturgical language is not a question about what God will have least difficulty understanding; rather it is a question about the symbolic representation of the believer's relation to God. Similarly, a decree that civil servants should write 'thank you for your letter' instead of 'your communication of the 5th *inst.* is hereby acknowledged' does more than just make the message clearer and save government stationery. It sends a message about the function-ary's role in relation to the public, marking it as less distant, less formal and less hierarchical than the alternative. (Gowers's golden rule, tellingly, was 'be short, be simple, be human'.) In these cases, using a certain style of language becomes a *moral* matter, to do with recognizing obligations to others and representing them in the form as well as the content of the language you use.

The idea that style norms have a strong moral element is developed by the philosopher Berel Lang in a thought-provoking collection of essays, *Writing and the Moral Self* (Lang 1991). In an essay called 'Strunk, White and grammar as morality' (Strunk and White are the authors of a classic writing handbook, *The Elements of Style* (1979)), Lang detects a 'structural analogy' between discourse about good writing and discourse on ethical conduct. One striking similarity can be found in the canonical syntax of stylistic prescriptions, which tend to the bald imperative (e.g. Strunk and White's famous 'omit needless words') and the axiomatic statement (e.g. 'brevity is always a virtue'). Like moral precepts ex-pressed in similar form ('thou shalt not kill'; 'eating people is wrong'), these prescriptions discourage the question 'why?'. As Lang remarks (1991: 15), 'the reader [of Strunk and White] is constantly ordered about, and if the orders do not persuade by their own force they will not persuade at all.'

The core of the analogy for Lang, however, is the strong connection we make between the stylistic qualities of writing and the moral qualities of the writer. Consider for example the commonplace argument that even the most trivial spelling mistakes are to be deplored because they show that the writer is 'careless' and 'sloppy' – they are, in other words, outward signs of a deeper flaw in character. In handbooks such as *The Elements of Style*, readers are shown how to construct an acceptable moral self by conforming to certain stylistic norms: 'to summarize the ideals of written style for Strunk and White … is to compose a model of human character: honest, plain, forthright, patient, simple' (Lang 1991: 17). As Lang points out, this is not the only conceivable model either for good writing or good character. If Strunk and White's prescriptions do 'persuade by their own force' it is not only because people share their conviction that style *is* character, but also because they admire the same virtues (and deplore the same vices) as Strunk and White do.

It is in this light that we must consider the consensus that currently seems to exist on the virtues of a plain and transparent style. The way of writing recommended by modern authorities has come to signify not merely the aristocratic good taste championed by A.S.C. Ross or the old-fashioned Yankee virtues Berel Lang detects in Strunk and White, but the values we cherish as essential to democracy, and conversely opposition to values we regard as inimical to democracy. For example, in spite of its aristocratic associations, plainness often stands symbolically against elitism. It is not acceptable in modern society for class or professional elites to address people in a way they find unintelligible, pretentious or suggestive of very distant and authoritarian social relations. But in addition, plainness has acquired another, even more morally compelling symbolic function. It has become a symbol of the struggle against totalitarianism.

## References

CROWLEY, T. (ed.) (1991) *Proper English? Readings in Language, History and Cultural Identity,* London: Routledge.

GOWERS, E. (1973) *The Complete Plain Words* (revised by Sir Bruce Fraser), London: HMSO.

GREGORY, K. (1989) *The Last Cuckoo: The Very Best Letters to The Times Since 1900,* London: Unwin Hyman.

LANG, B. (1991) *Writing and the Moral Self,* New York: Routledge.

LOCKE, J. (1975) *An Essay Concerning Human Understanding* (1690), ed. P.H. Nidditch, Oxford: Clarendon Press.

NUNBERG, G. (1990) 'What the usage panel thinks', in RICKS, C. and MICHAELS, L. (eds) *The State of the Language,* London: Faber.

ORWELL, G. (1946) 'Politics and the English language', in *The Collected Essays, Journalism and Letters of George Orwell, Vol. 4, In Front of Your Nose, 1945–50,* (1968), ed. ORWELL, S. and ANGUS, I. Harmondsworth: Penguin.

ROSS, A.S.C. (1954) 'Linguistic class indicators in present-day English', *Neuephilologische Mitteilungen,* Vol. 55.

STRUNK, W. and WHITE, E.B. (1979) *The Elements of Style,* 3rd edn, New York: Macmillan.

THIESMEYER, E.C. and THIESMEYER, J.E. (1990) *Editor: A System for Checking Usage, Mechanics, Vocabulary and Structure, Version 4.0. MLA Software for Students and Scholars,* New York: Modern Language Association.

THE TIMES (1970) *The Times Style Book,* rev. edn, London.

THE TIMES (1992) *The Times English Style and Usage Guide,* London: Times Newspapers.

Source: Cameron, 1995, pp. 28, 64–8

---

# Reading B
# SELLING IN SINGAPORE

*Anthea Fraser Gupta*

Commercial organizations and the government build on common techniques to promote their products or services, and to create an acceptance of government policies in Singapore. They also build on and develop stereotypes and myths of Singapore, its history and its people. The two cartoons examined here appeared in the *Straits Times*, Singapore's leading English language newspaper, in 1995, and portray a similar image of Singapore, manipulating images of ethnic identity, gender and language. The texts cannot be understood without prior access to these stereotypes, which allude to other cartoon and media sources, including those portrayed in comic strips, in textbooks and on television.

Figure 1 shows 'Kampong Days 1965', an advertisement for a shopping mall (Northpoint) in one of Singapore's large government housing estates (Yishun). 'The House-hunters', in Figure 2, is a lavish, full-colour spread, which guides Singaporeans through the complexities of applying for government housing. Eighty-five per cent of Singapore's population were living in housing development board (HDB) flats in 1990 (Lau, 1992b, p. 16): the procedures concern nearly the whole population of Singapore. Although apparently designed by staff from the *Straits Times*, 'The House-hunters' appears to be a public-service announcement: in Singapore the media are regularly used for public-service announcements in this way.

## 'Kampong Days 1965': a commercial advertisement

'Kampong Days 1965' manipulates an icon of Singapore: the kampong. The term *kampong* (from Malay *kampung*, 'village') refers to an area of traditional housing, sometimes but not necessarily rural, where houses were (and in one or two places, are) made of wood and roofed with tin or attap thatch. The mythic landscape is said to have been recreated at a promotion of a shopping mall inside one of the government housing estates that represent modern Singapore.

The advertisement manipulates both the English text and pictures to recreate the mythic past of kampong life – a source of nostalgia. The two main characters of the cartoon text are a stereotypical Chinese and a stereotypical Malay, both middle-aged males. They are ostensibly reflecting on their shared kampong youth, and the most striking feature of their language is the incorporation of many words, mostly of Malay origin, that are seldom used in modern Singapore English, and which refer to games played in the kampong past. Another mythic figure, a nonya (a woman from the ethnic Chinese community of long residence in the Malay peninsula, with distinctive customs of language, dress and culture), is represented in one frame.

Further examination reveals a much more complex text. The time reference is complex. On the one hand, the middle-aged men are supposed to be in present-day Yishun, and they are holding plastic carrier bags; yet they are dressed in a way (the Chinese man in shorts and singlet, the Malay man in sarong and songkok) that is seldom seen in the modern environment, but would have been more common in the adults of the kampong past. Similarly, on the one hand the archaic vocabulary of their English is supposed to recall the past, yet on the other, the Singaporean reader knows that the real kampong children of the past would have been unlikely to talk to each other in English. The magician who appears in the imagined kampong is actually in the present time period – a magic show is advertised below.

The nature of the recreated kampong does not correspond to that of the real kampong that formerly occupied the site of the present shopping mall, nor indeed to any actual kampong of Singapore's past. The promotion that is advertised here includes pictures of the historical kampong, which was a Chinese kampong specializing in pig farming. Most historical kampongs were ethnically homogeneous (Malay or Chinese or Eurasian). However, modern housing estates

Figure 1    'Kampong Days 1965'
(Sunday Times, 17 September 1995)

are (by government policy) ethnically mixed. The imagined kampong reflects the multiracial aspect of the modern Yishun, not the ethnically segregated housing of the historical past. In the picture of the kampong, the humans are identified as multiracial, while the animals portrayed do not include pigs and dogs, which were ubiquitous in Chinese kampongs but absent from Malay kampongs. The animals shown are the racially inoffensive cats, ducks, chickens and a cow. The cow has a European appearance and is historically implausible.

## 'The House-hunters': a public-information advertisement

'The House-hunters' takes the form of a cartoon narrative of a coach trip, with a tour guide who explains to passengers as they move around Singapore the complex rules for applying for flats. In the original advertisement, from which the frames in Figure 2 have been selected, only three frames show scenes exterior to the coach. One frame shows the coach setting off, while an Australian couple (thrown off for being foreigners) watch it depart. The HDB skyline is shown on

*Figure 2*
*Part of ' The House-hunters'*
*(Sunday Times,* 17 September
1995)

the horizon, although the hen in the foreground appears to suggest that we are in a non-HDB area. Another exterior frame shows a stereotypical 'mature estate' while a third portrays a private condominium, to illustrate the future HDB 'executive condominiums'.

The focus of the text, then, is on the passengers in the coach; these visually and linguistically represent Singapore types who fulfil certain of the requirements of HDB buyers. As in 'Kampong Days 1965', care is taken to portray multiracial Singapore, with characters being visually identified for race. In this text, ethnic identity is conveyed mostly by skin colour, with the Chinese (the tour guide and eighteen of the passengers) being portrayed as pink, and the Indians and/or Malays as dark brown. The Australians are portrayed with the same pink skin as the Chinese, but with blond hair. A dark-brown couple is identified as Sikh by means of dress, as the man wears the instantly recognizable turban, while the woman has a pigtail and a puttu on her forehead. There is a hint of her wearing a sari or a dopatta, in the material across her right shoulder. No other characters are identified ethnically by dress, with all other males portrayed in trousers and T-shirts, and all other females (implausibly) in dresses. Although Sikhs (known in Singapore as 'Bengalis') are a small minority among Indians in Singapore (officially only 7 per cent of all ethnic Indians in 1990; Lau, 1992a, p. 57), they

appear in disproportionate numbers in the media, as the turban creates an instant recognition. They also (it must be said) feature in nursery rhymes, as bogeymen, and as figures of fun, as in the following news item:

### British–Bengali Bungle

British health workers carrying out a survey about psychological well-being were puzzled by the results they were getting from the Bengali-speaking population in a London district.

According to New Scientist, all became clear when they realised that they had failed to check the translation into Bengali of the self-administered questionnaire.

The respondents must have been equally confused. 'I'm feeling on edge' became, in translation, 'I'm walking along', 'I'm finding it hard to make contact with people' turned out as 'I don't have a phone and can't write', and 'I feel there is nobody I am close to' became, regrettably, 'All my immediate family are dead.'

Happily, the questionnaire has since been corrected.

(*Straits Times*, 1 June 1994)

Unusually, there is no clear representation of Malays. As eighteen out of the twenty-three coach passengers, the Chinese are represented in a proportion as close as possible to their actual representation in the population (officially 78 per cent in 1990; Lau, 1992a, p. 5). This care over multiethnic representation is characteristic of all governmental materials.

The skin differences between Chinese and Indians/Malays are exaggerated visually in this cartoon, as is usual, with Indians and Malays being portrayed as of darker skin colour than is plausible (notably in the case of a Sikh family, for example), and the Chinese being portrayed as paler than is plausible. Sex roles are clearly demarcated, both by dress and by behaviour. Serious questions are put in the mouths of both males and females, but two Chinese females are shown in the stereotypical role of nagging wife – one demands a 'long-overdue first anniversary diamond ring' and another (not shown here) rebukes her husband for admiring a scantily dressed younger woman. Conversely one Chinese male is shown as obsessed with gambling, and another as lecherous. The only children are fat, greedy boys. These are all intertextual references: they recall familiar stereotypes from other texts (see, for example, the cartoon in Figure 3).

The explication of the HDB rules is given to the tour guide, portrayed with sunglasses and permed hair. Visually, this guide reminds the acculturated reader of the smooth guides and salesmen common in comic strips and in television comedy (for an example see Figure 4). This seems an inappropriately negative stereotype to invoke here, and may be intended to be humorous.

In the speech bubbles of 'The House-hunters', characters generally speak Standard English. All questions and answers relating to the HDB rules are in resolutely formal Standard English. For Chinese male characters, this may be Standard English with one of the pragmatic particles (*ah, lah*) associated with the nonstandard variety usually known as Singlish. Singlish is regularly quoted as an emblem of Singapore (as, for example, in the National Day Issue of the *Straits Times* for 9 August 1994). In 'The House-hunters', two Chinese males are portrayed as speaking only Singlish (although in reality, many speakers switch between Standard English and Singlish; see Gupta, 1994). However, these two characters are given no substantive comments: Singlish is a possibility only for asides, which are intended to lighten the tone of the cartoon, and which also relate to our expectations of a cartoon strip. While his wife asks for information,

Figure 3   A popular stereotype: the Chinese love of gambling

Figure 4   Another familiar stereotype: the tour guide

one man makes a personal response in Singlish (*Wah – not bad: live near parents can get extra money, and also use them as babysitters*). In another couple's interaction, the man again uses Singlish (*But cheap or not?* and *Got one-room only? Don't want to pay so much, lah!*) while the woman uses Standard English for both her substantive remarks and her asides (demanding a diamond ring).

At other points English is manipulated to invoke a foreign national identity. As the coach leaves the Australian foreigners behind, its passengers are shown calling the stereotypically Australian *G'day mate*. As in the case of the Sikh family, it would appear that Australians have been chosen because of the possibility of linguistic satire of this type.

Like 'Kampong Days 1965', 'The House-hunters' is a self-conscious portrayal of multiracial Singapore. A striking omission from the content is any reference to the racial policy of HDB allocation, which aims to keep blocks, sections of estates and whole estates racially mixed within a fixed proportion. This has been the subject of much discussion (Ooi et al., 1993; Tremewan, 1994) and is seen by many as discriminating against the minorities, who have a need to congregate in order to have sufficient numbers for ethnically based cultural events. The majority Chinese will always have such numbers.

## Advertising techniques

The fostering of consent to government policies and the conscious creation of an ideology for Singapore has long been a major concern of the Singapore government (Tremewan, 1994, p. 2f.; Chua, 1995). The primary aim of 'The House-hunters' is to inform readers of the rules and to convince them that these rules are beneficial. A secondary aim is to portray a harmonious multiracial Singapore. 'Kampong Days 1965' is attempting to persuade readers to visit a shopping mall. In both texts the use of an informal format encourages readers to read the text, which looks attractive and raises expectations of humour. Both texts use elements from Singlish, a Singapore identity marker. However, in both cases the conversationalization turns out to be superficial: Standard English remains the vehicle for the substantive content. Gender roles are clearly distinguished, with men being more central than women. Both texts choose characters with care to convey the impression of a multiracial Singapore, and use icons of skin colour and of dress that exaggerate ethnic stereotypes to allow for instant recognition. They are operating in the same mythic Singapore. In the real Singapore, sex roles are less clearly defined, dresses are not the sole (or even the principal) dress style for women, and the colour difference between Chinese and non-Chinese is not so sharp. The mythic Singapore has been created partly from the official ideology of a multiracial Singapore, where men are the head of household, and partly from popular cartoons published in both Singapore and Malaysia, which build on stereotypes and strengthen them.

Although the public-service advertisement would appear to be using many of the norms of advertising, it could be said that the government strategies have also influenced the commercial advertisement. The portrayal of multicultural Singapore is conscious and obligatory in government publications, but commercial advertisers are at liberty to represent whatever individuals they wish. However, the minorities are sensitive to their own visual absence and are likely to react negatively to advertisements in which they do not appear. This advertiser is building on government documents in its consciously multiracial portrayal. The influence is not in one direction only.

## Acknowledgement

I would like to thank my English as a World Language class (1995) for their full discussion of this text, and especially the following, who contributed important points: Imelda Chang; Caroline Ching; Feisal Abdul Rahman; Harn Siow Ping; Patricia Ho; Dinah Ong; and Laura Yzelman.

## References

CHUA, BENG-HUAT (1995) *Communication Ideology and Democracy in Singapore*, London, Routledge.

GUPTA, A.F. (1994) *The Step-Tongue: children's English in Singapore*, Clevedon, Multilingual Matters.

LAU KAK EN (1992a) *Singapore Census of Population 1990*, Statistical Release 1, *Demographic Characteristics*, Singapore, Department of Statistics.

LAU KAK EN (1992b) *Singapore Census of Population 1990*, Statistical Release 2, *Households and Housing*, Singapore, Department of Statistics.

OOI GIOK LING, SIDDIQUE, S. and CHENG, S.K. (1993) *The Management of Ethnic Relations in Public Housing Estates*, Singapore, Institute of Policy Studies/Times Academic.

TREMEWAN, C. (1994) *The Political Economy of Social Control in Singapore*, Basingstoke/London, St Martin's.

This reading was specially commissioned for this book.

---

## Reading C
## THE MARKETIZATION OF PUBLIC DISCOURSE: THE UNIVERSITIES

*Norman Fairclough*

[This paper] is a text-based examination of the marketization of discursive practices as a process which is pervasively transforming public discourse in contemporary Britain, with particular reference to higher education ...

The case I shall focus upon is the marketization of discursive practices in contemporary British universities ... by which I mean the restructuring of the order of discourse on the model of more central market organizations. It may on the face of it appear to be unduly introspective for an academic to analyse universities as an example of marketization, but I do not believe it is; recent changes affecting higher education are a typical case and rather a good example of processes of marketization and commodification in the public sector more generally.

The marketization of the discursive practices of universities is one dimension of the marketization of higher education in a more general sense. Institutions of higher education come increasingly to operate (under government pressure) as if they were ordinary businesses competing to sell their products to consumers ...

In what follows I wish to take up the discussion of 'promotional' culture ... I suggest that the discursive practices (order of discourse) of higher education are in the process of being transformed through the increasing salience within higher education of promotion as a communicative function ...

The ... example I want to look at specifically in terms of promotion – and more exactly self-promotion – is an extract from a curriculum vitae (CV). Such data are sensitive for obvious reasons, and I have therefore used an extract from a CV I prepared myself in 1991 for an academic promotions committee. The form of submissions to this committee is controlled by procedural rules which specify the maximum length of a CV and the categories of information it should contain, and require a 'supporting statement' of no more than 'two sides of A4 paper'. The extract I have chosen is a paragraph from the supporting statement. Unlike the CV proper, the content of the supporting statement is not specified in the procedural rules. I had to make informal enquiries to find out what was expected. I was able to look at previous submissions by colleagues, and I received advice from a colleague with experience of the committee. From these sources, I gathered that the supporting statement had to be a compelling account of one's contribution to, if possible, all of the categories of activity in two overlapping schemes of categorization: to research, teaching and administration; and to the department, the university, and the wider community (these categorization schemes are actually spelt out in the procedural rules, though not specifically with reference to the supporting statement). The advice I received was that one had to 'sell' oneself to stand any chance of success. The following extract from an internal memorandum, produced shortly after I had prepared the submission, gives a sense of the prevailing wisdom at the time:

> To succeed, departments have to 'sell' their candidates. One cannot expect merit to gleam with its own halo; the halo has been assiduously polished up! Put differently, this means that one has to hone one's application to give an impression of all-round excellence, preferably over a period of time, with feedback from others.

This easily extends to an emphasis on the need for extended preparation for the well-honed application – for instance, it is helpful to have favourable student feedback on one's courses, ideally over several years. One's future promotability may become a significant factor in the planning of one's current activities. Here is the extract:

### Contributions to the Department

I have I believe played a significant role in the academic and adminis-trative leadership of the Department over the past eight years or so. I was Head of Department from 1984 to 1987 and again for one term in 1990, and I have carried a range of other responsibilities including MA and undergraduate programme coordination and admissions. I helped to set up and now help to run the Centre for Language in Social Life. Through my coordination of the Language, Ideology and Power research group and in other activities, I have stimulated research (e.g. on critical lan-guage awareness) among colleagues and postgraduate students, and helped form what is now being recognized nationally and internationally as a distinctive Lancaster position on and contribution to study of language and language problems in contemporary British society. I am currently helping to edit a collection of Centre for Language in Social Life papers for publication.

Some of the self-promotional properties of the extract are obvious enough. There is a series of claims realized as clauses with past tense, present perfective and present continuous verbs and *I* as subject and theme. These are mainly claims which are categorical in their modality, positive assertions without explicit modalizing elements, though there is a subjective modality marker in the first clause (*I believe*) which (a) foregrounds the subjective basis of judgement in the whole paragraph in that the first clause is a summary formulation of the paragraph, but also (b) foregrounds (one might say rather brazenly) the self-promotional nature of the activity. (For the analytical terminology used here see Halliday, 1985, and Fairclough, 1992.) Except for one relational process (*I was Head of Department*), all clauses in the extract contain action processes. It would seem that material actional process verbs are consistently being selected even where other process types would be just as congruent with or more congruent with the happenings and relationships reported – for instance, although I am indeed one of the five co-directors of the Centre for Language in Social Life, it receives practically no 'running' from anyone, and I might well (indeed better) have worded this *am now an active member of*. Similarly *played a significant role in* might have been *been a significant part of*, *carried a range of other responsibilities* might have been *had a range of other responsibilities*, *helped to set up* might have been *was a founding member of*, and so forth. These changes would, I think, reduce the sense of dynamic activity conveyed in the extract. A noteworthy lexical choice is *leadership* in the first sentence. The wording of academic relationships in terms of *leadership* belongs, in my view, to a managerial discourse which has come to colonize the academic order of discourse recently, and which I actually find deeply antipathetic. In terms of the characteristics of promotional discourse discussed earlier, the extract is very much a signification/construction of its subject/object rather than just referentially based description, and meaning would seem to be subordinated to effect.

I suppose I saw the preparation of the submission as a rhetorical exercise. By which I mean that I was consciously using language in a way I dislike, playing with and parodying an alien discourse, in order to 'play the game' and convince the committee of my merits. That is rather a comforting account of events, and a common enough one; the self stands outside or behind at least some forms of discursive practice, simply assuming them for strategic effects. I felt embarrassed about the submission, but that is, I think, compatible with the rhetorical account. There are, however, problems with this account. In the first place, it assumes a greater consciousness of and control over one's practice than is actually likely to be the case. For instance, while I was quite conscious of what was at stake in using *leadership*, I was not aware at the time of how systematically I was 'converting' all processes to actions, although I *could* have been (and perhaps I ought to have been) – unlike most people I have the analytical apparatus. More seriously, the rhetorical account underestimates the incorporative capacity of institutional logics and procedures. Whereas the average academic rarely has contact with promotions committees, contact with other organizational forms whose procedures are based upon the same logics are necessary and constant. Doing one's job entails 'playing the game' (or various connected games), and what may feel like a mere rhetoric to get things done quickly and easily becomes a part of one's professional identity. Self-promotion is perhaps becoming a routine, naturalized strand of various academic activities, and of academic identities.

# References

FAIRCLOUGH, N. (1992) *Discourse and Social Change,* Cambridge, Polity.

HALLIDAY, M. (1985) *An Introduction to Functional Grammar,* London, Edward Arnold.

Source: Fairclough, 1993, pp. 133, 143, 151–3.

# 5 GLOBAL ENGLISH, GLOBAL CULTURE?

*David Graddol*

## 5.1 INTRODUCTION

The English language seems set to take over the world in the course of the twenty-first century, and become *the* global language. A press release from the British Council (a governmental agency responsible for supporting British cultural activities around the world) suggested in the mid 1990s that:

> World-wide, there are over 1,400 million people living in countries where English has official status. One out of five of the world's population speak English to some level of competence. Demand from the other four-fifths is increasing ... By the year 2000 it is estimated that over one billion people will be learning English. English is the main language of books, newspapers, airports and air-traffic control, international business and academic conferences, science, technology, diplomacy, sport, international competitions, pop music and advertising.
>
> (British Council, English 2000 press release, 23 March 1995)

How did English come to be such a dominant world language? Umberto Eco, an Italian novelist and cultural theorist, has summarized the explanations usually given in the following way:

> The predominant position currently enjoyed by English is a historical contingency arising from the mercantile and colonial expansion of the British Empire, which was followed by American economic and technological hegemony. Of course, it may also be maintained that English has succeeded because it is rich in monosyllables, capable of absorbing foreign words and flexible in forming neologisms, etc.; yet had Hitler won World War II and had the USA been reduced to a confederation of banana republics, we would probably today use German as a universal vehicular language, and Japanese electronics firms would advertise their products in Hong Kong airport duty-free shops (*Zollfreie Waren*) in German.
>
> (Eco, 1995, p. 331)

The growing world supremacy of the English language is clearly seen as a positive process by the British Council, although they could be said to represent native-speaker vested interests. It does seem to be true, however, that very many people who do not speak English as a first language see English as a language of economic opportunity, one that will help improve both their individual position and, because of the importance of English in international trade and technological research, their countries' economies.

There are, of course, less positive ways of viewing what seems to be the inexorable spread of a single language across the globe. Some people say it is implicated in a major human disaster, involving the destruction of linguistic and cultural diversity on a scale far larger than the parallel ecological destruction of biodiversity. English is, according to such views, a language of economic opportunity only for a few: for the rest it creates a new, global mechanism for structuring inequality both between 'the west' and 'the rest' and within the populations of nonwestern countries.

In this chapter I explore some of these ideas critically, and examine a variety of at times contradictory views and experiences of English as a global language. One of the main themes of the chapter is that the global spread of English has complex roots and is not a simple and unstoppable process that will lead ultimately to a single, homogeneous global culture. I draw attention, for example, to some of the ways in which the spread of English creates difference, as well as similarity, creates fragmentation as well as uniformity.

This chapter argues that although colonization was responsible for the first stages of the spread of English, and provided a basis for its further global development, in the twentieth century new forces and processes came into play. Technological developments, economic globalization and improved communications have all played a role in the new global flows of English. And with these new flows have emerged a changing pattern of identities and social relations – on both an individual level and on a global scale:

> The impetus and support for such diffusion [of English] no doubt came from the extended period of colonization … After all, the sun never set on the British Empire, and the English language was naturally basking in that global sunshine. Once English was adopted in a region, whether for science, technology, literature, prestige, elitism or 'modernization,' it went through a reincarnation which was partly linguistic and partly cultural. It was essentially caused by the new bilingual (or multilingual) setting, and by the new context in which English had to function.
>
> (Kachru (ed.), 1983, pp. 5–6)

Later, in the same volume, Kachru adds: 'For the first time a natural language has attained the status of an international (universal) language, essentially for cross-cultural communication. Whatever the reasons for the earlier spread of English, we should now consider it a positive development in the twentieth-century world context' (Kachru (ed.), 1983, p. 51).

The chapter brings together many of the strands of argument that have appeared in earlier chapters in this volume, and sets them in a longer history of global economic and technological development. I explore the new mechanisms that promote the diffusion and use of English worldwide, and examine the extent to which the positive attitudes of the British Council, Kachru and others can be justified.

## 5.2   THE UTOPIAN DREAM AND THE GLOBAL RISE OF ENGLISH

The dream of a shared world language, which could act as a neutral vehicle of communication between peoples of different nationalities and interests, which could serve the purposes of diplomacy and commerce and provide a rational and logical vehicle for science, has been a western dream since the European Renaissance. This was the period when scholars began to understand the social world as being shaped by people rather than some divine power, and that human destiny could therefore be controlled and brought to perfection. Ideal and rational forms of social institution and government were discussed and created. The beginnings were put in place of a European sociopolitical structure that was not to achieve full maturity until the nineteenth century. In particular there arose the idea that territory should be divided up into autonomous countries, each with a designated language which would be symbolic of a unified national identity.

These 'national' languages, which could serve as foci for national identity and provide the resources for the construction of national cultures and government, had to be created. What existed at that time was a diversity of spoken languages

The first book in this series, *English: history, diversity and change* (Graddol et al. (eds), 1996), discusses this period in the history of English in greater detail.

none of which provided necessary genres and discourses for government and administration, for literature or science. The English language was, during the sixteenth and seventeenth centuries, expanded and developed, raised from vernacular status to a vehicle for literature, science and government. During the eighteenth century (the period sometimes referred to as 'the Enlightenment') the English language received its major instruments of regulation and documentation, including Samuel Johnson's *Dictionary.*

These various processes of redesign and regulation of language for national purposes are embraced by the term 'standardization'. The creation of national languages was a method of managing the linguistic diversity (particularly dialectal but in some cases also including distinct languages) which fitted the ideas of the times, through the creation of regulated and reasonably uniform, high-status language varieties which could be used as internal lingua francas within countries. It gave rise to a new problem, however: that of effective communication *between* the peoples in the new Europe.

At the beginning of the Renaissance, there existed two transnational (insofar as we can talk of transnationality at that time) lingua francas in Europe. The first was the Latin language, which – although spoken by no one as a first language – served as an effective lingua franca for elite groups. The second lingua franca was Sabir, a pidgin based on southern Romance languages, and used for trade between Europeans, Turks, Arabs, and others in the Levant. Sabir is the oldest documented pidgin based on European languages and emerged at the time of the crusades (between the eleventh and thirteenth centuries).

Largely as a consequence of national language development, knowledge and use of Latin declined. Latin thus acquired a dual function: it permitted communication between elite groups in different European countries, but it also increasingly served as a 'secret language', which created barriers of access to knowledge by the unlearned. Of all the professional groups in the seventeenth century, the medical profession was perhaps the most notorious for its deliberate refusal to conduct transactions in the national language in order to prevent knowledge falling into the hands of ordinary people. The role of Latin in permitting the creation of elite social groups who have access to privilege and power and who can communicate with each other over national borders provides an informative precedent. In the world today, the English language can be seen to serve a similar function.

The European modernizers of the seventeenth century recognized a new need for an international language that could replace Latin. Not only was the use of Latin declining, it was also increasingly unsuitable for dealing with the new domains of knowledge and new forms of international transaction. A number of scholars proposed that an **artificial language** be created: one that was capable of representing the new ideas and concepts generated by scientific enquiry and that could be employed as a **universal language**. Britain was the main location for such work, partly – ironically – because it was thought that modern English would be a marginal European language of little use beyond the shores of Britain. The titles of these seventeenth-century British philosophical works demonstrate something of the idealism and aspirations of the age: Francis Lodwick's *The Groundwork or Foundation (or so Intended) for the Framing of a New Perfect Language and a Universal Common Writing,* 1652, or John Wilkins's *An Essay towards a Real Character, and a Philosophical Language,* 1668.

Interest in the idea of an international language slackened in the eighteenth century because French emerged as an international language that linked both scholars and diplomats. An eighteenth-century landowner in the south of England wrote to his son:

The first book in this series, *English: history, diversity and change* (Graddol et al. (eds), 1996), discusses the nature of pidgins and the processes of standardization in more depth.

A man who understands French may travel all the World over without hesitation of making himself understood, and may make himself perfectly agreeable to all Good Company, which is not the case of any other Language whatever.

(Cited in Large, 1985, p. 44)

By the end of the eighteenth century, however, ideas were being put forward by French scholars for a simplified form of French which could be more easily learned by speakers of other languages. Thus arose the idea that an international lingua franca did not have to be a completely new invention (such as John Wilkins's *Real Character*), but could be created by simplifying and rationalizing an existing language.

However, several hundred artificial languages were also devised in the period from 1850 to World War Two, including some, like Esperanto, whose supporters continue to speak the language today. Such artificial languages were often referred to as **auxiliary languages** in order to make it clear that they were not expected to replace any natural language or to become the property of any one nation. The reasons for this rapid growth in the auxiliary language movement are complex. In retrospect, we can see that this period represented an important shift in the relationships of nation states, which arose as a result of a combination of factors: increasing industrialization and a consequent increase in international trade; the development of communications technology (such as the telegraph, first patented in England in 1837); the expansion of European colonial territories (particularly in Asia and Africa); and increasing armed conflict (made more disastrous by improved technologies of war) between European nation states both within Europe and in colonial theatres of war. These developments gave rise to a natural anxiety about international stability at a time when industrialization had created a necessity for international trade.

You might imagine that the invention of artificial languages was a kind of idle professional activity akin to 'fantasy football' (in which football fans imagine their 'dream team') or that of model railway enthusiasts who design but never build their ideal layout. The artificial languages that were created were, however, by no means all the work of eccentrics. The nineteenth century was the period in which linguistics became recognized as one of the new sciences and acquired a confidence in its methods and understanding of human language. The drive to create and implement an auxiliary language was regarded by some linguists as a professional responsibility to help solve one of the pressing social and political problems of their age. Jespersen, for example, the inventor of Novial, was a well-respected Danish linguist (1860–1943) who published a number of grammars and other works on the English language.

The most ironic point about the international auxiliary language (IAL) movement, however, is that so many languages were invented – a veritable artificial Tower of Babel was created. Not only did several of the languages find themselves in competition with each other, but many languages proved to be unstable in form – under constant development and 'improvement' (like modern computer software, a new version would be released before users had quite mastered the preceding one). Furthermore, the individual language movements typically depended on a charismatic leader and consequently the language died when he died – or else stultifying arguments and schisms developed over the succession.

With hindsight, we might regard the whole idea as being in many ways naive. At the very least, it was an essentially European project, though one intended to be usable beyond Europe. It arose from the European experience of nation-state creation and was encouraged by the knowledge that most European languages had evolved from a common ancestral language. Indeed, many of the created languages attempt to identify a common denominator among natural languages in terms of grammatical and lexical structure. 'It is the European root material, its elements, and its grammatical structure which provide the language builder with the basis for a precise, a simple, and an economic language' (Jacob, 1947, p. 21).

What lay behind this explosion of interest in what might be called 'bricolage' languages (made up from bits and pieces of existing languages) was an unspoken recognition of a fundamental rivalry between English and French. French, during the eighteenth and much of the nineteenth centuries, was without doubt the main language of diplomacy and international commerce. Not until World War Two did businesses in Britain give up the habit of employing French native speakers to correspond with clients in other countries. But by the second half of the nineteenth century, English was clearly challenging French as an international language – not least because of the increased trade that resulted from Britain's major role during the industrial revolution, and the consolidation of the British empire which created a major world trading network administered through English.

The international auxiliary language movement recognized a need for an international lingua franca that did not economically or culturally privilege one country. The language was to be a utilitarian, rational language, sufficient only for the communication of ideas. It was recognized that such languages, unlike national languages, were not a suitable medium for great works of literature, but that was to be regarded as one of their strengths: an auxiliary language should not be used as a vehicle for cultural values. It should never become threatening to any national language. The growing influence of English was thus a cause of concern for some. Particularly after World War One, it was thought to represent too much of a threat to other major European languages – not only French but also German – ever to become fully accepted. Rather than help prevent armed conflict through the spread of international cooperation and understanding, it might actually aggravate rivalries between European nations. In 1921, in the aftermath of World War One, the British Association published a report on the question of an auxiliary language, intended as a contribution to a major debate on the problem by the League of Nations. The British Association concluded that 'The adoption of any modern national language would confer undue advantages and excite jealousy ... [t]herefore an invented language is best' (cited in Jacob, 1947, p. 27).

The auxiliary language movement was largely abandoned because the English language became, de facto, the international lingua franca. Indeed, the designers of artificial languages began to recognize the pre-eminent position of English. Although one of the first artificial languages of the nineteenth century (Volapük) was ostensibly based on English (the fact that its name meant 'World Speak' demonstrates how untransparent that basis was), the majority of proposals were based on Romance vocabulary and morphology – perhaps a reminiscence of the role of Latin, or else the recent dominance of French in international relations. Gradually there appears to have been a shift towards English-based languages. Finally, in the 1920s emerged various plans for modifying English itself: for creating a simpler, more logical form of English which could be easily learned, serve as a lingua franca for basic communication, yet not overtly act as a carrier for British or American culture. Hence a movement that began with proposals for a simplified French, and then gave rise to scores of artificial languages that had mixed roots, ended with suggestions for simplified English (see the box overleaf).

---

**Some artificial languages**

Volapük (World Speak) (Schleyer), 1879
Esperanto (Zamenhof), 1887
Ido (a revised Esperanto) (de Beaufort or Couturat), 1907
Novial (Jespersen), 1928
Interglossa (Hogben), 1943
Tutonish or Anglo-German union tongue (Molee, Chicago), 1902
Anglo-Franca (Hoinix, London), 1889

**Some reduced Englishes**

Simplified English (Startschewsky, St Petersburg), 1889
World English (Brandley, Washington), 1910
World English (Hamilton, St Pauls, USA), 1924
Anglic (Zachrisson), 1930
Basic English (Ogden), 1920s/1930s
Nuclear English (Quirk), 1981

---

## C.K. Ogden's Basic English

I want to look more closely at one of the last such proposals: **Basic English** created by C.K. Ogden in the late 1920s (see Ogden, 1932), and popularized in the 1930s and 1940s. This case study illustrates issues involved in both the implementation of an artificial language and the use of an existing natural language as an international lingua franca. Basic English is also worth examining not as an example of failure (which, as an auxiliary language it ultimately was) but because of how influential it became in other ways. The linguistic analysis on which it was based, for example, was closely linked to the development of systemic-functional linguistics and the framework of analysis of which Michael Halliday is probably now the best-known exponent. Furthermore, the idea of creating a specialized subset of English as a limited medium of international communication has, to some extent, been achieved through the restricted report-and-control language of 'Airspeak' (used for air traffic control) or 'Seaspeak' (used in maritime navigation). Lastly, linguists have never quite abandoned one of the ideas behind Basic English – is it possible to define a set of 'core' vocabulary and grammatical structures which could be learned easily and serve as a basis for international communication? Indeed, has such an international English already emerged as a natural consequence of the increasing use of English as a medium of communication between speakers of different languages?

Chapter 2 of this book discusses Halliday's ideas in greater detail.

Basic English was motivated by both a social idealism and linguistic curiosity. I.A. Richards, one of the main popularizers and supporters of Basic English, wrote in an introduction to the language:

> Let us be clear about some political essentials from the outset. However desirable a common language for all the world may be, as a means of communication between peoples who in their homes speak different tongues, it neither can nor should be imposed by one nation or group of nations upon others. It must come into use freely, as a general convenience, under the urge of the everyday motives of mankind. It must be taken up because men see it to be useful to them – too useful to be neglected. It must serve, and serve immediately, their economic, cultural and social needs. It must give them, right away from the start, a reward in increased possibilities and power. It must spread as the automobile, the electric light, and the telephone or airplane have spread. Only so can it

get behind it the drive required to carry through such a gigantic stride toward increased rationality in human affairs.

Secondly, it must be clear from any threat to the economic, moral, cultural, social, or political status or independence of any persons or any people. It must carry no implications of intellectual, technological, or other domination. No one in learning the world language must have excuse for even the least shadow of a feeling that he is submitting to an alien influence or being brought under the power of other groups.

(Richards, 1943, p. 9)

However, there was from the beginning an ambiguity in the Basic English project: was it really intended as a neutral lingua franca or merely a means of promoting the position of natural English in the world? Many of the ardent supporters of Basic seemed a little confused on this issue. H.G. Wells, for example, the author of both science fiction (such as *The Time Machine*) and idealist social commentaries (such as *The Work, Wealth and Happiness of Mankind*) published a Utopian fictional history of the world, as written in the twenty-second century (*The Shape of Things to Come*), in which he foresaw a triumphant future for Basic:

One of the unanticipated achievements of the twenty-first century was the rapid diffusion of Basic English as the lingua franca of the world and the even more rapid modification, expansion and spread of English in its wake … This convenience spread like wildfire after the First Conference of Basra. It was made the official medium of communication throughout the world by the Air and Sea Control, and by 2020 there was hardly anyone in the world who could not talk and understand it.

(Wells, 1933, pp. 418, 419)

Basic English was a remarkable linguistic project, based on over a decade's careful analysis of the English language. Its central idea was the identification of a limited vocabulary, of only 850 words, which could be used to express:

anything needed for the general purposes of everyday existence – in business, trade, industry, science, medical work – in all the arts of living, in all the exchanges of knowledge, desires, beliefs, opinions, and news which are the chief work of a language.

(Richards, 1943, p. 20)

One of the principles for reducing the vocabulary of English was the eradication of all emotive words.

When we use an emotive word we allow attitudes and subjective judgments about the referent to form part of our reference. Economy is achieved by symbolizing the referent and our attitude to it separately. For instance, if we have the word *opinion* we do not need such words as *conceit, modesty, diffidence*, all of which symbolize a high or low opinion of oneself *plus* the speaker's mental attitude. A mother who commends her child for its *modesty* is 'pleased that the child has not a very high opinion of itself', and one who chides her child for its *diffidence* is '*not* pleased that the child has not a very high opinion of itself.'

(Catford, 1950, p. 43)

By a similar principle, words with literary associations, such as *steed* and *casement*, would be abandoned in favour of straightforward words like *horse* and *window*. By these various means English was to be stripped of its cultural values and made into a transparent vehicle for communication. The main linguistic peculiarity of Basic, apart from the restricted vocabulary, lay in the use of verbs. Ogden identified just sixteen verb forms which were to serve for all communicative purposes. The entire language could thus be listed on a postcard (see Figure 5.1).

# BASIC ENGLISH WORD LIST

| OPERATIONS 100 | THINGS 400 General | | | | THINGS 200 Picturable | | QUALITIES 100 General | QUALITIES 50 Opposites |
|---|---|---|---|---|---|---|---|---|
| COME | ACCOUNT | EDUCATION | METAL | SENSE | ANGLE | KNEE | ABLE | AWAKE |
| GET | ACT | EFFECT | MIDDLE | SERVANT | ANT | KNIFE | ACID | BAD |
| GIVE | ADDITION | END | MILK | SEX | APPLE | KNOT | ANGRY | BENT |
| GO | ADJUSTMENT | ERROR | MIND | SHADE | ARCH | LEAF | AUTOMATIC | BITTER |
| KEEP | ADVERTISEMENT | EVENT | MINE | SHAKE | ARM | LEG | BEAUTIFUL | BLUE |
| LET | AGREEMENT | EXAMPLE | MINUTE | SHAME | ARMY | LIBRARY | BLACK | CERTAIN |
| MAKE | AIR | EXCHANGE | MIST | SHOCK | BABY | LINE | BOILING | COLD |
| PUT | AMOUNT | EXISTENCE | MONEY | SIDE | BAG | LIP | BRIGHT | COMPLETE |
| SEEM | AMUSEMENT | EXPANSION | MONTH | SIGN | BALL | LOCK | BROKEN | CRUEL |
| TAKE | ANIMAL | EXPERIENCE | MORNING | SILK | BAND | MAP | BROWN | DARK |
| BE | ANSWER | EXPERT | MOTHER | SILVER | BASIN | MATCH | CHEAP | DEAD |
| DO | APPARATUS | FACT | MOTION | SISTER | BASKET | MONKEY | CHEMICAL | DEAR |
| HAVE | APPROVAL | FALL | MOUNTAIN | SIZE | BATH | MOON | CHIEF | DELICATE |
| SAY | ARGUMENT | FAMILY | MOVE | SKY | BED | MOUTH | CLEAN | DIFFERENT |
| SEE | ART | FATHER | MUSIC | SLEEP | BEE | MUSCLE | CLEAR | DIRTY |
| SEND | ATTACK | FEAR | NAME | SLIP | BELL | NAIL | COMMON | DRY |
| MAY | ATTEMPT | FEELING | NATION | SLOPE | BERRY | NECK | COMPLEX | FALSE |
| WILL | ATTENTION | FICTION | NEED | SMASH | BIRD | NEEDLE | CONSCIOUS | FEEBLE |
| ABOUT | ATTRACTION | FIELD | NEWS | SMELL | BLADE | NERVE | CUT | FEMALE |
| ACROSS | AUTHORITY | FIGHT | NIGHT | SMILE | BOARD | NET | DEEP | FOOLISH |
| AFTER | BACK | FIRE | NOISE | SMOKE | BOAT | NOSE | DEPENDENT | FUTURE |
| AGAINST | BALANCE | FLAME | NOTE | SNEEZE | BONE | NUT | EARLY | GREEN |
| AMONG | BASE | FLIGHT | NUMBER | SNOW | BOOK | OFFICE | ELASTIC | ILL |
| AT | BEHAVIOR | FLOWER | OBSERVATION | SOAP | BOOT | ORANGE | ELECTRIC | LAST |
| BEFORE | BELIEF | FOLD | OFFER | SOCIETY | BOTTLE | OVEN | EQUAL | LATE |
| BETWEEN | BIRTH | FOOD | OIL | SON | BOX | PARCEL | FAT | LEFT |
| BY | BIT | FORCE | OPERATION | SONG | BOY | PEN | FERTILE | LOOSE |
| DOWN | BITE | FORM | OPINION | SORT | BRAIN | PENCIL | FIRST | LOUD |
| FROM | BLOOD | FRIEND | ORDER | SOUND | BRAKE | PICTURE | FIXED | LOW |
| IN | BLOW | FRONT | ORGANIZATION | SOUP | BRANCH | PIG | FLAT | MIXED |
| OFF | BODY | FRUIT | ORNAMENT | SPACE | BRICK | PIN | FREE | NARROW |
| ON | BRASS | GLASS | OWNER | STAGE | BRIDGE | PIPE | FREQUENT | OLD |
| OVER | BREAD | GOLD | PAGE | START | BRUSH | PLANE | FULL | OPPOSITE |
| THROUGH | BREATH | GOVERNMENT | PAIN | STATEMENT | BUCKET | PLATE | GENERAL | PUBLIC |
| TO | BROTHER | GRAIN | PAINT | STEAM | BULB | PLOUGH | GOOD | ROUGH |
| UNDER | BUILDING | GRASS | PAPER | STEEL | BUTTON | POCKET | GREAT | SAD |
| UP | BURN | GRIP | PART | STEP | CAKE | POT | GREY | SAFE |
| WITH | BURST | GROUP | PASTE | STITCH | CAMERA | POTATO | HANGING | SECRET |
| AS | BUSINESS | GROWTH | PAYMENT | STONE | CARD | PRISON | HAPPY | SHORT |
| FOR | BUTTER | GUIDE | PEACE | STOP | CART | PUMP | HARD | SHUT |
| OF | CANVAS | HARBOR | PERSON | STORY | CARRIAGE | RAIL | HEALTHY | SIMPLE |
| TILL | CARE | HARMONY | PLACE | STRETCH | CAT | RAT | HIGH | SLOW |
| THAN | CAUSE | HATE | PLANT | STRUCTURE | CHAIN | RECEIPT | HOLLOW | SMALL |
| A | CHALK | HEARING | PLAY | SUBSTANCE | CHEESE | RING | IMPORTANT | SOFT |
| THE | CHANCE | HEAT | PLEASURE | SUGAR | CHEST | ROD | KIND | SOLID |
| ALL | CHANGE | HELP | POINT | SUGGESTION | CHIN | ROOF | LIKE | SPECIAL |
| ANY | CLOTH | HISTORY | POISON | SUMMER | CHURCH | ROOT | LIVING | STRANGE |
| EVERY | COAL | HOLE | POLISH | SUPPORT | CIRCLE | SAIL | LONG | THIN |
| NO | COLOR | HOPE | PORTER | SURPRISE | CLOCK | SCHOOL | MALE | WHITE |
| OTHER | COMFORT | HOUR | POSITION | SWIM | CLOUD | SCISSORS | MARRIED | WRONG |
| SOME | COMMITTEE | HUMOR | POWDER | SYSTEM | COAT | SCREW | MATERIAL | |
| SUCH | COMPANY | ICE | POWER | TALK | COLLAR | SEED | MEDICAL | |
| THAT | COMPARISON | IDEA | PRICE | TASTE | COMB | SHEEP | MILITARY | |
| THIS | COMPETITION | IMPULSE | PRINT | TAX | CORD | SHELF | NATURAL | |
| I | CONDITION | INCREASE | PROCESS | TEACHING | COW | SHIP | NECESSARY | |
| HE | CONNECTION | INDUSTRY | PRODUCE | TENDENCY | CUP | SHIRT | NEW | |
| YOU | CONTROL | INK | PROFIT | TEST | CURTAIN | SHOE | NORMAL | |
| WHO | COOK | INSECT | PROPERTY | THEORY | CUSHION | SKIN | OPEN | |
| AND | COPPER | INSTRUMENT | PROSE | THING | DOG | SKIRT | PARALLEL | |
| BECAUSE | COPY | INSURANCE | PROTEST | THOUGHT | DOOR | SNAKE | PAST | |
| BUT | CORK | INTEREST | PULL | THUNDER | DRAIN | SOCK | PHYSICAL | |
| OR | COTTON | INVENTION | PUNISHMENT | TIME | DRAWER | SPADE | POLITICAL | |
| IF | COUGH | IRON | PURPOSE | TIN | DRESS | SPONGE | POOR | |
| THOUGH | COUNTRY | JELLY | PUSH | TOP | DROP | SPOON | POSSIBLE | |
| WHILE | COVER | JOIN | QUALITY | TOUCH | EAR | SPRING | PRESENT | |
| HOW | CRACK | JOURNEY | QUESTION | TRADE | EGG | SQUARE | PRIVATE | |
| WHEN | CREDIT | JUDGE | RAIN | TRANSPORT | ENGINE | STAMP | PROBABLE | |
| WHERE | CRIME | JUMP | RANGE | TRICK | EYE | STAR | QUICK | |
| WHY | CRUSH | KICK | RATE | TROUBLE | FACE | STATION | QUIET | |
| AGAIN | CRY | KISS | RAY | TURN | FARM | STEM | READY | |
| EVER | CURRENT | KNOWLEDGE | REACTION | TWIST | FEATHER | STICK | RED | |
| FAR | CURVE | LAND | READING | UNIT | FINGER | STOCKING | REGULAR | |
| FORWARD | DAMAGE | LANGUAGE | REASON | USE | FISH | STOMACH | RESPONSIBLE | |
| HERE | DANGER | LAUGH | RECORD | VALUE | FLAG | STORE | RIGHT | |
| NEAR | DAUGHTER | LAW | REGRET | VERSE | FLOOR | STREET | ROUND | |
| NOW | DAY | LEAD | RELATION | VESSEL | FLY | SUN | SAME | |
| OUT | DEATH | LEARNING | RELIGION | VIEW | FOOT | TABLE | SECOND | |
| STILL | DEBT | LEATHER | REPRESENTATIVE | VOICE | FORK | TAIL | SEPARATE | |
| THEN | DECISION | LETTER | REQUEST | WALK | FOWL | THREAD | SERIOUS | |
| THERE | DEGREE | LEVEL | RESPECT | WAR | FRAME | THROAT | SHARP | |
| TOGETHER | DESIGN | LIFT | REST | WASH | GARDEN | THUMB | SMOOTH | |
| WELL | DESIRE | LIGHT | REWARD | WASTE | GIRL | TICKET | STICKY | |
| ALMOST | DESTRUCTION | LIMIT | RHYTHM | WATER | GLOVE | TOE | STIFF | |
| ENOUGH | DETAIL | LINEN | RICE | WAVE | GOAT | TONGUE | STRAIGHT | |
| EVEN | DEVELOPMENT | LIQUID | RIVER | WAX | GUN | TOOTH | STRONG | |
| LITTLE | DIGESTION | LIST | ROAD | WAY | HAIR | TOWN | SUDDEN | |
| MUCH | DIRECTION | LOOK | ROLL | WEATHER | HAMMER | TRAIN | SWEET | |
| NOT | DISCOVERY | LOSS | ROOM | WEEK | HAND | TRAY | TALL | |
| ONLY | DISCUSSION | LOVE | RUB | WEIGHT | HAT | TREE | THICK | |
| QUITE | DISEASE | MACHINE | RULE | WIND | HEAD | TROUSERS | TIGHT | |
| SO | DISGUST | MAN | RUN | WINE | HEART | UMBRELLA | TIRED | |
| VERY | DISTANCE | MANAGER | SALT | WINTER | HOOK | WALL | TRUE | |
| TOMORROW | DISTRIBUTION | MARK | SAND | WOMAN | HORN | WATCH | VIOLENT | |
| YESTERDAY | DIVISION | MARKET | SCALE | WOOD | HORSE | WHEEL | WAITING | |
| NORTH | DOUBT | MASS | SCIENCE | WOOL | HOSPITAL | WHIP | WARM | |
| SOUTH | DRINK | MEAL | SEA | WORD | HOUSE | WHISTLE | WET | |
| EAST | DRIVING | MEASURE | SEAT | WORK | ISLAND | WINDOW | WIDE | |
| WEST | DUST | MEAT | SECRETARY | WOUND | JEWEL | WING | WISE | |
| PLEASE | EARTH | MEETING | SELECTION | WRITING | KETTLE | WIRE | YELLOW | |
| YES | EDGE | MEMORY | SELF | YEAR | KEY | WORM | YOUNG | |

**SUMMARY OF RULES**

PLURALS IN 'S.'

DERIVATIVES IN 'ER,' 'ING,' 'ED' FROM 300 NOUNS.

ADVERBS IN 'LY' FROM QUALIFIERS.

DEGREE WITH 'MORE' AND 'MOST.'

QUESTIONS BY INVERSION AND 'DO.'

OPERATORS AND PRONOUNS CONJUGATE IN FULL.

MEASUREMENT, NUMERALS, CURRENCY, CALENDAR, AND INTERNATIONAL TERMS IN ENGLISH FORM.

Figure 5.1   (opposite)
Basic English vocabulary
and grammar

Despite these limitations, the language was not to be 'denatured'. Any text written in Basic was to look natural to a native speaker. Indeed, a native speaker should not be able to tell easily that a text had been constructed within the restricted vocabulary and grammar of Basic.

❖   ❖   ❖   ❖   ❖

## Activity 5.1

Below is printed an extract from a text written in Basic. Study it carefully. Does it appear to you to be 'natural' English? How many different verbs are used in this passage? What linguistic device is employed to extend the range of meanings?

The chief event of the past year in the history of the Institute was the opening of its new London Branch in Westminster on July 1st, 1934.

In 1928, when the work on Basic English was complete, a sound-testing room was taken, under a house in Frith Street, near the British Museum, so that work on Radio, recording, and the invention of sound-apparatus might go forward more quickly, and the experts whose help was needed for the word-lists of the special sciences might have a meeting-place at all hours of the day and night.

At first only one room was needed, then two; and a very strange place it was. For six years these rooms had been used by our friends Compton Mackenzie and Christopher Stone as the offices of 'The Gramophone Society,' which did so much for the development of public taste that good records are now put on the market regularly – as if there had not ever been any doubt that we are sometimes pleased to have a rest from dance music. In those days, however, things were very different, and the education of the Companies was a slow process; but the growth of the Society made it necessary for Mr. Mackenzie to go up higher. So Orthology had its chance, and a year later the Institute got four more rooms.

But with the expansion of Basic, even six rooms were not enough. Early in 1930, five others were taken over, and the house was ours. Three years more and space was again needed, so in June, 1934 the sound-apparatus and much of the printed material was moved to Highgate, and Basic was given a separate existence in Westminster, opposite the Passport Office, by St James's Park Station; so near to Big Ben that clocks and watches are not needed ... For some months before the move, new Basic books were kept waiting at the printing works, but from the end of June they have been coming out as before; and the day after the new office was open, we were able to send out another example of the art of short-story writing in Basic, *Death in High Society*, by Miss Inez Holden, whose picture (by Augustus John) is at the front.

Wide as the uses of Basic are, there is no suggestion that the works of great writers will have the same sort of value in Basic. Basic is able to give the sense of such writing and may be used for separating sense from feeling, but the full experience is open only to those who have a detailed knowledge of the language of the writer and of the conditions under which his work was produced.

It is foolish, however, to make water-tight divisions where all is so much a question of degree. At the highest levels, it is true, Basic is able to do little more than give an outline of what the writer said, his feelings when he said it, and the reactions desired in the reader.

(Orthological Institute, 1934, pp. 187–8))

## Comment

Ogden's research showed him that English has a tendency to **delexicalize** verbs. A delexicalized verb is one that has little referential meaning in itself, but retains a grammatical function by carrying markers for tense, aspect and so on. The burden of meaning is then placed on a noun or noun phrase. For example, one can say in English *contact someone* or one can *get in contact with them*; one can *note something* or one can *take note of something*; one can *outline something* or one can *give an outline of it.* In Basic only the latter formulations are possible.

Some forms in the text which may appear to be derived from verbs (such as *detailed, desired, separating,* etc.) are treated in Basic as derivatives from nouns (*-er, -ed* or *-ing* can be added to 300 nouns). You might regard this as 'cheating' on the part of Ogden or genuinely an interesting attempt to create a language in which the distribution of parts of speech was distinctively different.

## The emergence of English as an international language

The rise of English had been foreseen by many nineteenth-century commentators in America and Europe. In fact, rather wild speculations began to circulate about the growth of the number of English speakers in the coming century. Bailey (1992) reviews some of these accounts:

> The most extravagant projections were the most satisfying to the anglophone community and, therefore, the most popular. The Swiss botanist Alphonse de Candolle (1806–93) turned his attention to the question in the early 1870s ...
>
> > 'Now, judging by the increase that has taken place in the present century, we may estimate the probable growth of population as follows:
> >
> > In England it doubles in fifty years; therefore, in a century (in 1970) it will be 124,000,000. In the United States, in Canada, in Australia, it doubles in twenty-five; therefore it will be 736,000,000. Probable total of the English-speaking race in 1970, 860,000,000.'
>
> (Bailey, 1992, p. 111)

As one speculation became regarded as established fact, even larger figures began to circulate, until projections of English speakers for the year 2000 exceeded a billion. These were the expected figures for monolingual speakers – second language speakers were rarely mentioned or regarded as important.

From the late nineteenth century, those with experience of travel were beginning to appreciate that English was already a world language in the sense that many speakers of other languages spoke English as a second language. The following account, from before World War One, illustrates something of its spread:

> It was only on reaching Italy that I began fully to realize the wonderful thing that, for nearly six weeks, on a German ship, in a journey of nearly 10,000 miles we had heard little of any language but English ... In Japan most of the tradespeople spoke English. At Shanghai, at Hong-kong, at Singapore, at Penang, at Colombo, at Suez, at Port Said, all the way home, the language of the ship's traffic was English. The Chinese man-of-war's men who conveyed the Chinese prince on board at Shanghai received and exchanged commands with our German sailors in English. The

Chinese mandarins in their conversations with the ship's officers in-variably spoke English. To talk to our Japanese passengers they had to speak English. That, it seems to me, is a bigger fact than the British Empire. If, as some aver, the greatest hindrances to peaceful inter-national intercourse are the misunderstandings due to diversity of tongues, the wide prevalence of the English tongue must be the greatest unifying bond the world has ever known.

(A.M. Thompson, 1910, cited in Jagger, 1940, pp. 128–9)

The British empire, however, remained a 'big fact'. By this time it was said to cover one-fifth of the land surface of the Earth, making English the official administrat-ive language for one-third of the world's population. After World War One, some members of the international auxiliary language movement began to argue that English had become, in fact, the 'world language' and that some modest spelling reform would be sufficient to equip it as an international auxiliary language. A Swedish scholar R.E. Zachrisson, for example, proposed that one such re-formed English be called Anglic. In the 1930s he justified the adoption of English rather than Esperanto because:

No language has a better claim than English, which is spoken by more than two hundred million people, and is the administrative language of five hundred millions, *i.e.* one third part of the world's population. It is already the chief language of the sea and commerce. It is taught in practically all the secondary schools in most civilized countries, and for this reason it is already the common property of the whole world.

(Zachrisson, 1970, p. 7)

In Britain as well the experience of World War Two seems to have led to a more general change of mind about the future of English in the world. Its main European rivals (French and German) were now in no position to resist the rise of English. Most important of all, the USA had materialized as a world economic force and the process of war had introduced many parts of the world to US people, language and consumer goods.

Recognizing the need for the reconstruction of education within Europe after the war, the British Association now suggested 'the great political changes which have taken place ... point to the fact that any auxiliary means of communi-cation will have to be closely related to the English language and to be such that the learning of it is a direct step towards learning English' (Jacob, 1947, p. 27). Soon much of the idealism that inspired the auxiliary language movement faltered. Even supporters of Basic English began to emphasize its role in edu-cation as a first step towards 'proper' English. For example, Adolph Myers (1938) provided a worked-out curriculum for English teaching in India and Burma, endorsed by Jawaharlal Nehru and supported by a 'Times of India Guide to Basic English'.

## The world hierarchy of languages

There are many ways of evaluating the world status of languages and it would be wrong to suggest that English is the only language with claims to international status. I have already mentioned the position of French, but there are several other languages which could be considered as 'world languages' in some cases.

In the course of establishing the international order after World War One, six languages were given official status in the United Nations (UN): Arabic, Chinese,

English, French, Russian and Spanish. In practice, Arabic has not been adopted as an important 'working language' of the UN. The remaining five languages recur in lists of the working languages of international and intergovernmental organizations, with English and French the most frequent choices. Indeed, many international organizations have adopted a dual English/French policy. These include GATT (the General Agreement on Tariffs and Trade – the predecessor of the World Trade Organisation), OECD (Organisation for Economic Co-operation and Development), NATO (North Atlantic Treaty Organisation, for US/European defence cooperation, despite the fact that France has long not been a member), OAU (Organisation for African Unity), ILO (International Labour Organisation). The importance of French is often historical, though it serves the political purpose of avoiding obvious English hegemony in many international organizations. Many organizations use English exclusively but only one important international agency uses exclusively French (the UPU, Universal Postal Union). In terms of such intergovernmental forums, French remains an important language.

## English in Europe

Although the origins of English lie in Europe, this remains one of the world regions where it meets most resistance. Within Europe there are several countries besides Britain with colonial histories and aspirations to project their language, culture and economic activities worldwide – such countries include France, Spain and Germany. European history provides many cultural resources from which resistance to English, and English cultural products, can be built.

The creation of the European Union (EU) as a regional economic entity has provided a bureaucratic and intergovernmental framework designed precisely to ensure that none of the main languages of Europe takes undue precedence over others (specifically English, French and German) and that minority languages (including the national languages of smaller nations, such as Danish, but also minority languages within national borders, such as Basque) are given a certain degree of institutional support.

The project of a 'single Europe' is to establish a large economic area which can, in the twenty-first century, compete with the other large trading areas in the world, such as Asia-Pacific and the Americas. This places English in an ambiguous position within the EU: it is the language of Britain, which is widely seen as facing two ways – towards Europe and towards the USA, and with ambiguous commitments to the European project. German, however, is the language of the most economically dominant country in Europe. Since the integration of West and East Germany in 1989, German also has the largest number of native speakers within the EU.

**Table 5.1**  Numbers of European native speakers of the top five EU languages

|   | Language | Number of native speakers (in millions) |
|---|----------|------------------------------------------|
| 1 | German   | 78 |
| 2 | English  | 56 |
| 3 | French   | 54 |
| 4 | Italian  | 50 |
| 5 | Spanish  | 38 |

Although officially the nine national languages of the member states have equal status, there appears in practice to be a language hierarchy. Schlossmacher, for example, reports that 'French and English dominate as working languages in the political bodies of the EU. French is more important than English within the EU, while English is dominant in world-wide communication of the employees of the EU' (Schlossmacher, 1995, p. 1).

One study of small and medium-sized businesses in Europe (Hagen (ed.), 1993) found that English was probably the most used language of business, but that German was extensively used – particularly for informal communication – by many businesses across Europe, including especially those in Holland and Denmark. Ammon (1995) cites the recommendations made to their members by German chambers of commerce on which languages should be used for trade with each country in the world. German is recommended as the exclusive language of trade with only one other country (Austria), though it is suggested it can be used as a co-language for up to 25 (including Holland, Denmark and eastern European countries). English, however, leads the field, being recommended as sole language for 64 countries. French is second (25) and Spanish third (17). These figures show that while German has currency in Europe as a language of trade, even German companies have to do business with most of the world in English.

In the mid 1990s, then, German can probably be regarded as the third most important language in the EU, being used extensively for business. Then come the remaining national languages of the 12 member countries (Danish, Dutch, English, Finnish, French, German, Greek, Irish, Italian, Portuguese, Spanish, Swedish) somewhere in the centre, and below these, with varying degrees of recognition and support, over 40 local language varieties (including, for example, Welsh, Basque and Catalan). English, of course, exists at each level of this hierarchy: it is a local vernacular for some, a national language for Britain and the Irish Republic in standardized forms, and is used as a second language by many other European nationals.

The relative position of English, French and German may well change as the EU is enlarged and more languages join the hierarchy. In 1995 three more countries joined the EU (Austria, Sweden and Finland). Later, it is anticipated that countries from central and eastern Europe will join. The enlargement of the EU is likely to change the balance of power between the main languages, both because of the language preferences of the new members and because an increased membership will increase the need for communication in lingua francas (thus further privileging the 'big' languages).

The accession of Austria will support the position of German, as will the joining of eastern European countries which already use German extensively for international communication. But the inclusion of northern European countries may help English become a more dominant language of communication. This suggests that the dominance of French in Europe may decline in future and, although German is likely to remain an important language, some commentators see the adoption of English as the European lingua franca as an inevitable outcome:

> it is, in my view, likely that English will become the primary language of the citizens of the EC. Whether or not it is ever officially declared such, it will be even more widely used as a vehicle for intra-European communication across all social groups.
>
> (Berns, 1995, p. 9)

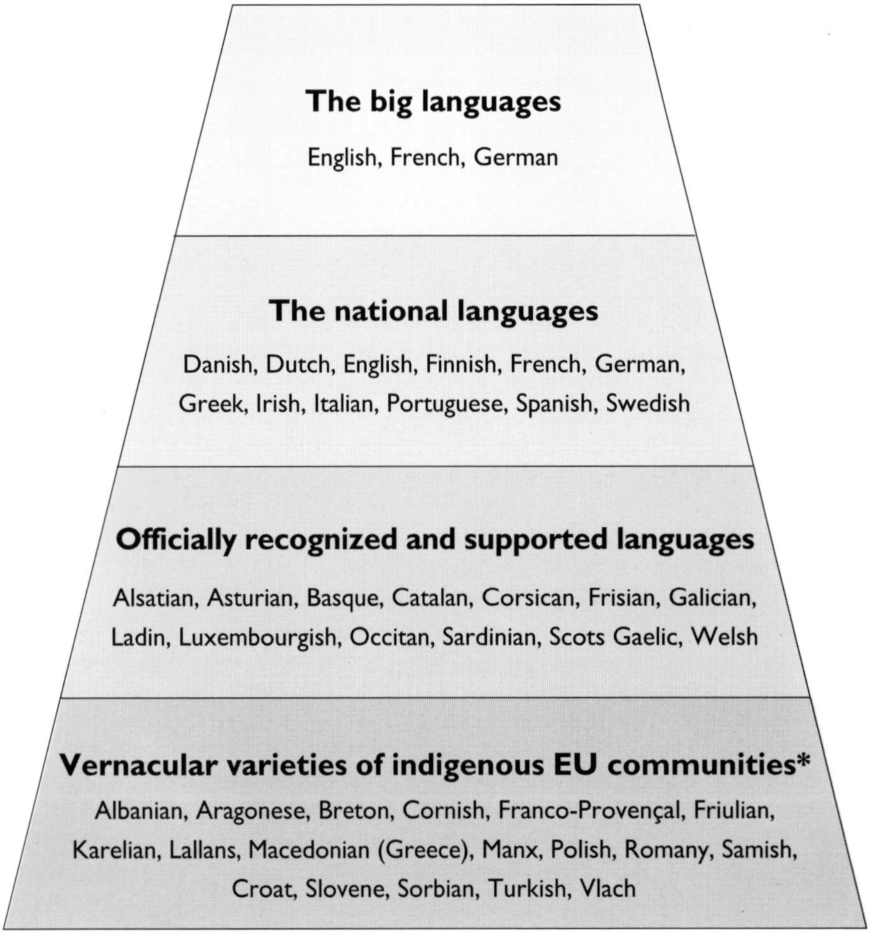

Figure 5.2    The European Union language hierarchy

Note: the official status of each language is different and categorization is thus difficult. Languages in the bottom layer enjoy least status and support.

*Some languages may be recognized in countries outside the EU.

(Includes information from Hearn and Button, 1994)

## World regions

The status of English in Europe shows how its relative position varies in different regions of the world. Spanish is in the second rank in the European hierarchy but is more common than English as the medium of communication in Central and South America. French is used as a lingua franca by many African countries that were former colonies and in Indo-China (though the use of English seems to be increasing). Arabic is used widely in West Asia and North Africa. Russian is now used as an international language in the Commonwealth of Independent States (CIS). English is used as the lingua franca in most parts of South and East Asia. It is most commonly the preferred language for communication *between* regions.

The use of English is thus far from uniform across the world. Within different countries there are many differences in how people speak English and what

alternative languages they have at their disposal. For example, despite experiencing 150 years as a British colony, Hong Kong never established an extensive
English-speaking community as occurred in India or Singapore. Now, Mandarin is
regarded by many Chinese speakers in Hong Kong as the more important second
language to learn.

Nevertheless, at the close of the twentieth century, English enjoys a position
in the world well beyond that which might be expected by the number of its native
speakers. It is undoubtedly at the apex of the complex political, economic and
cultural hierarchy of languages in the world. French is probably still the world's
second international language, but Spanish, Russian, Arabic and Chinese are
next in rank, though each with special influence in particular regions.

Below these in the world hierarchy, one might place the over 50 languages
recognized by the UN as national languages and below that the many more
languages recognized as official languages in the world's nation states. Yet lower
are the many languages that have regional status within countries, for purposes of
education or in the public media. And below that are thousands more languages
with small numbers of speakers and little institutional support or protection.

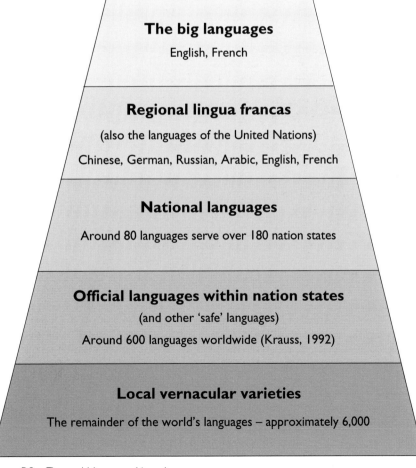

Figure 5.3   The world language hierarchy

## 5.3  ENGLISH AS A KILLER LANGUAGE

### Endangered languages

'I consider it a plausible calculation', wrote one linguist at the beginning of the 1990s, 'that – at the rate things are going – the coming century will see either the death or the doom of 90% of mankind's languages. What are we linguists doing to prepare for this or to prevent this catastrophic destruction of the linguistic world?' (Krauss, 1992, p. 7).

Calculations of linguistic diversity and the current viability of languages are fraught with problems, but Krauss argued that there would be around 6,000 languages still spoken in the world at the close of the twentieth century. Some linguists might argue with that figure plus or minus a few hundred, but few would take issue with it in round terms. The majority of these languages, however, are located in a few countries; they tend to be spoken by small groups of people who have little political or cultural power within the sovereign states in which they live. For example, in 1983 a report to Unesco calculated that 20–25 per cent of the world's languages are to be found in Oceania (that is, the islands of the Pacific, together with Australia and New Zealand) but that they were spoken by between only 0.1 and 0.2 per cent of the world's population (cited in Dixon, 1991). Overall, over 80 per cent of the world's languages are spoken by fewer than 5 per cent of its population.

Such small communities of speakers maintain a precarious foothold on their traditional ways of living, language and culture. They often become targeted by development agencies for 'modernization' and improvement. In many cases, such small communities of speakers cease to be viable in the face of such modernization. Alternatively, they may become dispossessed of their traditional lands as a consequence of exploitation by large companies and drift to the cities in search of employment. Such trends are visible throughout the developing world and affect tribal groups and small communities in the Amazon, in Africa, India, Australia and many other countries in remarkably similar ways. Pattanayak describes the process in India:

> It is interesting to see how 'development' affects multilingual pluricul-tural countries. The many languages result in small zones of communi-cation. When one or two languages are chosen for mega-communication, the small communication zones wither away, resulting in loss of culture. The land-holding pattern in the developing countries presents a similar picture. The average land size is five hectares in the tropical belt and three hectares in Asia. When superfarm technology is imposed on them the smallholdings become uneconomic. The tribal communities present a tragic case of death of language and loss of culture. The tribals live in small clusters in the midst of large forests. In the name of development, the erection of bunds (dams) for electricity generation, opening of the land for tourist promotion, exploitation of minerals located in hills and jungles all result in the tribals being dispossessed and dislocated. This in turn, results in the death of their language and cultures.
>
> (Pattanayak, 1996, p. 145)

**Table 5.2**   The 22 countries that account for around 5,000 of the world's 6,000 languages, showing their national official languages and their preferred language for international communication

| Country | Number of languages | National languages | International languages |
|---|---|---|---|
| Papua New Guinea | 850 | English/Tok Pisin/Hiri Motu | English |
| Indonesia | 670 | Bahasa Indonesia (Malay) | English |
| Nigeria | 410 | English/Yoruba/Ibo/Hausa | English |
| India | 380 | English/Hindi | English |
| Cameroon | 270 | English/French | English/French |
| Australia | 250 | English | English |
| Mexico | 240 | Spanish | English/Spanish |
| Zaire | 210 | French | French |
| Brazil | 210 | Portuguese | English/Portuguese |

The following countries each account for 100–160 languages:

| | | |
|---|---|---|
| Philippines | English/Pilipino | English |
| Former USSR | Russian | Russian/English |
| USA | English | English |
| Malaysia | Bahasa Malaysia (Malay) | English |
| People's Republic of China | Putonghua (Mandarin) | English |
| Sudan | Arabic | English |
| Tanzania | Swahili/English | English |
| Ethiopia | Amharic/English | English |
| Chad | French/Arabic | French |
| Vanuatu (New Hebrides) | English/French/Bislama | English/French |
| Central African Republic | French/Sango | French |
| Myanmar (Burma) | Burmese | English |
| Nepal | Nepali | English |

The map (Figure 5.4) shows that many of the lesser used languages are within the Asia-Pacific zone, which is experiencing rapid economic development.

The English language is rarely the direct cause of such language loss, despite the fact that English is an official language in many of the countries where endangered languages exist. There exists in most of these highly multilingual countries a complex linguistic hierarchy. English may be at, or near, the top of that hierarchy but its influence may not be felt directly by speakers whose languages

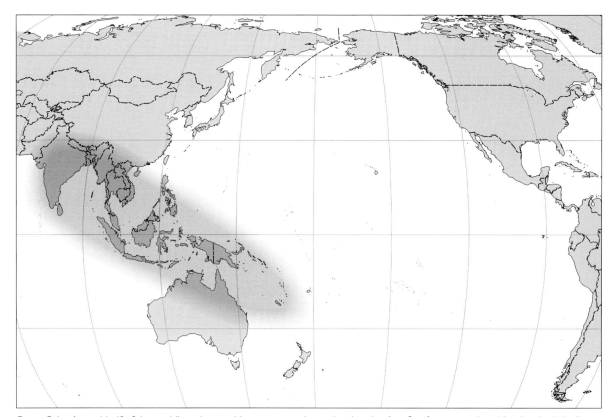

*Figure 5.4    Around half of the world's endangered languages are located within the Asia-Pacific area enclosed by the shaded ellipse*

are at the bottom. In India, for example, there exist over 190 recognized languages, 87 of which are used in the media, 58 taught as a school subject, 41 used as a medium of instruction in schools, 18 recognized for the purposes of government in the states, and two (Hindi and English) recognized as national languages. Language shift usually occurs from a small, low-status vernacular to one of the languages higher in the hierarchy, usually one with a larger number of speakers and wider currency in the region.

In India, even though English is an official language and relatively widely spoken, the speakers of the disappearing tribal languages are turning not to English, or even Hindi, but to regional languages such as Bengali or Marathi. One study of language loss in Africa came to a similar conclusion:

> European languages are very often labelled as being the primary danger to African languages and cultural heritage. A closer look at the reality in most African nations today reveals, however, that it is African *linguae francae* and other African languages with a national or regional status which spread to the detriment of vernaculars. Minority languages are still more likely to be replaced by those relatively few 'highly valued' African languages, than by imported ones. However, modern attempts reflected by, for example, the 'efforts towards indigenisation' of English in East Africa … are suitable to clear the way for English becoming more commonly accepted and used in more domains. This is how English finally may spread, even as a mother tongue.
>
> (Brenzinger et al., 1991, p. 40)

However, although the English language is not directly responsible for much of the threat to global diversity, it is intimately connected with the processes of economic globalization which are indirectly causing lesser used languages to disappear.

The English language has more direct responsibility for language loss in its native speaking countries. Canada, the USA and Australia each have a large number of indigenous languages within their borders which have already been lost or are on the verge of disappearance. In Australia, for example, more than 200 languages are thought to have been lost in recent years. The following reading describes in greater detail the process of language shift to English over several generations.

## Activity 5.2 *(Reading A)*

Read 'Language loss in Australian Aboriginal languages' (Reading A) by R.M.W. Dixon. Note what seem to be the main factors affecting language loss. How many of these factors might apply to lesser used languages in countries where English is *not* in such widespread use?

### Comment

The process Dixon describes is similar to that reported from elsewhere in the world, such as in the USA and Canada in relation to native American languages. The stages are likely to apply whatever language is replacing the minority language, but some of the factors described by Dixon refer especially to colonial or ex-colonial situations (where English has been firmly established as the majority language).

It is also worth looking briefly at some of the limitations of Dixon's account, which is too schematic to include some important details. For example, communities in which both English and language X are known will typically exploit the resources of both languages in codeswitching. Also, Dixon leaves vague the nature of the English variety that is learned by Aborigines. Aboriginal English is not just a form of Standard English with some vocabulary from language X: it is recognized as a pan-Australian variety in its own right. There are, in addition, forms of English creole spoken in some Aboriginal communities – such as Kriol in the Northern Territories. This is a useful reminder of the way that new varieties of English often emerge from contact situations. Indeed, there is often a new hierarchy of Englishes grafted on to the existing language hierarchy. In India, for example, there are typically many local forms of Indian English which reflect characteristics of regional languages, together with a national variety of Indian English and an 'international' one, which has fewer identifiable Indian usages.

Finally, Dixon's schematic description of language loss refers to the 'community' as if it maintained its physical integrity during the course of the process of language loss. That may, in some cases, be true. But in many cases the community may itself become dispersed as speakers drift to the towns in search of employment, or when they become dispossessed of their land. In other words, the traditional way of life and the social relations, social interactions and cultural practices from which a 'community' is constructed may themselves be broken up.

## 5.4 ENGLISH AND THE CREATION OF SOCIAL INEQUALITY

English is seen in many countries, at an individual, institutional or national level, as representing the key to economic opportunity. For example, in 1995 the British Council surveyed 2,000 people worldwide who were actively involved in the teaching of English. Respondents were asked to register their agreement or disagreement with a series of statements about the role of English. The results indicated that 'English is recognized and accepted as the world's language and is not, on the whole, associated with elitism' (British Council, 1995, p. 4). The majority of respondents agreed with statements that claimed English was important to modernization in developing countries:

2.1 English is a major contributor to economic and social advance in most countries (73 per cent agreed)

2.11 English is essential for progress as it will provide the main means of access to high-tech communication and information over the next twenty-five years (95 per cent agreed)

Interestingly, most respondents seemed to disagree that the demand for English had negative effects:

1.2 Competence in English encourages elitism and increases socio-economic inequalities (59 per cent disagreed)

It is probably to be expected that members of the English-teaching profession will see their role in a favourable light, but there is increasing evidence that in many countries fluency in the English language is required for access to better jobs and opportunities. Access to English, however, is rarely uniformly available. The other side of the coin of economic opportunity is thus the complex mechanism whereby English language structures usage inequality. Pattanayak, who has long been an active figure in language education, describes how this mechanism works in India:

> English is backed by international groups which treat English as an instrument of colonisation and as a commodity for trade. Intra-nationally it is the support system for the managerial mini-sector for the preservation of privileges. It promotes the generation, sustenance, and socialisation of a conspicuously consumeristic life style. It interprets skill migration as brightening life chances, and it accentuates the divide between (1) rural and urban, (2) the developing and the developed, and (3) elites and masses. It permits better education for a minuscule minority. At the same time, it inhibits interaction between science and society and it inhibits the creation of appropriate technology. As an adversary to many languages sharing communication, it promotes alienation, anomie, and blind spots in cultural perception. It is the carrier of values antithetical to indigenous cultures and results in the atrophy of cultures. It makes non-English cultures permanent parasites on English and English-speaking countries. In the process, indigenous languages become anaemic and move towards certain death ...
>
> It may thus be seen that there is a parallel between, on the one hand, English as a colonial imposition supported by a segment of the elite and receiving stiff nationalist opposition, and, on the other, the current elitist imposition acclaimed by a segment of the population aspiring to achieve access to elitist privileges and opposed by a larger segment of the population.
>
> (Pattanayak, 1996, pp. 150–1)

Tickoo (1993) studied the position of the Kashmiri language in north India. Although by no means at the bottom of the Indian linguistic hierarchy, being one of the 15 'scheduled' languages and spoken by 3–4 million people, Tickoo argued that educational policies rendered Kashmiri an inferior language, while the emphasis on English caused many students to fail:

> Kashmiri, like many other languages of similarly small reach in India, has to live in the shadow of larger languages or, more truly, at the bottom of a hierarchy of languages. In such an hierarchical arrangement what often happens is that the child's first language, which operates at the bottom of the educational ladder, is viewed as a mere stage on the way to gaining the mastery of the larger languages which are known to serve more import-ant national goals. It thus becomes a transactional language rather than a true language of learning or a dependable resource towards lasting literacy.
> (Tickoo, 1993, pp. 232–3)

Many students learn English in what Tickoo called an 'acquisition poor environ-ment' (APE): one where the teacher is not fully proficient in the language, where the schools and classrooms are under-equipped, and where there is no real communicative use of the language in the community.

> [T]he truth is that the vast majority of Indians are taught English in an APE, and as a result the language does not become a usable means of communication. This is eminently true for those who live in villages where there are no opportunities to hear the language spoken. It is almost equally true of a majority of those who learn it in the bulk of schools in cities and towns where English is learnt in a class hour of 35 minutes each working day.
> (Tickoo, 1993, p. 234)

Tickoo's study raises several important points. One is the way that the existence of English in the upper hierarchy positions languages lower down as everyday vernaculars. Although Kashmiri has experienced standardization, many languages that are low in a linguistic hierarchy never get the opportunity to be expanded, standardized and used for wider social functions in the way the European languages have been since the seventeenth century. Robert Phillipson argues that this is a common situation in postcolonial countries:

> It seems highly likely that the language policies followed in postcolonial societies have served the interests of [the] North far better than the South, in particular the masses in South countries. There are parallels between economic and linguistic underdevelopment. Use of dominant western European languages (English in Nigeria, French in Senegal, etc.) has prevented local languages from going through the extension of range and repertoire that many European languages went through as recently as in the nineteenth and early twentieth centuries.
> (Phillipson, 1994, p. 20)

The second point is that educational policy (which establishes the languages to be used as a medium of education at primary, secondary and university level) is a key factor in determining how successful speakers of the lesser used languages are within the education system. Tickoo argued that the pressure to attend English-medium education in cases where students had no real need for English and

**National languages**

Hindi/English

**Scheduled languages**

(in order of size)
Hindi, Telegu, Bengali, Marathi, Tamil, Urdu,
Gujarati, Kannada, Malayalam, Oriya, Punjabi,
Kashmiri, Sindhi, Assamese, Sanskrit

**Languages with widespread currency**

41 languages used for education
58 taught as school subjects
87 used in media

**Local vernaculars**

Over 190 recognized language varieties
1,652 'mother tongues' were recorded in 1961 census

*Figure 5.5   The Indian language hierarchy*
(Data taken from Mahapatra, 1990)

where the education system could not support quality learning through English, had disastrous consequences for both students and for the Kashmiri language. The reading in Activity 5.3 describes the fate of students emerging from the English-medium education system in Papua New Guinea, where English is the official national language, and Tok Pisin and Hiri Motu are co-official lingua francas.

**Activity 5.3**   *(Reading B)*

In 'The products of English-medium education in Papua New Guinea' (Reading B) Naihuwo Ahai and Nicholas Faraclas examine the effect of English-medium education in a country that probably contains greater linguistic diversity than any other in the world. They provide a critique of the effects of English-medium schooling in producing illiteracy and social and economic problems. The people who gain most, they claim, are the expatriate 'experts'. Before you read, look back at Pattanayak's criticism that English has created a social elite in India who are alienated from local culture. Bear this in mind as you read the account from Papua New Guinea. How similar are the arguments being put forward?

## Comment

Like Tickoo, Ahai and Faraclas argue that expecting students 'to learn to read and write in a language that most of them do not know in its oral form' results in a devastating toll, 'both in terms of rates of school leaving and declining standards for the few who manage to continue'. Like Pattanayak, they suggest that 'along with English language comes European culture' and 'a corresponding distaste for their own culture and village life'. Somewhat similar concerns about the role of English-medium education in producing low achievement have been voiced in many postcolonial contexts. An educational report in Hong Kong (Education Commission, 1995, p. 12), for example, claimed that compulsory English educa-tion 'has helped spread English more widely in the community, but, on the other hand, has increased the number of low achievers'.

❖   ❖   ❖   ❖   ❖

It must be admitted that it seems to be extremely difficult to find the mix of language education and language planning decisions that will work for everyone in a postcolonial and multilingual society. Each context is unique in the combi-nation of languages and the local cultural politics of English. The readings so far demonstrate the hazards of emphasizing English-medium education. One of the key questions to be asked here is: who benefits? Is the role of English in such countries an unfortunate colonial legacy, which has defied all attempts by the newly independent state to dismantle it? Or is the position of English maintained because it serves the interests of local elites?

The latter explanation has often been put forward. Tollefson (1991), for example, claims that arguments about the relative position of English and Pilipino in the Philippines reflect power shifts within the country, and that those who promote English do so less because they recognize its instrumental economic value and more because it serves their internal group interests:

> elites resisted surrendering the dominance of English because they owed a major part of their professional success to their proficiency in English. Similarly, leading members of the Aquino government graduated from elite universities where they became fluent in English, and they enjoy the benefits of their education in relatively well-paid jobs requiring advanced English proficiency ... For the government to shift toward an indigenous language in key areas of Philippine life, Aquino and her supporters would have to be willing to give up the enormous advantages provided by their proficiency in English. In doing so, they would risk encouraging the rise to power of a new elite.
>
> (Tollefson, 1991, p. 156)

Not all ex-colonies followed the same path after independence. Like many countries, Malaysia was faced with a dilemma: it wished to throw off the colonial ties and institutional structures, and create a new national identity which would provide unity and consensus among different ethnic and linguistic groups. It was decided to promote the Malay language, in the form of Bahasa Malaysia – a project that required the 'extension of range and repertoire' which Phillipson argues is denied many regional languages. New textbooks and materials had to be developed in order to implement the plan.

The establishment of Bahasa Malaysia as the new national language has been successful. Although its introduction might simply seem to be a commendable attempt to reassert local cultural values in the place of old colonial ones, some commentators have suggested that it is better understood as part of an internal struggle for power within the new nation state. The Malaysian nation is made up of several ethnic groups, of which the most prominent are Malay, Chinese and Tamil. For a variety of reasons, the English language was perceived by Malays (who were numerically the largest group) to be serving the interests of the Chinese and Tamils (see Pennycook, 1994, for an interesting discussion of this). The introduction of Bahasa Malaysia was thus not just a rejection of a colonial language, but an attempt to redistribute cultural and economic power within Malaysia.

Recently, there has been concern that the standard of English in Malaysia is falling and that this is having a detrimental impact on Malaysia's position in the global economy and in international negotiating forums. In December 1993, the prime minister of Malaysia announced that greater stress would be put on English as a second language, and that English-medium teaching would be encouraged once more in some university subjects. This led to a continuing debate about the future of English and Bahasa Malaysia. This might be seen as an example of a country whose national project to replace English could not, ultimately, be fully sustained because of the global pressure to acquire competence in English and the increasing demand for English from multinational and private-sector companies. In reality, the situation is probably more complex than this. Just as the adoption of Bahasa reflected the desire of Malays to assert greater power, so there is now growing concern that the Bahasa language policy is causing Malays to lose their position. Typical of this view is the following comment taken from one of the many discussion articles in the English language press in Malaysia:

> Ironically, the main victims of the slide [in English proficiency] have turned out to be the Malay students. They are the ones being punished when it's time to enter the job market. Non-Malays are basically trilingual and tend to cope slightly better. It is a tremendous disadvantage.
> (*New Sunday Times*, 2 January 1994)

While language planning can effectively support local languages (provided they are not too low within the internal hierarchy), economic globalization makes it increasingly difficult to prevent the spread of English and to discourage the natural desire of parents and students for an English education.

But the case of Malyasia shows that globalization is not a simple process in which global forces dominate countries and cultures in turn. In each locality there are different and complex outcomes.

## English proficiency testing and immigration
## to western countries

I conclude this section by looking at another way in which English proficiency is used as a gatekeeping mechanism on a global scale. One of the consequences of the unequal economic world order is an increased flow of people wishing to migrate or study in English-speaking countries. In many Asian countries, including Malaysia, the desire to study overseas is regularly given as a prime motive for learning English.

Students and others who wish to spend time in western English-speaking countries are routinely subjected to tests of English language competence – such as the Test of English as a Foreign Language (TOEFL) used in the USA, or the International English Language Testing System (IELTS) used in the UK. Such tests are used as a screening mechanism to allocate scholarships and visas.

Refugees and immigrants to English language countries also often find that their position in society depends not on their education and professional experience but on their fluency in English. Furthermore, they may be prevented from attaining fluency through the gatekeeping mechanisms that control entry to English-teaching programmes.

In the next reading Patricia Tomic and Ricardo Trumper, Chilean refugees who migrated to Canada in the 1970s, document the way that their competence in English was used to stream them into an unskilled, impoverished, working class despite their middle-class, professional position as economists in Chile. They argue that control of access to English as a second language (ESL) programmes by new immigrants and refugees was used as a racist mechanism to position immigrants in a low socio-economic status: 'language is a major determinant of an immigrant's future. In our case, this key was held by an unsympathetic bureaucrat … Denying us access to language training made us ineligible for other than unskilled and poorly paid work.'

## Activity 5.4   *(Reading C)*

Now read 'Canada and the streaming of immigrants' (Reading C) in which Patricia Tomic and Ricardo Trumper describe how they see access to English language training as a mechanism for streaming Canadian immigrants. Do you see any similarities in the nature of this gatekeeping mechanism with that which operates in countries where English is a second language?

### Comment

Regrettably, Tomic and Trumper's experience would not have been uncommon in other English-speaking countries. In this case, English proficiency is not only used to screen people for entry into the country, but is also used as a mechanism to reposition immigrants socially – so that a professionally trained and experienced immigrant is expected to take up a position in the working class of the destination country. Like the educational mechanism described in postcolonial countries, this seems to have two components. First, proficiency is used as a filtering mechanism. Second, only certain groups of people are given access to the quality of English language education that would allow them to pass through the screening mechanism.

## 5.5   ENGLISH AND COMMUNICATIONS MEDIA

Improved communications within and between countries has transformed patterns of human interaction. It has encouraged international travel, for business and leisure, but has also led to more information about distant parts of the world being available through local media. The global electronic media, however, have been dominated by English-speaking interests from their very beginnings in the eighteenth century. Here I want to explore some of the complex reasons behind the dominance of the media and international trade by English.

The first technology to wire up the world was the electric telegraph. Although various electric devices had been experimented with since the 1750s, it was not until 1837, with the patenting of the telegraph by William Cooke and Charles Wheatstone in Britain, and Samuel Morse in the USA, that a practical and commercial technology appeared. The telegraph did not allow the human voice to be transmitted, but it did permit the relatively slow transmission of written messages by means of coded signals representing the letters of the alphabet. The invention of the telegraph coincided with the development of the railway system in Britain, and the two expanded together. Railways not only created an ever-growing need for rapid messaging (to control and synchronize the movements of rolling stock and people) but also provided ready-made protected routes for cables between main cities.

In fact, the key to understanding the impact of the telegraph and how English grew up around it as the global lingua franca for trade, international news and technology itself lies in simultaneous and related developments in the political, technological and economic spheres. At the end of the nineteenth century there began a process of global restructuring, of a change in the social and economic relations between the peoples of the world. This process continues today, and is affecting the lives of an increasing proportion of the world's population, some in a positive way but many negatively. The global pattern of language loss, and new forms of social inequality within countries, must be seen as a part of this greater process of **globalization** – a term that embraces both economic and cultural spheres, and that expresses the increasing interdependence of geographically diverse countries and peoples. Indeed, the term 'globalization' is often used to express a changing perception of the world as a

*Figure 5.6   The world's first long-distance telegraph machines*
(Courtesy of Cable & Wireless Archive)

smaller, more compressed space, in which some people, at least, can project their agency and will over large distances.

## The development of the telegraph

By 1865 a telegraph link between Britain and India was operational, helping the British government administer its new imperial territory. Within the first nine months some 22,866 messages were conveyed to India. The link was by land through Turkey (submarine cable technology had proved not yet up to the task) and was composed of many separate stretches, with numerous operators along the way who decoded and retransmitted the messages. The Indo-Ottoman Telegraphic Convention of 1864 stipulated that the Turkish administration would employ clerks 'possessing a knowledge of the English language sufficient for the perfect performance of that service' and that the Constantinople office would have officials 'thoroughly conversant with the English language' (cited in Headrick, 1991, p. 21). Despite this, messages took up to a month to be transmitted (five to six days was the average) and often arrived garbled. But an important precedent had been set in establishing international conventions which required the use of an international language throughout the links. And since the greater proportion of the world's telegraph cables were controlled by Britain, the operating languages always included English. In the 1930s, when telephone calls across Europe still had to be set up manually by operators, only three languages were recognized (by international agreement): French, German and English, and by the 1950s German seems to have been rarely used. Callers could, of course, use whatever language they wished once the call was established.

Improvement in marine cables permitted a working transatlantic cable to be laid in 1866 which united the two major English-speaking countries. Further links were established with India by different routes, including an underwater route through the Mediterranean and Red Sea. Britain's desire was to establish an 'all red' route across the world which used imperial possessions as staging-posts and which would be safe from interference by any other country. By 1870 a cable ran from Britain via Gibraltar, Malta, Suez and Aden to Bombay. A year later an extension from India reached Australia via Penang and Singapore. At the same time, other extensions were made to China and Japan. In 1876 a link between Sydney and New Zealand provided a through link from New Zealand to North America, via London.

As is still the case with new technology, rhetoric and vision constantly ran ahead of what could yet be achieved. There are frequent references among early telegraph enthusiasts to the way in which the technology would 'render distance of no importance'. As early as 1816 one commentator was prophesying that 'by means of the electric agency we shall be enabled to communicate our thoughts instantaneously with the uttermost ends of the earth' (cited in Crutchley, 1938, p. 131). This appreciation of the telegraph not just as a piece of technology but also as a means of projecting subjectivity and agency was surprisingly well developed. Postmodern-sounding references to the 'annihilation of time and space' appeared in nineteenth-century reports as distant as India and Australia. William O'Shaughnessy, for example, experimented with what was probably the first underwater telegraph transmission (along the Hooghly river in Calcutta) and gleefully reported in 1838:

> A conquest still greater than all which I have quoted would be the annihilation of time and space in the accomplishment of correspondence. That a signal can be passed between places 1000 miles apart in less

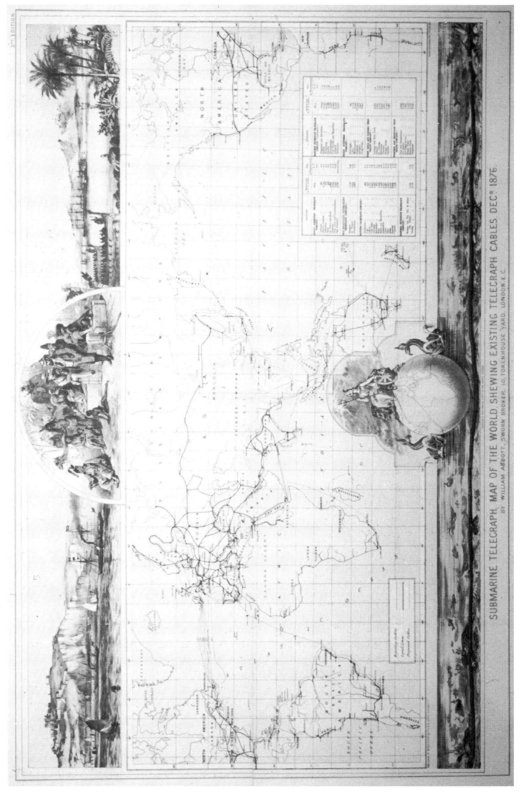

Figure 5.7   The global telegraph network at the end of the nineteenth century
(Courtesy of Cable & Wireless Archive)

time than the motions of solar light through the firmament, is no less
startling to assert than it is demonstrably and practically true.
(Cited in Headrick, 1991, p. 14)

Nearly 20 years later, an Australian newspaper picked up the phrase:

> Take the telegraph, that servant of man, which literally annihilates time
> and space. We shall shortly have the wires completed connecting all the
> important points within these colonies; and the hour is not distant when
> we shall have the same instantaneous agency linking us in communi-
> cation with friends in England.
> (Melbourne *Age*, 16 September 1857, cited in Harcourt, 1987, p. 14)

Early developers of the telegraph had a keen sense of the social and political
importance of their inventions. One of the early pioneers, for example, asked in
the 1820s (over a decade before the first practical telegraph was patented) 'Why
… should not the government govern at Portsmouth almost as promptly ·as in
Downing Street?' (Francis Ronalds, cited in Kieve, 1973, p. 17). The public
imagination was seized by such events as the arrest in 1845 of John Tawell, who
travelled to London by train after murdering his mistress in Slough but whose
description was telegraphed ahead. (The man was disguised as a Quaker and the
message was not at first understood by the London police owing to the lack of 'Q'
in the telegraph code then in use.) The telegraph provided new possibilities for
social control and remote surveillance. It could permit a railway company to
monitor its employees' work from headquarters as easily as it permitted an
imperial power to exercise central control on its colonial administrations. It was
also the technology that allowed, for the first time, a large transnational corporation to coordinate its commercial operations in different countries.

Those who controlled the telegraph effectively controlled the world. By the
end of the nineteenth century, Britain was the hub of a global telegraph network.
Over half the world's extensive cable traffic was said to flow through a single
building in London, carrying international news, commercial information and
diplomatic dispatches. Britain achieved this position because of the extraordinary
advantages conferred by colonial possessions, early industrial expansion and the
development of financial systems which could provide the capital needed for
large-scale enterprises. British interests not only owned the cable, they also held a
monopoly on the technology, including submarine cable manufacture, ships for
laying cables and repair facilities:

> Until the 1890s, only Great Britain had a commercial and financial
> organization and a level of demand sufficient to warrant a cable industry.
> Moreover, only Britain had colonies and islands in every ocean suitable
> for cable relay stations. In 1887 Britain owned 70 percent of the world's
> cables; from 1894 to 1901, it still retained a 63 percent share … More
> important, Britain's share of the world's cables included the trunk lines
> to India, East Asia, Australasia, Africa, and the Americas. Though other
> countries had feeder cables, most of the world's important business
> traffic traveled over British lines. The period from 1866 to 1895 was one
> of British hegemony in international communications.
> (Headrick, 1991, p. 28)

The international business which the telegraph made possible required standard
working practices not just for the maintenance of the messaging systems but also
for the diverse commercial interests involved in the trade. As well as facilitating

**Table 5.3**   Who controlled the world's telegraph cables?

|            | 1892 | 1908 | 1923 |
|------------|------|------|------|
| British    | 66.3 | 56.2 | 50.5 |
| American   | 15.8 | 19.5 | 24.2 |
| French     | 8.9  | 9.4  | 11.0 |
| Danish     | 5.3  | 3.8  | 2.6  |
| Others     | 3.7  | 11.1 | 11.7 |

Figures show percentage of world telegraph cables

(Data taken from Headrick, 1991)

trade in goods, the telegraph also encouraged the rapid growth in international services, such as news agencies and financial dealing:

> The development of world produce markets, involving uniformity of usage, trading conditions, the distribution of information and the practice of arbitrage, depended upon the efficiency of the telegraph. Metal markets, shipbroking and insurance all grew to service the international economy. The cable companies made their greatest impact on the international money markets; funds flowed across Europe and the world. Without rapid communication it would have been impossible for the industrial and commercial world to have absorbed vast increases in the supply of gold or to have provided the enormous subscription of English capital to foreign loans, whereby the development of Canada, Brazil and Australia was possible.
>
> (Kieve, 1973, p. 238)

Largely because of the British control of the telegraph network, the English language became firmly established as the key lingua franca for international trade and services – a position it has never lost.

## Development of global media

Use of the telegraph began to decline in the 1920s, particularly for domestic communications where the telephone was rapidly proving more popular – permitting as it did direct interaction between communicating parties.

Long-distance telephony was made possible by the invention of radio (radio-telephony was the only way of communicating by voice between the USA and Britain until the laying of the transatlantic telephone line in 1956). Here the USA gradually overtook Britain in the exploitation of the technology worldwide. All countries were able to develop their own national communications systems, and some, such as France and Germany, became notable producers of equipment. But the international network of links *between* countries, and later facilities such as satellite, which can simultaneously reach whole continents, have been largely controlled by English-speaking interests to this day. The timeline (see box) shows some key milestones in the development of communications media and demonstrates the extent to which new technology was first invented or exploited in English-speaking countries.

# A timeline for electronic global communications

| | |
|---|---|
| 1759 | First experiments with electronic signalling |
| 1837 | Telegraph patented by William Cooke and Charles Wheatstone in Britain and Samuel Morse in USA |
| 1844 | First commercial telegraph (between Washington and Baltimore) |
| 1850 | First submarine cable – across English Channel |
| 1852 | Transmission of hourly Greenwich time signals electrically signalled to major British cities |
| 1866 | First successful Atlantic cable |
| 1868 | Nationalization of British telegraph companies brings lower uniform rate permitting general public use. Buying out the private companies makes them cash-rich and eager to set up new international ventures |
| | International Bureau of Telegraph Administration established in Berne – the world's first permanent international organization |
| 1876 | Alexander Graham Bell patents the telephone |
| 1905 | Marconi establishes first commercial transatlantic radio link |
| 1906 | First public cinema opens (France) |
| 1915 | First thermionic valve amplifier makes long-distance telephone possible (USA) |
| 1919/ 1920 | RCA (Radio Corporation of America) and ITT (International Telephone and Telegraph) founded – the first transnational American communications conglomerates |
| | First public service broadcasting (USA and Britain) |
| 1924 | Marconi demonstrates 24-hour voice communication between Britain and Australia by short-wave radio. This heralds cheap, global voice communication |
| | BBC broadcasts GMT time signals |
| 1926 | First commercial transatlantic telephone service (by long-wave radio) |
| 1929 | Cable & Wireless Ltd founded, merging all British international communications interests, controlling over half the world's cables and 253 cable and wireless stations worldwide |
| | First public television broadcast (Britain) |
| 1941 | First colour television service (USA) |
| | First television advertisement broadcast (USA) |
| 1948 | Transistor invented (USA) |
| 1956 | First transatlantic telephone cable |
| 1964 | First electronic mail (USA) |
| 1965 | First commercial geostationary communications satellite (Early Bird/INTELSAT) |
| 1970 | International direct dialling between London and New York first introduced |
| 1985 | CNN International launched |
| 1989 | Sky satellite TV launched |
| 1991 | BBC World Service Television opens Asia service |
| 1992 | Reuters Television launched |
| 1995 | Reuters Television provides 24-hour news service for Sky |

Improved availability of international communication, through better technology and falling prices, has given rise to two rather different cultural trends. Originally, someone wishing to communicate at a distance had to visit or send a messenger to a Central Telegraph Office, and numerous other intermediaries stood in the path of the message. Now, the majority of people in the developed world can dial directly to one another, from home, office, public or mobile telephone. The breakdown of centralized and hierarchically controlled communication systems that this represents can be regarded as a 'centrifugal' cultural force in the sense that it encourages diversity of language and communication practices. The international organizations that negotiate the standard technology protocols may rely on English, but the day-to-day users can use whatever language they choose.

Like the Internet (see Chapter 3), however, improved global communication also increases the number of interactions between speakers of different languages. One consequence of globalization is that an increasing number of people in organizations or different sections of a multinational company have to communicate directly with one another. Such communication requires the use of a shared language. In many cases, that language is English. This creates a centralizing or 'centripetal' cultural trend in which speakers of different languages converge upon English for certain communications. English emerged as the 'default' language for communication between speakers of different languages in the telegraph era.

Improved technology allowed not just private but also public communications, in which a message or programme from a central source can be received by a dispersed audience. The first radio broadcasts were made in the 1920s. By the mid 1990s some kinds of television programming were being seen around the world, courtesy of satellite television. Such shared global experience of media also represents a centripetal, unifying force.

You will remember that one of the factors contributing to language loss according to Dixon (Reading A) is 'media pressure'. I want now to examine the extent to which the rise of global media – particularly satellite television – is leading to greater use of English worldwide.

## Media and the construction of national cultures

Terrestrial media, particularly television, with its relatively short transmission ranges, has long served a function in every country in constructing a sense of shared national identity and culture. In some countries this is done explicitly through state control of the media, but terrestrial television, with its limited number of channels and mixed programming, probably has this effect everywhere by providing a common entertainment experience and representations of the world to a wide population. As one analyst has remarked, 'We can say that (on both sides of the Atlantic) broadcasting has been one of the key institutions through which listeners and viewers have come to imagine themselves as members of the national community' (Robins, 1995, p. 249).

Two features of satellite television encourage the breakdown of 'national' media cultures. One is the way that, in most countries, scores, if not hundreds, of satellite television channels are available, each carrying a specialist content strand. Viewers 'channel hop' between them, picking whatever seems of most interest. In this sense, satellite television has a divisive effect (sometimes within families as well as cultures), since few viewers have a shared experience. Secondly, many satellite television channels rely on films and programmes bought on the global market for audiovisual products. Such programmes are likely to reflect a global media culture rather than a national or local one:

> Audio-visual geographies are thus becoming detached from the symbolic spaces of national culture, and realigned on the basis of the more 'universal' principles of international consumer culture. The free and unimpeded circulation of programs – television without frontiers – is the great ideal in the new order. It is an ideal whose logic is driving ultimately toward the creation of global programming and global markets – and already we are seeing the rise to power of global corporations intent on turning ideal into reality.
> (Robins, 1995, p. 250)

In the days of the telegraph and radio, ownership of the means of transmission permitted English-speaking interests effectively to control what flowed across their networks. In the late twentieth century, things are a great deal more complicated. Patterns of ownership (as we will see in the next activity) are themselves complex, as are the relationships between the television channel operators and those who make or distribute the programmes.

## Activity 5.5   *(Reading D)*

Read 'The new spaces of global media' (Reading D) in which Kevin Robins, a British geographer, describes the recent development of a new global media order, arguing that English language programming is increasingly dominating world satellite television. Which countries dominate the new global order? What reasons are given for believing that local and regional programming will continue to thrive?

### Comment

Robins argues that a pattern of global media has emerged in which there are relatively few players, with the market dominated by US, British, Australian and Japanese corporations. This allows a few huge corporations to distribute their material – news, entertainment and sports – throughout the world. The main players in this market are again English speaking. CNN International uses a dozen or so satellites to deliver its news service worldwide. BBC World now offers television services to over 140 countries. Sky News, supplied by Reuters Television, provides a 24-hour news service in Europe and Asia. You may be surprised to learn that Japanese corporations are also among the most important global players. This demonstrates how there is now no simple relationship between ownership and source language of material. The Japanese corporations have become global players in audiovisual distribution largely through buying up Hollywood companies and film achives. Their presence in the market is thus leading to greater distribution of American product than of Japanese.

What does the new global order mean in terms of language? Will everyone who watches television eventually accept programmes in English and become at least passively competent in the English language? As is so often the case, the answer to this question seems to be 'it depends'. Some speakers of lesser used languages certainly feel vulnerable, faced with extensive English language programming.

## Activity 5.6   *(Reading E)*

Read 'English in Sweden in the age of satellite television' (Reading E). Olle Findahl concludes that 'In the satellite age, linguistic boundaries are more important than national boundaries, as far as television is concerned', and says 'today, many Swedish children find it perfectly natural to watch television in English, and some say that English "isn't really foreign any more"'. 'In one hundred years' time,' she asks, 'will we still speak Swedish?'

## Comment

Findahl is concerned with the impact of English language satellite television in areas such as Sweden where English proficiency is already widespread. She argues that writing competence in English makes the influence of English television more powerful, especially among the young. Although she voices a concern felt by many, there is, as yet, too little evidence to predict what the fate of Swedish will be. One particularly interesting prediction is the idea that, as bilingualism in English increases, there will be a corresponding fall in bilingualism with other European languages (for example, Swedish–German, or French–Spanish). This would increase the role of English as a European lingua franca, since it would increasingly be the only language that countries had in common.

There is, however, no immediate danger of the world's television programming becoming English language only. Too many tendencies – political, cultural and economic – exist to counteract the linguistic hegemony of English language broadcasting. For example, some countries, such as China, have tried to restrict the reception of satellite television by requiring receivers to be licensed. In many other countries, people do not have private satellite dishes but receive satellite television via cable networks. These cable companies, however, are subjected to national regulation. In most developing countries, satellite television in English tends to reach the privileged sectors of the population who are the ones most likely to speak English anyway (the main audience for CNN International in many countries is, for example, in the international hotels). This means that the bulk of the population in most countries is not yet as exposed to 'raw' satellite programming as might be imagined.

There is also, as Robins pointed out, an economic logic which encourages programming for 'segments' and 'market niches'. Hence the most likely outcome of the global corporate order will be English established at the head of the world hierarchy, allowing some programming streams (such as international news, western pop music and sports coverage) to be beamed into every country. But each region will have a range of programming in other languages for audiences of various sizes. Indeed, satellite television can be used to distribute cultural products to dispersed members just as well as to maintain a cultural hegemony. In Britain, for example, there are several Asian satellite channels which provide programming for Indian, Chinese and Islamic communities. Hence minority languages and cultures may be sustained by the new global order, but kept safely in a position of less cultural and economic power.

An insight into how the English language fits into the new relations between global and local in televisual media is provided by Pennycook (1994), who describes how English language programming is increasing in Malaysia because the national broadcasting authorities have been under pressure to 'corporatize' and become increasingly dependent on advertising revenue.

> This is one of those particularly interesting and complex interconnections between English and global relationships. The move to corporatize is of course connected to shifts both in the global economy and, more importantly, recent discourses on economics, discourses which, once again, are supported by and supportive of the spread of English. In the case of Malaysian television, American movies and TV programmes, and the advertising that they attract, are a far better financial proposition than locally made programmes. The advertising also tends to follow the programmes, so that Chinese and Malay programmes may attract more local commercials aimed at a specific clientele, while US programmes attract some of the larger international sponsors such as McDonalds, Kentucky Fried Chicken ... and the cigarette manufacturers.
> (Pennycook, 1994, p. 215)

## Indirect cultural influence from English language programming

The global corporations sell their material to terrestrial television services as well as to satellite operators, as the quotation above from Pennycook shows. But many countries set quotas for foreign programmes. In Europe, according to European Union law, over 50 per cent of the programme content must be European in origin. In addition, in many European countries it is usual for US programmes to be dubbed into the national or local language.

However, the influence of English on other languages is often indirect. English language media texts bring with them images of lifestyle, expected social relations and ways of representing the world, which go beyond verbal communication and which survive translation. Pennycook, in the quotation above, referred to 'discourses on economics', which arise first in English-speaking countries (primarily US) and which then circulate the world in many languages, becoming an orthodox view on how national economics should be managed. Often these discourses are directly reinforced through the (English-speaking) international economic agencies such as the International Monetary Fund and the World Bank, with whose economic ideas many developing countries must comply. Chapter 4 in this book explores the changing discourses of selling and promotion, and how such discourses are penetrating other kinds of texts. Such promotional discourses, and their propensity to colonize other text types, are increasingly influencing texts in other languages. I want to examine now some of these indirect ways in which the English language is affecting the development of other languages.

Many television formats, such as game shows, have been licensed from the USA, with local language versions being produced, and these frequently reproduce social values and forms of public behaviour. Similarly, the dubbing of English films into a local language does not destroy their capacity for cultural imperialism. The plot, characterization and visual imagery remain the same. And regular dubbing may even influence the local language itself in unexpected ways.

**Activity 5.7**   *(Reading F)*

Read 'Dubbing American in Italy' (Reading F), by Nigel J. Ross, which shows how the dubbing of US films into Italian has given rise to new Italian expressions that conform to US verbal behaviour and that synchronize well with the lip movements of English speech. What have been the main effects on the Italian language?

**Comment**

Ross describes several ways in which English can influence other languages indirectly, such as in word order and morphology. The need to follow the lip movements of the original English makes film dubbing a particularly potent form of language contact. Pragmatic aspects of language – which include politeness formulae, turn-taking habits such as interruptions, and other linguistic patterns through which interpersonal relations are signalled, seem particularly affected by dubbing. In this way, the recipient language may not be transformed just at the linguistic level, but also in terms of the expected social relations between colleagues, family, friends and strangers.

## English and the creation of a global consumerist culture

In many countries, the social elites with disposable income are those who are bilingual in English. English-medium advertising can thus effectively target higher income groups. Increasingly, in Asian advertising fragments of English are used symbolically in what linguists refer to as 'language display': to connote western cultural values and status.

In a study of 543 advertisements in East Asian magazines (Hong Kong, Japan, South Korea and Taiwan) Neelankavil et al. (1995) found that 74 per cent contained some foreign language words, virtually all of which were English. They concluded that:

> the use of Western languages in the advertisements of the four East Asian countries is pervasive, attesting perhaps to the fact of globalization of advertising communications ... As globalization of markets continues, there is going to be a convergence of ideas, cultures, values and even language in advertisements.
>
> (Neelankavil et al., 1995, pp. 34, 36)

It is, however, important not to overemphasize the standardizing cultural role of the English language. There are many ways in which globalization brings about new forms of diversity and identity. Indeed, in corporate terms, globalization is often very much a process of exploiting local cultural resources in order to promote and market products. We can thus expect the English language to have rather different meanings in different parts of the world: it can be used as a resource for constructing new forms of identity as well as a mechanism for destroying traditional ones. It *may* be that English is making the world a more homogeneous place: it may also be that the world is making English more diverse in its forms, functions and cultural associations.

## 5.6   CONCLUSION

This chapter has examined a number of opposing tendencies and contradictions associated with the global spread of English. On the one hand, the continuing expansion in the use and learning of English and the loss of lesser used languages around the world might suggest that there is some kind of homogeneous global culture emerging, fostered by the growth of global mass media and the activities of transnational companies. Yet it seems that the English language itself is becoming fragmented as it spreads into different speech communities. Other books in this series have documented the new varieties of English which have arisen in many parts of the world and which have led some linguists to suggest that the designation 'English' should now be thought of as that of a language group (like 'Germanic' or 'Romance') rather than a single language. Furthermore, the English language often has a very different social significance to different people in different parts of the world. In each territory it finds a cultural niche which is exploited by advertisers and global corporations and used by local elites to maintain their positioning power.

We are living through a period of rapid economic and technological change during which a new global economic and cultural order is emerging. It seems likely that English will maintain its position at the top of this world linguistic hierarchy, but this does not mean that everyone in the world will end up speaking English, or that cultural materials will not continue to be produced in other languages. The process of economic modernization transforms patterns of living, education and livelihood in ways that make it impossible to maintain the kind of very small and largely isolated linguistic communities that still account for thousands of the world's stock of languages. The logic of economic globalization, however, actually encourages the maintenance of some local and regional identities and languages. There is no discernible trend towards complete cultural and linguistic homogeneity, but there is unlikely to be room for many of the smallest languages in the new world hierarchy.

Reading A
# LANGUAGE LOSS IN
# AUSTRALIAN ABORIGINAL LANGUAGES

*R.M.W. Dixon*

Language loss in Australia can be attributed to a number of factors, including:

1.  *White insistence*: in many missions and government settlements there was an 'assimilation policy' with children being separated from their parents at an early age and placed in boys' and girls' dormitories where only English was allowed; children heard speaking their native language would be punished. Even where this did not happen, the local language might be banned in the school; and adults employed by a European were often forbidden to communicate in their own language during work.

2.  *Aboriginal choice*: many Aborigines have decided to make the best out of the situation they find themselves in, a minority group in a European-type society. Parents who want their children to 'succeed' may speak to them only in English.

3.  *Shift of cultural emphasis*: people who speak two languages generally use them in different circumstances. Aborigines might, a few generations ago, have used their autochthonous language when hunting together and at corroborees and other social gatherings, but switched to English at work, in a dancehall, or in a school meeting. Gradually, less time was devoted to hunting and social interaction of the traditional type. As these social domains dropped out of use, so did the language that was used in them.

4.  *Media pressure*: English is used almost exclusively in radio, TV, videos, newspapers, magazines, books and school instruction. This media barrage naturally encourages a child to speak English, rather than any other language to which he or she may be exposed at home.

Languages can die suddenly or gradually. Sudden death can take place in the space of a single generation; the children of parents who had an Aboriginal tongue as their first language may grow up speaking only English. When the loss is more gradual we can distinguish a number of stages in the Australian situation:

*Stage 1*:    Language X is used as the first language by a full community of at least some hundreds of people and is used in every aspect of their daily lives. Some of these people will also know another language (another Australian language, or English, or both) but only as a second language. Everyone thinks in language X.

*Stage 2*:    Some people still have X as their first language (and think in it) but for others it is a second language, with English as the preferred medium (and these people may think in English, or in a mixture of English and X). At this stage the language is still maintained in its traditional form, with the original phonetics, grammar and vocabulary (although the second language speakers will not have so wide a vocabulary as traditional speakers).

*Stage 3*:    Only a few old people still have X as their first language. For most of the community, English is the dominant language (which they think in).

Some of those with X as a second language may still speak it in a fairly traditional way, but younger people tend to use a simplified form of the language, perhaps putting together words from X in English word order.

*Stage 4*:    Nobody now knows the full, original form of X. Some members of the community speak a modified version of X, with simplified grammar; at most they will know a few hundred words. The younger people speak a variety of English that includes just a few words from X.

*Stage 5*:    Everyone in the community speaks, and thinks in, English. There may be a few words from X still used but these are treated as if they were English words (with plural -*s*, past tense -*ed*, and so on).

Source: Dixon, 1991, pp. 236–7

## Reading B
## THE PRODUCTS OF ENGLISH-MEDIUM EDUCATION IN PAPUA NEW GUINEA

*Naihuwo Ahai and Nicholas Faraclas*

The education system in PNG [Papua New Guinea], through its enforcement of the 'English Only Policy', the levying of school fees, and the use of 'eliminatory' examinations, has managed to produce for the neo-colonialist system the two classes upon which it thrives: a very large number of losers or 'School Leavers' ('pushouts' – who are alienated and powerless in the context of industrial society) and a very small number of winners or 'Elites' (graduates, who are alienated but powerful in the context of industrial society). In overview, the pattern of participation in PNG looks like this: 34 per cent of school-aged children never attend school in the first place. These children usually grow up to become 'well-adjusted' community members in villages that are marginal to the 'modern' economy. Of the remaining 66 per cent, less than 25 per cent will attend high school (Grades 7–10) and less than 17 per cent will complete Grade 10, the minimum legal grade at which students may leave school in most industrialized countries.

### Icons of the products of the educational system

The products of the PNG education system are popularly conceived of in terms of images or icons. The many who fail in school are usually dissatisfied with traditional life and often leave their villages to become plantation workers or low-skilled wage earners (Icon Number One: the School Leavers). Many find themselves among the unemployed, some of whom make their living illegally (Icon Number Two: the Rascals). Because so few Papua New Guineans are given the opportunity to get a formal education, vast numbers of expatriate skilled labourers, professionals, business-people, and consultants are imported into PNG at an astronomical cost to the PNG Government (Icon Number Three: the Experts). The few Papua New Guineans who do graduate usually join the small and relatively privileged group of indigenous business-people, professionals, and senior public servants (Icon Number Four: the Elites). Each of these icons has the force of a guiding myth in educational discourse in PNG, and thus each deserves some elaboration.

## Icon number one: the 'school leaver'

In PNG society, the 'School Leaver' is typically a young person in a rural area who has had some formal schooling but has 'left' school because he or she couldn't cope with the English Only curriculum or the eliminatory examinations, or because his or her parents could not find a classroom space and/or could not afford to pay school fees. School Leavers are often viewed as misfits who have learned neither the skills that they need for well-paid work in the towns nor the skills that they need for work in the village. Because they cannot survive in the industrial economy and because they often lack the desire and the skills needed to contribute to the traditional economy, they are seen, and often see themselves, to be 'useless' individuals, who represent a bad investment of their parents' hard-earned school fee monies.

In a few years' time, if not already, School Leavers will constitute the majority of the population of PNG. For most of these school leavers or 'pushouts', school has been an experience of progressive alienation from their traditional way of life. We prefer the term 'pushout' to 'dropout' because the former term appropriately allocates the agency for the phenomenon. In place of this traditional way of life, little in the way of skill-acquisition has been provided that might help the student to cope with the industrialized society for which the school has simply whetted the appetite.

Despite the newly adopted National Language and Literacy Policy (described below), the great majority of school students in PNG are still expected to learn to read and write in a language that most of them do not know in its oral form – English. Attempts by teachers and students to use languages with which the students are familiar – to lessen the confusion resulting from giving lessons in English – have been and continue to be vigorously repressed. Confusion builds on confusion and the toll is devastating, both in terms of rates of school leaving and declining standards for the few who manage to continue. Parents' inability to find classroom spaces or to pay school fees for their children, which may amount to over 50 per cent of their earnings, and students' inability to pass eliminatory examinations in Grades 6 and 10 make it impossible for some of even that group of students who have managed to cope with the English Only curriculum to stay on.

Along with English language comes European culture. Students see Europeans in the pictures in their school-books, and they learn about European culture, history, science, and literature. Although the use of English in schools makes it almost impossible for most students to learn much of the content of their lessons, one lesson comes through loud and clear: European language, culture, and way of life are superior to Papua New Guinean languages, cultures, and ways of life. Very few primary school students in PNG can read or write or achieve basic mathematics with confidence, but nearly all of them have cultivated a taste for European culture, European dress, European food, 'town life', and a corresponding distaste for their own culture and village life.

When they are finally pushed out of primary school the great majority of PNG students lack both the skills needed to do town work and the desire and many of the skills needed to do village work. Defeated and frustrated, many 'pushouts' stay on in the rural areas, trying to integrate themselves into traditional life or just hanging on as perpetual misfits. Others travel out to find low-paid wage work. Some, however, join the ranks of the Rascals.

### Icons number two and three: the 'rascal' and the 'expert'

In PNG society, a 'Rascal' is typically a young School Leaver who has turned to criminal activities to make enough money to survive in town and enjoy what is euphemistically called 'town life' – a life largely imported from Europe, and characterized by such activities as drinking beer, driving an automobile, and gambling. Rascals are perhaps the most despised members of PNG society and they are the target of constant and intense criticism and invective in the media as well as in common conversation; it is the Rascals who are deemed to have caused the 'law and order problem' or 'law and order crisis' in PNG.

The crime rate in PNG is not nearly as great as in the United States, Europe, or Australia, yet the international media and international agencies have characterized PNG as one of the most dangerous and crime-ridden countries in the region. What makes the 'law and order problem' in PNG so much more unacceptable to expatriates in PNG than the more serious law and order problems in their own countries? Why are Papua New Guinean Rascals so much more dangerous than Australian, American, or European criminals?

'Racism' is perhaps one obvious and justified answer to these questions, but a careful analysis of the economic realities reveals that the basis for rascalism in PNG is quite different from that of criminality in, for example, Australia or the US. The average Papua New Guinean does not yet believe, as do the average Australian and American, that the few deserve to have most of society's resources under their control, while the great majority have little or no power over those resources. When this strong sense of justice and equality is confronted by the extreme inequalities and injustices produced by the economics of neocolonialism and the neocolonial education system, Rascalism becomes not only understandable but may even be considered 'positive social action'.

An illustration is in order here to support this claim – an archetypal narrative icon to be deconstructed, but also a genuine case: a security guard works twelve hours a day, ten days on and four days off every fortnight to protect the tenants of one of the luxury apartment buildings in Port Moresby against intrusions by Rascals. The tenants of this building include an Australian 'Expert' who has been hired by the PNG Government to help solve the 'law and order problem' in PNG. The Government pays over K1,000 per week (in 1990, 1 PNG Kina roughly equals 1 US Dollar) for the rental of the Expert's apartment, as well as K600 per month for the Expert to send his three children to private schools. The Expert also receives a salary of K2,000 per week plus paid home leave, with air tickets, for himself, his wife, and his children. The Expert enjoys a much higher standard of living in PNG, often including luxury automobile, maid service, yacht club membership, than he would in Australia, where he might not have been able to find work at all.

Despite the long hours and the risk of being attacked by Rascals on the job, the security guard's salary of K72 per week is not enough to pay even the least expensive private rental, which averages about K100 per week in Port Moresby and the other major towns of PNG. Such rental costs are indeed themselves related to the large numbers of well-paid expatriates competing for limited housing with Papua New Guineans. The security guard therefore lives in an illegal settlement house made of bits of timber, tarpaulin, and discarded building materials with his wife and three children. He finds it nearly impossible to find places for his children in the government primary schools and to save the K150.00 each year that it costs to pay his children's school fees. The number of available places in government schools and hospitals has been reduced and the school fees and medical fees have been increased as part of the International Monetary Fund/World Bank (IMF/WB) 'restructuring' package imposed on PNG to deal with the 'debt crisis'. As his eldest son completes Grade 6, there is no money to pay the even more expensive high school fees.

The security guard's son goes out to find work, but there are no jobs, since the IMF/WB imposed cuts have caused extensive retrenchments in the public sector, with ripple effects into the private sector. There are relatively well-paid jobs in the Defence Force, but many soldiers are, at this time, engaged in battles against fellow Papua New Guineans in order to protect the interests of an Australian-owned mining company in Bougainville. The son disappears for some time but is later found beaten to death by security guards who caught him trying to steal an expatriate Expert's automobile.

Rascals are often the School Leavers who refuse to define their condition in terms of defeat and frustration. They are the ones who are not willing to become security guards, work long hours, and live in distress and without hope for their children so that an expatriate can be sure that his or her automobile will be in the garage the next morning to take his or her children to private school at the PNG Government's expense. Their sense of justice and equality is too strong to allow them to accept this state of affairs.

Rascalism is one of the most dramatic expressions of the threat that a country like PNG, where most of the land is still communally owned by the people, poses to the neocolonial order. This is why the 'Rascal problem' and the 'law and order problem' are constantly being discussed and deplored in the media and among expatriates. This is also why Port Moresby is alive with expatriate Experts from the most lawless countries in the world who have been hired by the PNG Government to solve the 'law and order problem' in PNG.

## Icon number four: the 'elite'

The 'Elites' are typically the few people who manage to graduate from the PNG education system. Their success is often due either to the fact that they come from one of the few homes where English is commonly used in everyday activities, or to the fact that they were willing to so thoroughly reject their own culture and so thoroughly adopt European culture that they were able to succeed against all odds in a European education system. The Elites may be thought to be the winners in the system, and take on the highest-paying jobs available to Papua New Guineans, usually alongside expatriates who are making double or triple the salary for the same work.

In a fundamental way, however, the Elites are the biggest losers of all. They are completely alienated from their languages, their cultures, their people, and themselves. Most Papua New Guineans live with the security of guaranteed work, housing, and food on their traditional lands. This sense of security and identity, long lost by the peoples of Europe and the industrialized countries of the world through a long history of expropriation and exploitation, is the basis for the considerable power that the people of PNG have compared to their counterparts in other countries, both industrialized and non-industrialized. The Elites in PNG pay the highest price possible for their 'success' – the complete loss of their traditional cultural-economic power base.

Elites are often reluctant to return to their villages, because they are ashamed of their inability to speak the languages of their origin or to participate in traditional ways of living. Elites are not so reluctant, however, to enter into deals with plantation owners or with international logging and mining companies to sell their traditional lands, often without the informed consent of their own blood relatives still living on these lands. The alienation of the Elites is so complete that many are willing to sell the present and future well-being of their immediate and extended families for the possibility of securing the trappings of affluent European society.

Source: Ahai and Faraclas, 1993, pp. 82–6

## Reading C
# CANADA AND THE STREAMING OF IMMIGRANTS

*Patricia Tomic and Ricardo Trumper*

We expected to have access to English as a second language (ESL) training because we had been offered it [by the Canadian Embassy] in Mexico. One of us did not speak English, and the other had learned English at primary school twenty years before but had seldom used it. We belonged to the large group of non-English speakers who arrive in Canada every year. We required English training to be able to work in jobs relatively similar to the ones we had before and for which we had been trained. We were naive enough to believe the promises made to us by the Canadian government.

However, the next immigration officer we met offered us no training whatso-ever. He had been a Czech refugee and made it clear to us from the beginning that he did not like 'communists.' He then proceeded to deny us English training. The political aspect, no doubt, was important. Perhaps another bureaucrat would have acted differently, and we know that in the case of other Chileans many did. However, the usual practice in Canada was, and still is, to offer fewer opportunities for language training than the number of applicants. For example, in a recent study commissioned by the Ontario government, the systematic streaming of immigrants away from their previous skills through denial of English training is clear: Let us quote some of the findings:

> Acquiring a new language is one of the greatest problems facing a foreign-trained individual who arrives in Ontario without speaking English or French ... Yet, although this skill (some level of fluency) is essential for integration into the workplace, and although there are available numerous programs, it appears that language training is not meeting the need. Among the problems conveyed to the Task Force were the long delays in gaining admission to programs; the shortage of training allowance and support; the emphasis on training in general fluency rather than on occupation-specific proficiency development; and the difficulty that some categories of immigrants have qualifying for language training ...
>
> Time after time, in briefs from foreign-trained individuals, in meet-ings with the immigrant communities and in interviews with the pro-fessional bodies, the fact of language was raised before the Task Force as

posing a significant barrier to the entry of immigrants into the Ontario workplace …

All professional associations, to some degree, consider fluency essential to safe practice, and thus some assessment is necessary for registration … In the trades, too, fluency can be viewed as essential to public safety, and the level of language proficiency must be ascertained (Cumming et al., 1983).

The discretion given to government officials to make decisions regarding who gets access to training and who does not needs examination. The Labour Market Entry Language Training Program purchases spaces in ESL programs in several colleges. However, 'officers of the Canada Employment Commission are given broad discretion to determine who is eligible to be enroled in a course,' and thus, 'of the 30,000 immigrants to Ontario in 1988 who spoke neither English nor French, less than one-fifth received any language training from CEIC' (Cumming et al., 1989).

Language is considered to be an 'objective' measurement of one's ability to perform in work and everyday life. As a Hungarian Canadian poet pointed out at a conference we attended, it is also Canadian common sense. The gist of what he said was, 'If you speak with an accent, it is believed you think with an accent.' Although race, colour, size, gender, or age cannot be taken officially into account in a hiring process, it is accepted that a certain level of fluency is essential to work in certain jobs. Of course, the worst paid and most alienating jobs are not considered to require a great deal of language proficiency.

Language proficiency is also considered a must for university admittance. The Test of English as a Foreign Language (TOEFL) and the Michigan English Language Test (MELT) are not challenged by anyone as 'objective' indicators of a 'non-English speaker's' basic ability to function in a university environment. Take the York University graduate faculty calendar for 1988–90 as an example:

> Because facility in the English language is essential to the pursuit of advanced studies at York University, an applicant will normally be required to demonstrate competence in English to the satisfaction of the Faculty of Graduate Studies and the sponsoring graduate programme as a condition of admission and continuance in the programme. The following minimum guidelines will be used when English Language tests are required: (a) Normally, for … Science and Mathematics … Test of English as a Foreign Language (TOEFL): 550, Michigan English Language Test (MELT): 85-90. (b) Normally, for … Humanities and Social Sciences … Test of English as a Foreign Language (TOEFL): 600, Michigan English Language Test (MELT): 92. (c) Normally, for … Economics, Computer Sciences and Biology … Test of English as a Foreign Language (TOEFL): 575, Michigan English Language Test (MELT): 88 (p. 26).

Therefore, in practice, in discourse, and in legal terms, language is a major determinant of an immigrant's future. In our case, this key was held by an unsympathetic bureaucrat. The immigration officer's prerogative to give or deny us the right to government-sponsored language training was clear in the Immigration Act. As late as 1987,

> an officer may, on the request of an adult, arrange for the enrolment of that adult in a course, if the officer is satisfied … that the course is suited to the needs of the adult and is likely to increase his [sic] earning and employment potential (National Training Act, 1985).

In our case, the officer also made it clear that he would make sure we entered the work force as soon as possible in a factory where minimum skills and wages were the rule. Indeed, he had the legal power to enforce these regulations. Moreover, he also had the power to withhold our survival allowance should we refuse to do as he saw fit. He was also even more powerful in our eyes because we had no knowledge of our rights. Access to information was denied to us. Here language was used against us, as the officer knew he could stream us into lower rungs of society by using language skills as an objective measure. Denying us access to language training made us ineligible for other than unskilled and poorly paid work. Today this is still 'common sense.'

Our case was certainly not unique. This practice continues to this day. For example, in October 1989, articles in the *Toronto Star* clearly showed how immigrant workers are, for a period of time, disciplined and streamed into the worst paid jobs and become part of the reserve army of labour whose salaries are at the lowest possible levels.

## References

Cumming, P.A., E.L.D. Lee and D.G. Orepoulos (1989) *Access! Task Force to Professions and Trades in Ontario*, Toronto, Ontario Ministry of Citizenship.

National Training Act (1985) *Revised Statutes of Canada*, Ottawa, Queens Printer.

Source: Tomic and Trumper, 1992, pp. 175–8

---

## Reading D
# THE NEW SPACES OF GLOBAL MEDIA

*Kevin Robins*

## Introduction

In the 1990s, we are seeing dramatic transformations in media industries and media cultures. In geographical terms, these transformations may be seen in terms of the shift from national to global media systems. Taking the example of broadcasting and audio-visual media, I want to consider the nature and the significance of those new spaces of global media ...

## The new media order

What we are seeing is the construction of the media order through the entrepreneurial devices of a comparatively small number of global players, the likes of Time Warner, Sony, Matsushita, Rupert Murdoch's News Corporation and the Walt Disney Company ... For viewers, the new media order has become apparent through the emergence of new commercial channels such as BSkyB, CNN, MTV, or the Cartoon Network. What we are seeing is the development of a new media market characterized by new services, new delivery systems (satellite and cable), and new forms of payment ... In place of the mixed-programming channels of the 'traditional' broadcasters, we now have the proliferation of generic channels (sport, news, music, movies). It is estimated that the 59 channels licensed to operate in the UK in 1992 will increase to around 130 by 2002 (Booz-Allen & Hamilton 1993, p. 9). In the United States, there are likely to be more than two hundred. It is, of course, the global media players that are investing in these channels (and the UK is only one small part in their global jigsaw).

Global corporations are presently maneuvering for world supremacy. There are three basic options open to media corporations: 'The first is to be a studio and produce products. The second is to be a wholesale distributor of products, as MTV, CBS, and HBO are. The third is to be a hardware delivery system, whether that hardware is a cable wire or a Walkman' (Auletta, 1993b, p. 81). The objective for the real global players is to operate across two or even all three of these activities. It is this ambition that has motivated the recent takeovers of Hollywood studios (Universal by Matsushita, Columbia/TriStar by Sony, Fox by Rupert Murdoch, and currently Paramount, which is attracting rival bids from both the US cable giant Viacom, and the home-shopping cable channel, QVC). As Steven Ross (1990) observes, 'mass is critical, if it is combined with vertical integration and the resulting combination is intelligently managed.' The issue for media corporations now is to decide what scale of integration they need to achieve, and are capable of managing, in order to build globally …

In describing the development of a global cultural order, I have emphasized that it will be a global corporate order. Global corporations are securing control over programming (production, archives), over distribution, and over transmission systems. The developments described above indicate that the flow of images and products is both more intensive and more extensive than in the past. What should also be emphasized is how much American cultural domination remains a fundamental part of this new order, though now American or American-style output is also the staple fare of non-US interests too (Schiller 1991). As a writer in the *Financial Times* recently observed, 'soon hardly anywhere on earth will be entirely safe from at least the potential of tuning in to cheerful American voices revealing the latest news or introducing the oldest films' (Snoddy 1993).

What corporate maneuvers and machinations are seeking to bring into existence is a global media space and market. In the mid-1980s, the global advertising company Saatchi and Saatchi was talking about 'world cultural convergence,' and arguing that 'convergences in demography, behaviour and shared cultural elements are creating a more favourable climate for acceptance of a single product and positioning across a wide range of geography.' Television programs such as *Dallas*, or films such as *Star Wars* and *E.T.*, were seen to 'have crossed many national boundaries to achieve world awareness for their plots, characters, etc.' (Winram 1984, p. 21). Theodore Levitt, whose influential book *The Marketing Imagination* helped to shape the Saatchi outlook, was, at the same time, pointing to the increasing standardization and homogenization of markets across the world. 'The global corporation,' he argued, 'looks to the nations of the world not for how they are different but for how they are alike … it seeks constantly in every way to standardise everything into a common global mode' (Levitt 1983, p. 28). Of course, if it is profitable to do so, global companies will respond to the demands of particular segments of the market. In so doing, however, 'they will search for opportunities to sell to similar segments throughout the globe to achieve the scale economies that keep their costs competitive' (ibid., p. 26). The strategy is to 'treat these market segments as global, not local, markets' (Winram 1984, p. 19).

This would still seem to be the logic at work in the 1990s. American movies – now it is *The Flintstones* and *Jurassic Park* – are still breaking box-office records across the world (hence the keen struggle to acquire Hollywood studios and archives). Satellite and cable channels are also making headway in marketing a standardized product worldwide. MTV, recently invited into Lithuania to help promote democracy, and CNN, now on twelve satellites beaming 'global village' news the world over, seem to have come close to finding the answer to global marketing. The new 'super-highways,' still in their early stages of development, seem set to push processes of standardization further. But they are also likely to add more complexity, delivering 'personalized' and 'individualized' services to specialized and niche markets. Such strategies, it should be emphasized, 'are not denials or contradictions of global homogenization, but rather its confirmation … globalization does not mean the end of segments. It means, instead, their expansion to worldwide proportions' (Levitt 1983, pp. 30–1).

So much for the logic of corporate ambition. The question that we must now consider is how this logic unfolds as it encounters and negotiates the real world, the world of already existing and established markets and cultures. Let us first take the example of CNN, which might be seen as the very model of a global operator. Launched in 1980 by the American entrepreneur Ted Turner, its phenomenal success has been achieved through the distribution worldwide of a single, English-language news service. Increasingly, however, the channel is confronting the accusation that it is too American in its corporate identity. CNN's global presence is interpreted as an expression of American cultural domination, and this clearly raises problems as to its credibility as a global news provider. Back at company headquarters, this also translates into a fundamental dilemma over market strategy and position. CNN's present news service has been successful in reaching the world's business and political élites, but it has not significantly penetrated mass markets, where local affiliations and attachments are far stronger. To reach such viewers, 'CNN would have to dramatically change its vision of a single, English-speaking global network,' and 'to effect that change Turner would need to seek partners and would need to localise' (Auletta 1993a, p. 30). What CNN is having to recognize is that the pursuit of further success will entail the production of different editions, in different languages, in different parts of the world. To this end, collaboration with local partners will be essential. In the context of growing competition – from, among others, Sky News, BBC World Service Television, and Reuters – CNN must learn to reconcile global ambitions with local complexities.

The case of Star TV provides another good example of the necessary accommodation between global and local dynamics. As part of their strategy for global hegemony, media corporations have sectioned the world into large geoeconomic regions. Star, a Hong Kong-based company which began broadcasting in August 1991, has effectively constructed the Asia region; stretching from Turkey to Japan, from Mongolia to Indonesia, it encompasses 38 countries (though only 13 receive Star signals at present). The station combined pan-Asian programs and advertising with a certain amount of material targeted at 'spot markets,' such as India or Taiwan. It also sought to balance Asian programming (Indian or Chinese pop music and films, for example) with 'Western' channels (MTV, BBC World Service Television, Prime Sports), many of which are highly popular and welcomed as forces of internationalization and 'modernization' (Poole 1993). Acknowledgment of its success across this vast region came in July 1993 when Rupert Murdoch's News Corporation paid $525 million for a controlling share of Star TV. For Murdoch, the Asian region was part of his 'global dream,' and he will clearly seek to market his Sky channels there. But he also recognizes the enormous cultural and linguistic differences within the region, and is planning to create separate services for India and China, and possibly also for Indonesia (Snoddy 1993). Given the diversity and complexity of this market, and given the enormous political (China, Indonesia) and religious (Malaysia) sensitivities, Murdoch's 'local' partners are crucial to the future success of Star. Success will depend on finding the right balance between market integration and market diversity.

The new media order involves, then, the articulation of both global and local factors (Robins 1990) ... Anxious to avert charges of cultural homogenization and domination, global corporations are concerned to develop local credentials and credibility (though in this context, of course, 'local' may amount to a multi-national region).

## References

AULETTA, K. (1993a) 'Raiding the global village', *The New Yorker*, 2 August, pp. 25–30.

AULETTA, K. (1993b) 'The last studio in play', *The New Yorker*, 4 October, pp. 77–81.

BOOZ-ALLEN & HAMILTON (1993) *The changing environment for UK broadcasters and its economic implications*, London, ITV Network Association.

LEVITT, T. (1983) *The Marketing Imagination*, New York, Free Press.

POOLE, T. (1993) 'Star in the East heralds TV revolution', *Independent on Sunday*, 18 April.

ROBINS, K. (1990) 'Global local times' in ANDERSON, J. and RICCI, M. (eds) *Society and Social Science: a reader*, Milton Keynes, Open University.

ROSS, S. (1990) Worldview address, delivered at the Edinburgh International Television Festival, 26 August.

SCHILLER, H.I. (1991) 'Not yet the post-imperialist era', *Critical Studies in Mass Communication*, 8, pp. 13–28.

SNODDY, R. (1993) 'The film that can erase itself', *Financial Times*, supplement on cable TV and satellite broadcasting, 6 October.

WINRAM, S. (1984) 'The opportunity for world brands', *International Journal of Advertising*, 3 (7), pp. 17–26.

Source: Robins, 1995, pp. 248, 252, 253–9

## Reading E
## ENGLISH IN SWEDEN IN THE AGE OF SATELLITE TELEVISION

*Olle Findahl*

Today, we have a dozen or so satellites overhead that carry some twenty television channels broadcast from the major nations of the world. They are available to cabled neighbourhoods and areas throughout Europe. For Sweden and several other small nations of Europe, most of the programming offered is in foreign languages.

This development is not entirely new; for years many Europeans have been able to watch television across national frontiers. What is new is the accessibility of programmes from a variety of countries, plus the dominance of Anglo-American programmes from the start.

What does this portend? First of all, the pressures tending toward commercialism in broadcasting may be expected to increase. Satellite transmissions are expensive, and the money to be made is expected to come from advertising revenues. This is an important aspect of satellite broadcasting that warrants more attention than it has received to date. Commercial programming is completed by a number of state-sponsored channels that were launched for propaganda reasons and their 'PR' value (e.g. Horizon from the Soviet Union, Worldnet produced by the United States Information Service, TV5 from francophone countries, Sat 1 from German-speaking countries).

Secondly, we may expect the influence of the major languages, particularly English (British and North American), to be reinforced, an effect which will be particularly noticeable in countries where knowledge of English is widespread. This is the case in Scandinavia and Finland, for example, and in the Netherlands.

The national languages of Europe have always been influenced by foreign languages. In earlier centuries French exerted a dominant influence; French was succeeded by German, and since the Second World War English has been paramount. In past centuries, however, interculturalism was restricted to social and educational élites, the vast majority of people remaining oblivious to foreign influence. Today, while the intelligentsia and professionals are still subject to the greatest influence from foreign languages, the lives of children are also full of foreign words and expressions. In the satellite age foreign languages will be heard daily in most people's living rooms. This prospect contains both dangers and possibilities. Will the accessibility of foreign television programmes promote international understanding? Will it improve our command and understanding of foreign languages? If so, then we may expect widespread viewing of satellite channels to strengthen the prospects of world peace, and we will take a giant step toward bi-, tri- or multi-lingualism.

But what content will satellite channels carry, and what programmes will Swedes and other minor-language nations choose to watch? Is it actually possible to learn a language by watching television? Is it not more likely that we will simply grow accustomed to watching programmes we don't fully understand? The questions are many.

The present article concentrates on a single aspect of these developments, namely, on how small languages like Swedish may be expected to fare. It is already clear that English is in the ascendant in many parts of the world. This is true in science, commerce, finance and, not least, in the transnational media industry. Swedish children and youth will be spending an hour or more a day with the English language via satellite television. What impact will this have? What might it mean for our grandchildren and great-grandchildren?

A number of factors must be examined in order to be able to answer these questions. First, it is necessary to survey the present situation in areas with access to satellite television. In Sweden, some areas have had such access in the last couple of years; viewers in Belgium and the Netherlands have had satellite television for over ten years. Second, we need to know something about how languages live and develop, and under what conditions they shrink and fade into obscurity. We have to study linguistic history, and the growing dominance of the English language in recent decades.

Third, if we are to be able to make any kind of prediction regarding the future of, say, Swedish, we have to know something about language learning, about how we assimilate foreign languages. Finally, we should familiarize ourselves with the fates of languages that have been subject to strong pressure from other languages, particularly English. Are there parallels? What we can learn about our own situation may be summarized in three basic questions:

1   Will we Swedes, a minor-language nation, still speak Swedish in a hundred years' time, albeit highly seasoned with English loanwords and expressions?

2   Or will we be bilingual, equally at home in both English and Swedish?

3   Or will we have become English-speaking, but still with some knowledge of our quaint 'mother tongue', which we bring out on Swedish Flag Day and festive occasions? ...

## Knowledge of English in Sweden and Europe

Swedes' knowledge of foreign languages has improved considerably since the Second World War as a result of the rise in the general level of education. Today, English is obligatory in Swedish schools; most students have studied the language for at least six or seven years, and many for eight to ten years. Consequently, most Swedes today both understand English and can make themselves understood, if not always fluently, in English (see Tables 1 and 2).

As late as the 1950s only 15–20 percent of the Swedish people could understand and express themselves in English; today two out of three say they have a good understanding of English (Bergentoft, 1986). There are, however, differences in proficiency in English, particularly between young people and the elderly and the generation gap is greatest outside metropolitan areas (see Table 2).

**Table I**   Self-rated language abilities (percentages)

|  | How well do you understand: | | | | | |
|---|---|---|---|---|---|---|
|  | English | German | French | Russian | Norwegian | Danish |
| Well/Fairly well | 60-70 | 20 | 2-6 | 0-2 | 71 | 33 |
| Poorly/Not at all | 40-30 | 80 | 98-94 | 100-98 | 29 | 67 |

*Note:* Data based on telephone interviews of random samples (N = 500–700) conducted by Sveriges Radio/PUB.

**Table 2**   Self-rated command of English among Swedes of different ages (percentages)

| Understand English | Ages (years) | | | | | |
|---|---|---|---|---|---|---|
|  | Total | 9-14 | 15-24 | 25-44 | 45-64 | 65-79 |
| Well/Fairly well | 63 | 58 | 91 | 77 | 29 | 8 |
| Poorly/Not at all | 37 | 42 | 9 | 23 | 71 | 92 |

Source: SR/PUB, 1987, unpublished data.

Knowledge of other languages is much less widespread. Only small fractions of the population know any of the other satellite languages – French, German and Russian. Satellite transmissions cannot be expected to redress the balance. Rather, 'third languages' may be expected to recede even farther into the shadows as the dominance of English grows.

If we compare self-rated comprehension of English with understanding of other Scandinavian languages, we find that English is considered much easier to understand than Danish, but that Norwegian is considered easier than English. Here, too, marked differences between the generations may be noted. Elderly and middle-aged respondents have a better understanding of other Scandinavian languages, whereas some young people even find English easier to understand than Norwegian.[1] (A similar pattern occurs in Iceland, where schools teach both English and Danish in addition to Icelandic. Language tests show that pupils have a better command of Danish, but they say they know English better than Danish, see Börestam, 1984.)

A comprehensive study of Swedes' knowledge of English found that Swedish young people are very favourably disposed toward English (Ljung, 1986). They are much more accepting of English loanwords and English pronunciation. They also have more contact with the language than other groups. This is true of young people in general, regardless of whether they attend school or are working. However, when it comes to precise knowledge of the meaning of given loanwords and a sensibility for English grammar, education, not age, is the decisive factor. Consequently, we have reason to suspect that the self-ratings reported above are somewhat 'inflated'. A second factor, too, plays a part. Young people appear to base their judgements on 'functional' criteria; i.e. whether or not they know enough English to get by in simple conversations or, say, to watch American television series.

## Do language problems keep viewers away?

Even though many Swedes feel they have a fairly good command of English, it is still a foreign language and poses something of a hindrance. Do viewers' difficulties with foreign languages ever keep them from watching English-language satellite programmes? The short answer is yes. Studies in two cabled areas in different parts of Sweden found that one viewer in four sometimes refrains from watching satellite channels because of the language. This is especially common among older age groups and, not surprisingly, those who say they have poor knowledge of English.

About every second Swede between the ages of nine and fourteen reports finding it very difficult to understand the English spoken in the programmes, but only a quarter of this age group ever refrain from watching a programme for that reason … In other words, many watch the satellite channels despite the fact they do not understand the language. Where young people do refrain from watching, feature films are the programmes most often excluded (Westrell, 1987). Similar observations have been made in Norway, where again about a quarter of the satellite viewers who say they find English hard to understand watch Sky on an average day. Of those who say English is impossible to understand, only 18 percent watch Sky Channel programmes (Werner, Höst and Ulvaer, 1984).

What might the fact that many viewers watch programmes without fully grasping their verbal content mean? Will children and young people become accustomed to not understanding what they see? Will they learn to consider television a frivolous medium that need not be fully understood?

## Attitudes toward English among our youngest

As we have seen, young Swedes have a very positive attitude toward the English language, and very few refrain from watching satellite channels due to the language barrier. Only among the eldest group do a majority of viewers sometimes abstain for that reason.

But what about the very youngest? How do they react to programmes that are entirely in English? Studies have found that they do comment on the foreign language, but it does not keep them from watching the programmes. Only among the very youngest (3-year-olds) does the use of English turn as many as one-third away from Sky Channel programmes. Among 4-to-8-year-olds only about one in ten sometimes refrains.

Interviews with parents in a cabled suburb of Stockholm reveal surprisingly positive attitudes. The subjectively experienced language barrier between young Swedish viewers and English-language programming does not seem much of a problem. Even today children find it natural that English is spoken on television. This attitude is hardly likely to change as they grow up and study English in school, perhaps for as long as ten years. But we must not forget that about half the children sit quietly and watch without saying a word. What goes on in their minds is an equally important, and perhaps more urgent, question.

## A comparison with knowledge of English in other countries

When we compare English as a second language in Europe, only in the smaller countries with national languages in Western Europe do we find knowledge of English that is on a par with that of the Swedes ... [O]nly in Scandinavia and the Netherlands do a majority of the people know English. In German- and French-speaking nations English is not nearly as widely spread throughout society ...

## What future for Sweden?

[Although] language barriers still prevail in many countries, [in Sweden] the barrier toward English is crumbling. This brings us back to the question: How many Swedes will speak English as their native language in one hundred years' time? The question is provocatively phrased, and the time horizon is far more distant than is customary in questions relating to the media. When it comes to predictions regarding linguistic changes, however, generations are the proper unit of measure.

The direction of change is clear. The question is how much and how fast Anglo-American influence will continue to grow, and how vigorous and obdurate the Swedish language will prove to be.

In one hundred years' time, will we still speak Swedish, albeit with numerous loanwords from British and American English? Can Swedish be expected to survive, to proceed along the same course as major languages like French and German? Or, will Swedes of the 2080s be bilingual, with Swedish and English as native tongues? Or will we, few as we are, have become engulfed by the 'English empire' and keep Swedish in the family chest, a quaint relic to be dusted off, polished up and displayed on festive occasions? The questions remain unanswered.

The advance of English worldwide is reinforced by the fact that English has become the primary second language in a growing number of countries, as in Europe. In many countries English is the only foreign language taught in primary and secondary schools. The result is that, in future, people from different European countries will not be able to understand one another's languages, but will be forced to use English. This will happen when Frenchmen meet Spaniards, or Italians; it may also be the case between Danes and Icelanders and even between Swedes and Norwegians.

As noted above, there is ample evidence that the younger generation stands wide open to Anglo-American culture. In no other country do children and young people watch English-language satellite television to the extent Swedish young people do, and, when asked where they would move if they had to leave Sweden, the USA is the most popular choice. Even today, British and American expressions have already influenced the Swedish language, and this occurs in such diverse fields as the natural sciences, advertising, computer sciences, music and popular culture, and above all, in satellite television. In contrast to the other sectors, popular culture and, not least, satellite television are open to everyone. As more and more Swedish households are cabled, the contact surface grows.

Sweden will continue to be economically and culturally aligned with English-speaking countries. This is one prerequisite for comprehensive linguistic change. Further, the influence of English-language television via satellite can only be expected to increase. Sweden is not alone in this situation, but small countries, whose languages are spoken by relatively few people, feel the pressure more than others. If the orientation of our youth is any indication, Sweden appears to be more susceptible to the pressures than many other nations.

Swedish youth feel they have a good or very good command of English. Only a few say they ever refrain from watching English-language television because of the language. Only among Swedes over fifty years of age do as many as one in three experience a language barrier; among young people such frequencies are noted only among 3-year-olds. Even today, many Swedish children find it perfectly natural to watch television in English, and some say that English 'isn't really foreign any more'.

In the satellite age, linguistic boundaries are more important than national boundaries as far as television is concerned. While national television services in the smaller countries (and smaller markets) of Europe are experiencing a period of economic retrenchment, their audiences are being opened up to transnational television from England and the USA (Wedell and Luyken, 1986).

What this coincidence of trends will lead to in Sweden will depend on how we react to it, and the nature and quality of Swedish television services. In some small countries, such as Iceland, the level of public awareness and concern is high; in other countries, such as the Netherlands, the reaction has been one of equanimity (Blidberg and Thinsz, 1986). We in Sweden fall somewhere in between. Of one thing we can be sure: English dominance is expanding at a faster pace today than it has historically, and satellite television has been, and will continue to be, highly instrumental in this process.

## Notes

The author would like to thank Charly Hultén for the translation into English. The research was supported by the Draft Committee on grants for Programming and Technical Research and Development of Sveriges Radio and the National Telecommunication Administration.

1   The Scandinavian languages – Danish, Norwegian and Swedish – are closely related derivates of Old Norse. In principle they are mutually understandable, but de facto they are different enough so as to be a barrier to some. The languages share the greater part of their vocabularies, but pronunciation and spellings differ. Spoken Danish, for example, is more difficult for Swedes and Norwegians to understand than written Danish.

## References

BERGENTOFT, R. (1986) '... för att hjälpa skolan', *Språkvård*, 1: 35–6.

BLIDBERG, K. and THINSZ, I. (1986) 'Rapport Från Samtal med Represententer för Undervisning, Massmedia samt Massmediaforskning Under en Resa i Holland 9/4–16/4 1986'. Stockholm: Utbildningsradion (unpublished manuscript).

BÖRESTAM, U. (1984) *Språkförståelse och Språkpreferenser i Internordisk Kommunikation på Island*. Uppsala: FUMS, inst för nordiska språk vid Uppsala Universitet.

LJUNG, M. (1986) 'Hur ser det ut? Undersökningen Engelskan i Sverige', *Språkvård*, 3: 5–10.

WEDELL, G. and LUYKEN, G-M. (1986) *Media in Competition. The Future of Print and Electronic Media in 22 Countries*. Manchester: European Institute for the Media.

WERNER, A.S. HÖST and ULVAER, B. (1984) *Publikums Reaksjoner på Satellit og Lokalfjernsyn*. Oslo: Institut for presseforskning.

WESTRELL, C. (1987) *Satellit-TV:s publik. Vidareanalys av Kabel-TV Undersökningar i Borlänge och Kalmar Hösten 1985*. Stockholm: Sveriges Radio/PUB.

Source: Findahl, 1989, pp. 133–5, 143–7, 156–9

---

## Reading F
## DUBBING AMERICAN IN ITALY

*Nigel J. Ross*

A good deal has been written over the years about how English has influenced other languages. Vocabulary is clearly the main field of influence: other languages have adopted and adapted a whole range of English words, and nowadays many new products and trends are referred to by an English or English-based term the world over. Linguists are well aware of these processes, these 'mainstream influences'. There are, however, a number of much more subtle ways in which English has influenced other languages and these, too, can at times be quite significant.

The more subtle influences involve such aspects as word order, word forms, shifts in meaning and sentence structure. David Crystal (1988, p. 254) cites how an invitation in Spanish might have once begun *El señor Rodriguez y señora* ..., but is now more likely to follow the English pattern of *El señor y la señora Rodriguez* ...; an indefinite article may now be used in a Swedish construction mirroring English as in *Han är en läkare* (He is a doctor) (ibid); in Italian *permissivo* (relating to permission) has also come to mean 'tolerant', 'behaving freely' as in English, and so on. Many European languages keep the English plural when they borrow an English word, some examples being: *hooligans, fans* and *sandwichs* (sic). At times direct translations are made from English to provide a new concept in a foreign language: Italian has *maggioranza silenziosa* (the silent majority), *parola-chiave* (key-word), and *le pubbliche relazioni* (public relations). Translation is a subtle but effective influence and one that is perhaps all too often ignored.

A very specific kind of translation from English – dubbing – has had a number of effects on foreign languages that are worth taking a closer look at. Although some governments may wish it were not the case, in the main the world watches *American* movies and television series. In other words, the world watches films and programmes that were originally made in English. In some non-English-speaking countries they are shown with subtitles, but more often they are dubbed into the local language. This dubbing process – technically we should refer to it as 'post-synchronous dialogue dubbing' (Bobker, 1974, p. 89) – is a highly skilled tech-nique and often requires a rather imaginative translation if the dubber's words are to be successfully synchronized with the actor's lip movements. It is the subtle influence of this 'imaginative translation' that will be dealt with in this article, and although influences of English on the Italian language alone will be analysed here, the same kind of process clearly takes place with other languages.

A good dialogue translator is very much aware that some of the most noticeable lip movements come at the beginning of speech segments, especially when the actor is seen in close-up. Certain consonant sounds have particularly distinct lip movements, /m/ /b/ /p/ /f/ and /v/ being excellent examples. When a phrase begins with a /p/ sound, such as 'Please will you …' a translator should try to provide the dubber with a line that also begins with a /p/, though a /b/ sound would also suffice since no one but an expert lip-reader will distinguish the movements. Likewise, the number of syllables in the original and translated versions should be as similar as possible, and mid-line /m/ /b/ /p/ and other crucial lip movements should be matched if the lips may be subject to close audience scrutiny.

The need for a close match becomes particularly critical for short speech items, the most troublesome being short one-word expressions such as 'Great!' When Italians want to express similar approval, they normally say something like *Magnifico! Meraviglioso! Favoloso!* or *Splendido!* But none of these are successful translations for 'Great!' when lip and mouth movements are considered: they all have far too many syllables and start with very 'visible' sounds. Watch a few films or TV programmes in Italy that have been dubbed from English and you are bound to catch a *Grande!* (large) or a *Grandioso!* (grand) voiced over a 'Great!' But although they fit beautifully from a labial point of view, they have never been really suitable or natural Italian expressions. However, after years and years of hearing *Grande!* or *Grandioso!* on their screens, Italians have now begun to use them spontaneously.

Another very frequent one-word expression is 'Hello'. It is dubbed fairly well with *Ciao* in informal contexts, but the formal *Buon giorno/buona sera* alternatives are labially unsuitable. As a result, the general-purpose term *Salve* is often pressed into service, and this is probably the main reason for its increasing use nowadays (it also dubs the French *Salut* splendidly). In the same manner, the expression 'Sure!' is usually translated as *Sicuro!* (i.e. sure, secure, safe), and this perhaps explains why it seems to be gaining ground over alternatives such as *Senz'altro* or *Naturalmente!*

Just as one-word expressions lead to novel labial translations, short phrases also bring linguistic innovations when lip movements need to be matched. The common expression 'Call me tomorrow!' would usually translate into Italian as *Dammi un colpo di telefono domani!* (fairly literally: Give me a telephone call tomorrow!) or simply *Telefonami domani!* Once again the Italian equivalents are far too long, and lip movements could never be matched. Therefore, in order to ensure 'labial sync', the dubbed voice will probably say *Chiamami domani!* (literally 'Call me tomorrow!') which fits rather well, though it would hardly be the usual way of putting it … or would it? The repeated use of the phrase in films and TV programmes is very likely the reason why *chiamare* in the sense of 'to telephone' has recently come into fairly general use, especially among younger speakers.

An individual word that causes problems for labial translation is 'blame'. Scripts seem to have fairly frequent scenes when characters blame each other for things – especially in soap operas where close-ups are also extremely common. Purely from the point of view of meaning, Italian equivalents for 'to blame' are: *dare la colpa* (to lay the blame), *ritenere responsabile* (to hold responsible) or even *accusare* (to accuse), but none of them are suitable labial equivalents. As a result, the fairly rare verb *biasimare* is usually brought in to play, even though its meaning is more that of 'disapprove' or 'censure'. Nowadays, however, *biasimare* appears to be shifting its meaning and gaining a wider use – some Italians now simply use it in the sense of 'to hold responsible'.

In a similar manner, the verb *ritornare* (to return) also seems to have undergone a shift in meaning in recent years. 'Return' is now often translated by *ritornare* in all senses, although *ritornare* only ever used to have the relatively narrow meaning of 'going back' to a place. The more usual Italian verbs to express the idea of 'giving back' or 'sending back' are *restituire* and *rimandare*. But once again the influence of translation – either because of the need for labial parallelism or simply as a result of downright sloppiness – has deflected the meaning of a word.

Pronouns are another area where we can notice 'imaginative translations'. Although Italians usually miss out personal pronouns, saying *sono* rather *io sono* for 'I am', dubbers will very often include the *io* as it gives closer lip movements. The most awkward pronoun is 'she' which translates as *lei* in Italian, obviously a very poor labial match. When an actor says something like: 'She's not sure if he'll come,' it may be dubbed *C'è una possibilità che lui non venga* (literally 'There's a possibility that he won't come'). In fact *c'è* ('there is', pronounced rather like 'chair') is often used to dub an initial 'she'. If this is another case of discrimination against the female sex, it is surely quite involuntary.

Problems are not only caused by consonant sounds, of course. Anthony Burgess (1992, p. 29) has pointed out how the wide-lipped vowel sound of 'arse' (or 'ass') pairs so badly with the Italian rounded /u:/ sound in *culo*. Likewise, an English expression of pain such as 'Ow!' or 'Ouch!' cannot be dubbed very well with the usual Italian *Ahi!* or *Ahia!*, and so a less natural sound such as *Ohi!* is usually employed. The ubiquitous opening 'Well, …' is nearly always translated with *bè* (an abbreviation of *bene*), and this generally works reasonably well: the vowel sounds compare very successfully. However, while 'well' is used by all classes of English speakers, the shortened Italian *bè* would normally be avoided by upper-class Italian speakers, except of course on the screen. Consequently *bè* seems to be moving up-class thanks to the influence of dubbing.

The mentioning of 'arse' (or 'ass') brings us on to an important category of words that have been influenced by dubbing – swear words. Readers who object to hearing swear words in films may prefer to skip the rest of this paragraph. Actors tend to enunciate swear words loudly, distinctly and very visibly – close-ups are often used at such moments of anger to heighten tension. Consequently they need to be dubbed very accurately. But what do you do when the English 'Shit!'

corresponds to the Italian *Merda!*? They are evident labial enemies. Well, for once the answer is not too difficult: the translator goes for *Cazzo!* (literally 'prick' but a typical Italian expression for extreme anger). *Cazzo!* is also frequently pressed into service to dub a blasphemous cry of 'God!': it fits much better than the literal *Dio!*

Problems arise with an expression like 'fucking bastard!' – two words starting with the clearly visible sounds /f/ and /b/. 'Bastard' fortunately translates well as *bastardo,* but the Italians seldom use any form of *fottere* (fuck) as a swear word. Nevertheless, over the years thousands of movie 'fucking bastards' have been translated with the wonderfully labial *fottuto bastardo,* the adjective being put before the noun instead of in the usual Italian post-noun position. Exposure to this labial equivalent has introduced a new expletive expression to the Italian language which is now used on and off the screen. (Another example of English word order being maintained in translation was seen earlier with *le pubbliche relazioni,* and a recent letter in the 'Corriere della Sera' newspaper complained about this trend, calling it a 'rather too English influence' (Corriere della Sera, 27 April 1994) – the subtle influences to word order abound.)

Pronunciation is a final area where the dubbing process has actually had an impact on the language. This can be seen particularly clearly with names. Whereas in the past the standard Italian pronunciation of 'Canada' accentuated the final syllable, the English stress on the first syllable is now preferred. Likewise, the older pronunciation of 'Florida' with a stress on the middle syllable has been superseded by the English stress pattern. The name 'Nobel' in the expression *premio Nobel* has shifted its stress from the first to the second syllable, though this is perhaps less a direct influence of dubbing alone than the consequence of a range of influences. In the past, Italian generally used to follow French pronunciations of foreign names and words, but now the English pronunciation is taking over. 'Waterloo' is now usually pronounced in the English rather than the French manner (Gabrielli, 1977, pp. 47–8). The way an Italian says 'Titanic' now nears the English pronunciation.

Dubbing has evidently played a significant role in altering pronunciations. When an actor is actually dubbing a film, a silent version is shown in the recording studio but the actor hears the original sound-track through head-phones. Hearing the English pronunciation while dubbing the new sound-track naturally leads an actor to mimic the sounds and stress patterns of the English pronunciation, especially for words that are similar in both languages.

The dubbing process is obviously a fairly recent phenomenon, but other forms of written and spoken translation have long affected language development; dubbing has become just one more subtle influence. Although this brief survey has only concentrated on how dubbing from English can introduce new words and expressions into Italian, bringing about shifts in meaning, register and pronunciation in the language, there can be no doubt that similar processes are also underway in many other languages. Such influences clearly abound ... even in rather apt situations: the word 'dubbing' itself (from the French term *doubler*) in all likelihood originates from a rather mangled pronunciation of an over-literal translation (Foster, 1968, p. 75).

## Notes

The author wishes to thank friends and colleagues for their confirmations and suggestions during the preparation of this article, and in particular Vincenzo Bonini, Daniela Gervasi and Mike Sicoli.

# References

BOBKER, L.R. (1974) *Elements of Film, 2nd edition.* New York: Harcourt Brace Jovanovich.

BURGESS, A. (1992) *A Mouthful of Air.* London: Vintage.

CRYSTAL, D. (1988) *The English Language.* London: Penguin.

FOSTER, B. (1968) *The Changing English Language.* London: Macmillan.

GABRIELLI, A. (1977) *Il museo degli errori.* Milan: Oscar Mondadori.

Source: Ross, 1995, pp. 45–8

# REFERENCES

AHAI, N. and FARACLAS, N. (1993) 'Rights and expectations in an age of "debt crisis": literacy and integral human development in Papua New Guinea' in FREEBODY, P. and WELCH, A.R. (eds) *Knowledge, Culture and Power: international perspectives on literacy as policy and practice*, London, Falmer.

AMMON, U. (1995) 'To what extent is German an international language?' in STEVENSON, P. (ed.) *The German Language and the Real World*, Oxford, Oxford University Press.

ANDERSON, B. (1991) *Imagined Communities: reflections on the origins and spread of nationalism*, London, Verso.

ARNHEIM, R. (1970) *Visual Thinking*, London, Faber & Faber.

ARNHEIM, R. (1988) *The Power of the Center: a study of composition in the visual arts*, London, University of California Press.

ATKINSON, M. (1984) *Our Masters' Voices: the language and body language of politics*, London, Methuen.

BAILEY, R.W. (1992) *Images of English: a cultural history of the language*, Cambridge, Cambridge University Press.

BAKHTIN, M.M. (1981) *The Dialogic Imagination*, edited M. Holquist, trans. C. Emerson and M. Holquist, Austin, University of Texas Press.

BAKHTIN, M.M. (1986) *Speech Genres and Other Late Essays*, edited C. Emerson and M. Holquist, trans. V.W. McGee, Austin, University of Texas Press.

BELL, A. (1991) *The Language of News Media*, Oxford, Blackwell.

BERNS, M. (1995) 'English in the European Union', *English Today*, vol. 11, no. 3, pp. 3–11.

BOLINGER, D.L. (1946) 'Visual morphemes', *Twentieth Century Literature*, vol. 22, pp. 333–40.

BOLTER, J.D. (1989) 'Beyond word-processing – the computer as a new writing space', *Language and Communication*, vol. 9, nos. 2–3, pp. 129–42.

BOLTER, J.D. (1991) *Writing Space: the computer, hypertext, and the history of writing*, Hillsdale, N.J., Lawrence Erlbaum.

BOYD-BARRETT, O. (1980) *The International News Agencies*, London, Constable.

BRENZINGER, M., HEINE, B. and SOMMER, G. (1991) 'Language death in Africa' in ROBINS, R.H. and UHLENBECK, E.M. (eds) *Endangered Languages*, Oxford, Berg.

BREWER, W.F. (1985) 'The story schema: universal and culture-specific properties' in OLSON, D.R., TORRANCE, N. and HILDYARD, A. (eds) *Literacy, Language, and Learning: the nature and consequences of reading and writing*, Cambridge, Cambridge University Press.

BRITISH COUNCIL (1995) *English in the World: the English 2000 global consultation*, Manchester, British Council.

BROWN, R. and GILMAN, A. (1972) 'The pronouns of power and solidarity' in GIGLIOLI, P.P. (ed.) *Language and Social Context*, Harmondsworth, Penguin.

BURT SIR C. (1950) *A Psychological Study of Typography*, London, Cambridge University Press.

CAMERON, D. (1995) *Verbal Hygiene*, London, Routledge.

CAREY, J.W. (1987) 'Why and how? The dark continent of American journalism' in MANOFF, R.K. and SCHUDSON, M. (eds) *Reading the News*, New York, Pantheon.

CARTER, R., DAY, B. and MEGGS, P. (1985) *Typographic Design: form and communication*, New York, Van Nostrand Reinhold.

CATFORD, J.C. (1950) 'The background and origins of basic English', *English Language Teaching*, no. 28, pp. 36–47.

CHERNEY, L. (1995) 'Marie Disconnects: third person simple tense in MUD discourse', Georgetown University Round Table on Languages and Linguistics, Pre-session on Computer-mediated Discourse Analysis, Georgetown University.

COOK, G. (1992) *The Discourse of Advertising*, London, Routledge.

CORNER, J. (1995) *Television Form and Public Address*, London, Edward Arnold.

CRANE, G. (1991) 'Composing culture', *Current Anthropology*, vol. 32, no. 3, pp. 293–311.

CRUTCHLEY, E.T. (1938) *GPO*, Cambridge, Cambridge University Press.

CZERNIEWSKA, P. (1992) *Learning about Writing: the early years*, Oxford, Blackwell.

DEPARTMENT OF HEALTH (1991) *The Patient's Charter*, London, HMSO.

DERRIDA, J. (1976) *Of Grammatology*, Baltimore, Johns Hopkins University Press.

DERWING, B.L. (1992) 'Orthographic aspects of linguistic competence' in DOWNING, P., LIMA, S.D. and NOONAN, M. (eds) *The Linguistics of Literacy*, Amsterdam, John Benjamins.

DICKENS, C. ([1855–7] 1979) *Little Dorrit*, edited H.P. Sucksmith, Oxford, Clarendon.

DIXON, R.M.W. (1991) 'The endangered languages of Australia, Indonesia and Oceania' in ROBINS, R.H. and UHLENBECK, E.M. (eds) *Endangered Languages*, Oxford, Berg.

DONDIS, D.A. (1973) *A Primer of Visual Literacy*, Massachusetts, Massachusetts Institute of Technology (MIT).

DURKHEIM, E. (1964) *Division of Labour in Society*, trans. G. Simpson, New York, Free Press.

ECO, U. (1995) *The Search for the Perfect Language*, Oxford, Blackwell.

EDUCATION COMMISSION (1995) *Enhancing Language Proficiency: a comprehensive strategy*, Report no. 6, Hong Kong, Education Commission.

ERVIN-TRIPP, S.M. (1969) 'Sociolinguistics', *Advances in Experimental Social Psychology*, vol. 4, pp. 93–107.

FAIRCLOUGH, N. (ed.) (1992) *Critical Language Awareness*, London, Longman.

FAIRCLOUGH, N. (1993) 'Critical discourse analysis and the marketization of public discourse: the universities', *Discourse and Society*, vol. 4, no. 2, pp. 133–68.

FAIRCLOUGH, N. (1994) 'Conversationalization of public discourse and the authority of the consumer' in KEAT, R., WHITELEY, N. and ABERCROMBIE, N. (eds) *The Authority of the Consumer*, London, Routledge.

FAIRCLOUGH, N. (1995) *Media Discourse*, London, Edward Arnold.

FAIRCLOUGH, N. (1996) 'Border crossings: discourse and social change in contemporary societies' in *Change and Language*, BAAL 10, Clevedon, Multilingual Matters.

FINDAHL, O. (1989) 'Language in the age of satellite television', *European Journal of Communication*, vol. 4, pp. 133–59.

FOWLER, R. (1991) *Language in the News*, London, Routledge.

FRY, S. (1995) 'I fell into the safety net', *Daily Telegraph*, 13 November.

GADDIE, G.P. (1989) 'Homophony and paranomasia in America: on the validity of puns', unpublished PhD thesis, Ohio, Bowling Green State University.

GALTUNG, J. and RUGE, M.H. (1965) 'The structure of foreign news', *Journal of Peace Research*, vol. 2, no. 1, pp. 64–91.

GEIPEL, J. (1972) *The Cartoon*, Newton Abbot, David & Charles.

GOFFMAN, E. (1981) *Forms of Talk*, Philadelphia, University of Pennsylvania Press.

GOMBRICH, E.H. (1959) *Art and Illusion*, London, Phaidon.

GOODIN, R.E. (1980) *Manipulatory Politics*, New Haven, Yale University Press.

GOODY, J. and WATT, L. (1963) 'The consequences of literacy', *Comparative Studies in Society and History*, vol. 5, pp. 304–45.

GOWERS, E. (1973) *The Complete Plain Words*, Harmondsworth, Penguin.

GRADDOL, D., CHESHIRE, J. and SWANN, J. (1994) *Describing Language*, 2nd edn, Buckingham, Open University Press.

GRADDOL, D., LEITH, D. and SWANN, J. (eds) *English: history, diversity and change*, London, Routledge/The Open University.

GREGSTON, B. (1996) 'French connection', *Internet*, no. 15, 21 February, pp. 48–9.

HAGEN, S. (ed.) (1993) *Languages in European Business: a regional survey of small and medium-sized companies*, London, City Technology Colleges Trust/CILT.

HALLIDAY, M.A.K. (1970) 'Language structure and language function' in LYONS, J. (ed.) *New Horizons in Linguistics*, Harmondsworth, Penguin.

HALLIDAY, M.A.K. (1978) *Language as Social Semiotic*, London, Edward Arnold.

HALLIDAY, M.A.K. (1985) *Introduction to Functional Grammar*, London, Edward Arnold.

HALLIDAY, M.A.K. (1987) 'Spoken and written modes of meaning' in HOROWITZ, R. and SAMUELS (eds) *Comprehending Oral and Written Language*, New York, Academic Press.

HALLIDAY, M.A.K. and HASAN, R. (1989) *Language, Context, and Text: aspects of language in a social-semiotic perspective*, Oxford, Oxford University Press.

HAMMOND, P. and HUGHES, P. (1978) *Upon the Pun: dual meaning in words and pictures*, London, W.H. Allen.

HARCOURT, E. (1987) *Taming the Tyrant: the first one hundred years of Australia's international communication services*, Sydney, Allen & Unwin.

HEADRICK, D.R. (1991) *The Invisible Weapon: telecommunications and international politics 1851–1945*, New York, Oxford University Press.

HEARN, P.M. and BUTTON, D.F. (eds) (1994) *Language Industries Atlas*, Amsterdam, IOS.

HEATH, S.B. (1983) *Ways with Words: language, life and work in communities and classrooms*, Cambridge, Cambridge University Press.

HJARVARD, S. (1994), 'TV news: from discrete items of continuous narrative? The social meaning of changing temporal structures', *Cultural Studies*, vol. 8, no. 2, pp. 306–20.

HOCHSCHILD, A.R. (1983) *The Managed Heart*, Berkeley, University of California Press.

HOCK, E.T.B. (1995) 'English in cyberspace', unpublished BA thesis, National University of Singapore.

HUTT, A. (1967) *Newspaper Design*, 2nd edn, London, Oxford University Press.

JACOB, H. (1947) *A Planned Auxiliary Language*, London, Dennis Dobson.

JAGGER, J.H. (1940) *English in the Future*, London, Thomas Nelson.

KACHRU, B.B. (ed.) (1983) *The Other Tongue: English across cultures*, Oxford, Pergamon.

KACHRU, B.B. (1991) 'World Englishes and applied linguistics' in TICKOO, M.L. (ed.) *Languages and Standards: issues, attitudes, case studies*, Anthology 26, Singapore, SEAMEO Regional Language Centre.

KIEVE, J. (1973) *The Electric Telegraph: a social and economic history*, Newton Abbot, David & Charles.

KRAUSS, M. (1992) 'The world's languages in crisis', *Language*, vol. 68, no. 1.

KRESS, G. and VAN LEEUWEN, T. (1990) *Reading Images*, Deakin, Vic., Deakin University.

KRESS, G. and VAN LEEUWEN, T. (1996) *Reading Images: the grammar of visual design*, London, Routledge.

LABOV, W. (1972) *Language in the Inner City: studies in the black English vernacular*, Philadelphia, University of Pennsylvania Press.

LABOV, W. and WALETZKY, J. (1967) 'Narrative analysis: oral versions of personal experience' in HELM, J. (ed.) *Essays on the Verbal and Visual Arts (Proceedings of the 1966 Annual Spring Meeting of the American Ethnological Society)*, Seattle, University of Washington Press.

LARGE, A. (1985) *The Artificial Language Movement*, Oxford, Blackwell.

LEVINE, K. (1986) *The Social Context of Literacy*, London, Routledge & Kegan Paul.

LEVINSON, P. (1988) *Mind at Large: knowing in the technological age*, London, JAI.

LYNCH, M. and EDGERTON, S.Y. (1988) 'Aesthetics and digital image processing: representation craft in contemporary astronomy' in FYFE, G. and LAW, J. (eds) *Picturing Power: visual depiction and social relations*, London, Routledge.

MAHAPATRA, B.P. (1990) 'A demographic appraisal of multilingualism in India' in PATTANAYAK, D.P. (ed.) *Multilingualism in India*, Clevedon, Multilingual Matters.

MAYBIN, J. and MERCER, N. (eds) (1996) *Using English: from conversation to canon*, London, Routledge/The Open University.

McCLOUD, S. (1994) *Understanding Comics: the invisible art*, New York, Harper Collins.

McLUHAN, M. (1962) *The Gutenberg Galaxy: the making of typographic man*, London, Routledge & Kegan Paul.

MERCER, N. and SWANN, J. (eds) (1996) *Learning English: development and diversity*, London, Routledge/The Open University.

MORGAN, J. and WELTON, P. (1986) *See What I Mean: an introduction to visual communication*, London, Edward Arnold.

MYERS, A. (1938) *Basic and the Teaching of English in India*, Bombay, Orthological Institute.

NEELANKAVIL, J.P., MUMMALANENI, V. and SESSIONS, D.N. (1995) 'Use of foreign language and models in print advertisements in East Asian countries', *European Journal of Marketing*, vol. 29, no. 4, pp. 24–38.

NOP (NATIONAL OPINION POLL) (1995) 'NOP Research Group provides first profile of Internet users', http://www.maires.co.uk/inet/users.html (visited 27 September 1996).

OGDEN, C.K. (1932) *The Basic Dictionary*, London, Kegan Paul, Trench, Trubner.

OPEN UNIVERSITY (1994) *Presenting the Open University: a guide to visual identity*, Milton Keynes, The Open University.

OPEN UNIVERSITY (1996) U210 *The English Language: past, present and future*, Study Guide 1, Milton Keynes, The Open University.

ORTHOLOGICAL INSTITUTE (1934) 'Basic news', *Psyche*, no. 14, pp. 187–201.

ORWELL, G. (1987) *Animal Farm*, London, Secker & Warburg.

PAOLILLO, J. (1995) 'Mode switching in CMC discourse', Georgetown University Round Table on Languages and Linguistics, Pre-session on Computer-mediated Discourse Analysis, Georgetown University.

PATTANAYAK, D.P. (1996) 'Change, language and the developing world' in COLEMAN, H. and CAMERON, L. (eds) *Change and Language*, Clevedon, BAAL/Multilingual Matters.

PENNYCOOK, A. (1994) *The Cultural Politics of English as an International Language*, London, Longman.

PHILLIPSON, R. (1992) *Linguistic Imperialism*, Oxford, Oxford University Press.

PHILLIPSON, R. (1994) 'The spread of dominant languages (English, French and German) in multilingual Europe' in PHILLIPSON, R. and SKUTNABB-KANGAS, T. (eds) *Language Policy in Europe*, Rolig-Papir 52, Roskilde, Roskilde University Center.

POSTER, M. (1990) *The Mode of Information: poststructuralism and social context*, Cambridge, Polity.

RICHARDS, I.A. (1943) *Basic English and its Uses*, London, Kegan Paul, Trench, Trubner.

ROBINS, K. (1995) 'The new spaces of global media' in JOHNSTON, R.J., TAYLOR, P.J. and WATTS, M.J. (eds) *Geographies of Global Change*, Oxford, Blackwell.

ROSCH, E. (1978) 'Principles of categorization' in ROSCH, E. and LLOYD, B.L. (eds) *Cognition and Categorization*, Hillsdale, N.J., Lawrence Erlbaum.

ROSS, N.J. (1995) 'Dubbing American in Italy', *English Today*, vol. 11, pp. 45–8.

SCHLESINGER, P. (1987) *Putting 'Reality' Together: BBC news*, 2nd edn, London, Methuen.

SCHLOSSMACHER, M. (1995) 'Official languages and working languages in the political bodies of the European Union', *New Language Planning Newsletter*, vol. 9, no. 4, pp. 1–2.

SCHUDSON, M. (1987) 'When? Deadlines, datelines, and history' in MANOFF, R.K. and SCHUDSON, M. (eds) *Reading the News*, New York, Pantheon.

SCHUDSON, M. (1989) 'The sociology of news production', *Media, Culture and Society*, vol. 11, no. 3, pp. 263–82.

SNOW, J. (1995) 'All the news that fits on screen', *Guardian*, 19 September.

SPENDER, D. (1995) *Nattering on the Net: women, power and cyberspace*, Melbourne, Vic., Spinifex.

STREET, B.V. (1984) *Literacy in Theory and Practice*, Cambridge, Cambridge University Press.

SWANN, C. (1991) *Language and Typography*, New York, Van Nostrand Reinhold.

TANNEN, D. (1992) 'How is conversation like literary discourse? The role of imagery and details in creating involvement' in DOWNING, P., LIMA, S.D. and NOONAN, M. (eds) *The Linguistics of Literacy*, Amsterdam, John Benjamins.

TAYLOR, M.C. and SAARINEN, E. (1994) *Imagologies: media philosophy*, London, Routledge.

TICKOO, M. (1993) 'When is a language worth teaching? Native languages and English in India', *Language, Culture and Curriculum*, vol. 6, no. 3, pp. 225–39.

TOLLEFSON, J.W. (1991) *Planning Language, Planning Inequality*, London, Longman.

TOMIC, P. and TRUMPER, R. (1992) 'Canada and the streaming of immigrants: a personal account of the Chilean case' in SATZEWICH, V. (ed.) *Deconstructing a Nation: immigration, multiculturalism and racism in '90s Canada*, Halifax, NS/Saskatoon, Fernwood/Social Research Unit, University of Saskatchewan.

TREW, T. (1979a) 'Theory and ideology at work' in FOWLER, R., HODGE, B., KRESS, G. and TREW, T., (eds) *Language and Control*, London, Routledge & Kegan Paul.

TREW, T. (1979b) '"What the papers say": linguistic variation and ideological difference' in FOWLER, R., HODGE, B., KRESS, G. and TREW, T. (eds) *Language and Control*, London, Routledge & Kegan Paul.

ULMER, G.L. (1985) *Applied Grammatology: post(e)-pedagogy from Jaques Derrida to Joseph Beuys*, Baltimore, Johns Hopkins University Press.

VAN DIJK, T.A. (1988a) *News Analysis: case studies of international and national news in the press*, Hillsdale, N.J., Lawrence Erlbaum.

VAN DIJK, T.A. (1988b) *News as Discourse*, Hillsdale, N.J., Lawrence Erlbaum.

WALES, K. (1989) *A Dictionary of Stylistics*, London, Longman.

WALSH, K. (1994) 'Citizens, charters and contracts' in KEAT, R., WHITELEY, N. and ABERCROMBIE, N. (eds) *The Authority of the Consumer*, London, Routledge.

WELLS, H.G. (1933) *The Shape of Things to Come*, London, Hutchinson.

WERNICK, A. (1991) *Promotional Culture*, London, Sage.

ZACHRISSON, R.E. (1970) *Anglic: an international language*, Maryland, McGrath.

# ACKNOWLEDGEMENTS

Grateful acknowledgement is made to the following sources for permission to reproduce material in this book:

## Colour plates

*Plate 1:* © Open University; *Plate 2:* 'Femigraine', in *She*, December 1992, courtesy of Roche Consumer Health; *Plate 3:* reproduced by permission of the Social Contract Press; *Plate 4: Mighty Max* © 1996 Bluebird (UK), Film Roman, Inc., Canal and D.A. Under licence from Bluebird (UK); *Plate 5:* reproduced by permission of *The Sun*, 1 January 1993, Rex Features; *Plate 8:* 'Cutting queues' 1995, Post Office Counters Ltd; *Plate 9: CPF Newsline*, Issue 02/95 and 'Minimum Sum Scheme' April 1995, Central Provident Fund Board.

## Text

*Pages 7–8:* Labov, W. 1975, *Language in the Inner City*, University of Pennsylvania Press; *pages 27–8 and 28–30:* From *Reading the News* by Robert Karl Manoff and Michael Schudson, editors 'Deadlines, datelines, and history'. Copyright © 1986 by Michael Schudson. Reprinted by permission of Pantheon Books, a division of Random House, Inc.; *pages 30–2:* Carey, J.W. 1987, 'Why and how? The dark continent of American journalism', from Manoff, R.K. and Schudson, Professor M. (eds) *Reading the News*, Pantheon Books, a division of Random House, Inc.; *pages 46–7:* Swann, C. 1991, *Language and Typography*, Lund Humphries Publishers Ltd; *pages 109–11:* Courtesy of BBC Radio 4, *Woman's Hour*, first transmitted on 27 November 1995; *pages 134–5:* Fry, S. 1995, 'I fell into a safety net', *Daily Telegraph*, 13 November 1995, by permission of David Higham Associates Ltd; *pages 135–6:* Snow, J. 1995, 'All the news that fits on screen', *The Guardian*, 19 September 1995; *pages 137–40:* Poster, M. 1990, *The Mode of Information*, University of Chicago Press and Basil Blackwell Publishers Ltd; *pages 165–9:* Cameron, D. 1995, *Verbal Hygiene*, Routledge; *pages 177–80:* Reprinted by permission of Sage Publications Ltd from Fairclough, N. 'Critical discourse analysis and the marketization of public discourse: the universities', in *Discourse and Society*, 4(2) 1993, Sage Publications; *page 174:* 'British–Bengali Bungle', *The Straits Times* 1 June 1994, by courtesy of *The Straits Times*; *pages 218–19:* Dixon, R.M.W. 'The endangered languages of Australia, Indonesia and Oceania' in Robins, R.H. and Uhlenbeck, E.M. (eds) 1991, *Endangered Languages*, Berg Publishers; *pages 219–23:* Ahai, N. and Faraclas, N., 'Rights and expectations in an age of "debt crisis": literacy and integral human development in Papua New Guinea' from Freebody, P. and Welch, A.R. (eds) 1993, *Knowledge, Culture and Power: international perspectives on literacy as policy and practice*, Falmer Press, A member of the Taylor & Francis Group; *pages 223–5:* Tomic, P. and Trumper, R. 'Canada and the streaming of Immigrants: a personal account of the Chilean case' in Satzewich, V. (ed.) 1992, *Deconstructing a Nation: immigration, multiculturalism and racism in '90s Canada*, Social Research Unit, University of Saskatchewan; *pages 225–8:* Robins, K. 'The new spaces of global media', in Johnston, R.J., Taylor, P.J. and Watts, M.J. (eds) 1995, *Geographies of Global Change*, Blackwell Publishers; *pages 228–34:* Reprinted by permission of Sage Publications Ltd from Findahl, O. 'Language in the age of the Satellite Television', in *European Journal of Communication*, 4(2) 1989, Sage Publications; *page 234–8:* Ross, N.J. 'Dubbing American in Italy', *English Today*, 41, 11(1), January 1995. Copyright © 1995 Cambridge University Press.

## Figures

*Figure 1.1:* 'Protest cut short', *Evening Post*, 20 January 1995, Reuters, New Zealand; *Figures 1.2 and 1.3:* Bell, A. 1991, *The Language of News Media*, Blackwell Publishers; *Figure 2.1:* © Apple Macintosh; *Figure 2.9:* © 1994 Fins, Milton Keynes; *Figure 2.13:* The Imperial War Museum, London; *Figure 2.18:* Kress, G. and van Leeuwen, T. 1996, *Reading Images*,

Routledge; *Figure 2.19:* Courtesy of Fleetway Editions; *Figure 2.23:* (*left*) 'How do you keep from getting pregnant?' courtesy of Yuan-Liou Publishing Company, (*right*) 'One bottle of rice wine for my old man', cartoon by Chu Tey-yung; *Figures 2.24 and 2.29:* Excerpts from *Understanding Comics* by Scott McCloud. Copyright © 1993, 1994 by Scott McCloud. Reprinted by permission of HarperCollins Publishers, Inc.; *Figure 2.26:* Eisner, W. 1994, *Comics and Sequential Art*, p. 44, Poor House Press; *Figure 2.27:* Photo by Don McPhee. © The Guardian; *Figure 2.28:* Illustration from *Batman Adventures* # 22 © 1994 DC Comics. Used with permission. All rights reserved; *Figure 2.30:* reproduced by permission of *The Sun*, 6 February 1991, Rex Features; *Figure 3.1:* Ao, B. 1995, Letter, 14 November 1995, from *Linguist* list, Internet; *Figure 3.2:* Knappen, J. 1995, 'Linguistic diversity on the Internet' 19 November 1995, and Inoue, N. 1995, ' "Regarding Linguistic diversity on the Internet" ' 21 November 1995; *Figure 3.5:* Siivonen, T. 1995, 'Letter by Discussant 6', Friday 24 February 1995; *Figure 4.1:* © La Redoute UK; *Figure 4.2:* Bugis Junction advertisement, from *The Straits Times*, 22 April 1995, Straits Steamship Land (Singapore); *Figure 4.3:* Minimum Sum Scheme advertisement, April 1995, Central Provident Fund Board; *Figure 1 (p.171):* reproduced by permission of Centrepoint Properties Ltd; *Figure 2 (pp. 172–3):* By courtesy of *The Straits Times; Figure 3 (p. 175):* Reproduced by permission of Flame of the Forest Pte Ltd; *Figure 4 (p. 175):* From *Lat as Usual*, Berita Publishing, 1990. Reproduced by permission of the publisher; *Figure 5.1:* Richards, I.A. 1943, *Basic English and its Uses*, Kegan Paul, Trubner & Co. Ltd, by permission of Routledge; *Figures 5.6 and 5.7:* Courtesy of Cable & Wireless Archive.

# NDEX